MOB RULE IN THE OZARKS

Arkansas History

JEANNIE WHAYNE AND KELLY HOUSTON JONES
Series Editors

OTHER TITLES IN THIS SERIES

Better Living by Their Own Bootstraps: Black Women's Activism in Rural Arkansas, 1914–1965

Das Arkansas Echo: A Year in the Life of Germans in the Nineteenth-Century South

Arkansas Travelers: Geographies of Exploration and Perception, 1804–1834

Just and Righteous Causes: Rabbi Ira Sanders and the Fight for Racial and Social Justice in Arkansas, 1926–1963

KENNETH C. BARNES

MOB RULE IN THE OZARKS

THE MISSOURI AND NORTH ARKANSAS RAILROAD STRIKE, 1921–1923

THE UNIVERSITY OF ARKANSAS PRESS

FAYETTEVILLE · 2025

978-1-68226-261-0 (cloth)
978-1-68226-262-7 (paperback)
978-1-61075-828-4 (e-book)

29 28 27 26 25 5 4 3 2 1

Manufactured in the United States of America

Designed by William Clift

IMAGE CREDITS: Front cover, foreground: M&NA steam locomotive number 50. *Courtesy of Ray Hanley.* Front cover, background: The route of the Missouri and North Arkansas Railroad, and other lines in Arkansas, from a 1912 M&NA timetable. *Courtesy of Steven C. Hawkins.* Back cover: Crowd gathered around casket at M&NA depot in Harrison, Arkansas. *Courtesy of Ray Hanley.*

♾ The paper used in this publication meets the minimum requirements of the American National Standard for Permanence of Paper for Printed Library Materials Z39.48–1984.

Cataloging-in-Publication Data on file at the Library of Congress.

For my grandchildren—Cohen, Claire, Kai, and Mia—who loved their trains.

CONTENTS

PREFACE

I HAD JUST BEGUN THE research for this book, when, on Wednesday, January 6, 2021, I came home early to watch the television coverage of the counting of electoral votes at the US Capitol. Like millions of other Americans, I witnessed a mob of some ten thousand men and women push past the police and smash their way into the Capitol Building, with the intent to stop the transfer of presidential power. I wept as the violence unfolded over a period of six hours. I saw one rioter beat a Capitol policeman with the wooden pole extending from an American flag. Later I learned the man had traveled to Washington, DC, from my hometown.

This book examines a two-year-long strike on the Missouri and North Arkansas (M&NA) Railroad, 1921–23. The strike came to an effective end on January 15, 1923, when a mob of a thousand men converged on Harrison, Arkansas, the headquarters of the railroad, where most of the strikers lived. The mob dragged strikers away, ransacked their homes, and forced them to renounce the strike or leave the state. Several strikers and sympathizers were whipped or beaten. One striker was lynched, hanged from the railroad bridge south of town.

Like the nation since January 6, I have tried to understand how a mob assembles, how it functions, and who is responsible for its actions. More than fourteen hundred members of the January 6 mob at the time of this writing have been indicted for criminal actions, and it remains to be seen whether those who summoned and directed the mob will face any consequences. Of the rioters in 1923, no one was prosecuted for the hanging of a striker, and only four men were held criminally liable for publicly stripping and flogging strikers and sympathizers. One man paid a fine of fifty dollars for his crime; the others paid ten dollars each.

This project began with another book, *The Ku Klux Klan in 1920s Arkansas* (2021), in which I described the Klan's role in ending the M&NA Railroad strike. I decided that the story deserved more than a few pages. The strike tapped the significant issues of the post–Great War labor movement. It created an utter rupture within communities of the Arkansas Ozarks that would take years to heal, as the Civil War had done sixty years before. The strike and its end demonstrated how government officials at local, state, and federal levels could sanction illegal violence to protect the economic interests of some citizens at the expense of others.

In the three months following the strike, a joint committee of the Arkansas General Assembly investigated the actions that ended the strike, taking testimony from hundreds of individuals on all sides of the event. The committee produced a report that held no one accountable and was widely regarded as a whitewash. While the committee's work was of little consequence, the investigation left behind 1,400 pages of manuscript testimony, a gold mine for historians, with detailed information about all aspects of the strike and its violent conclusion. The transcripts of this testimony became the major source for this book.

The staff at the Arkansas State Archives, especially Brian Irby, made available the manuscript testimony and several other materials essential to this project. The folks of the Boone County Heritage Museum in Harrison, particularly Martha Wilson and former director Toinette Madison, graciously guided me through their large collection of materials concerning the M&NA Railroad. Charles Stuart and Paul Enos of the Cleburne County Historical Society and its museum in Heber Springs assisted with several documents and photographs in their collection. Christeen Waters of the Office of the Mayor in Harrison and Carolyn Thomas of the Boone County Clerk's Office gave me access to local records of interest. Tina Farmer guided me through materials held in the Boone County Library. Steven C. Hawkins and Ray Hanley kindly provided images. Mike Christeson shared a wealth of knowledge and images of Harrison in the 1920s. Nancy Hensley and James J. Johnston provided oral testimony and assisted with research concerning Searcy County. I thank archivists Harry Lah of the Bowen School of Law Library in Little Rock, Joshua Youngblood of the Special Collections Department of the University of Arkansas Libraries, and Daniel Klotz of the University of Central Arkansas Archives. Nita Gould shared her knowledge about Harrison and Boone County at various stages of this project, and she provided a helpful reading of the manuscript. I benefited from conversations about US labor history with my friend and colleague Mike Rosenow. I thank the two anonymous readers, whose advice made this a better book, and the staff of the University of Arkansas Press for their assistance in many ways. As always, I benefited from editorial suggestions and moral support from my wife, Debbie, who for the last several years has heard more than she wished about railroads, burned bridges, flogged strikers, and disingenuous government officials.

Individuals in 1920s America had the annoying tendency to refer to themselves only by initials for men, for example J. C. Doe for John Charles Doe. His wife might use Mrs. J. C. Doe. I relied on Ancestry.com to establish full names when possible. I especially used Social Security information or cemetery records as the final authority for names. World War I selective service registrations and the 1920 manuscript census returns were particularly useful for incidental biographical information that I did not cite, such as ages, occupations, addresses, and physical descriptions. While digital access to newspapers has greatly facilitated research, digitization services sometimes use later titles for newspapers in searches and headings than the name on the masthead for a particular date. In this book, citations provide the name of the newspaper actually used. The bibliography references the name that might appear in the digitized version of the newspaper.

KENNETH C. BARNES
Conway, Arkansas
May 2024

MOB RULE IN THE OZARKS

CHAPTER 1

A RAILROAD CUTS THROUGH THE OZARKS

ON THE MORNING OF January 15, 1923, a crowd of more than a thousand angry men assembled in the courthouse square in Harrison, Arkansas, the headquarters of the Missouri and North Arkansas (M&NA) Railroad. They were prepared to use any measure necessary to end a strike of railroad employees that had dragged on for nearly two years. The M&NA ran from Joplin, Missouri, to Helena, Arkansas, through the heart of the Ozark Mountains. Its management and local law officials had been unable to stop a campaign of sabotage by strikers against railroad property, including the burning of bridges, poisoning of water tanks, and cutting of hoses.

The mob arrived in downtown Harrison on foot, by automobile, and on board a special train. The men quickly organized a "citizens committee" of twelve men, mostly lawyers and businessmen, who adjourned upstairs to the rooms of the Rotary Club, overlooking the square below. Squads of armed men roamed the streets, apprehended strikers and sympathizers, and brought them to appear before the committee. This kangaroo court gave strikers a choice of surrendering their union cards or leaving town. After dark the crowd stormed Union Hall, on the east side of the square next to the M&NA offices, and carried out documents and furniture for a bonfire in the middle of the street. A few hours before dawn, three masked men burst into a room holding several strikers and took away railway shopman Ed C. Gregor. At morning light, he was found hanging from the railroad bridge south of town. The symbolism of a striker's body swinging in the winter air from the M&NA's property spoke for itself. Over the next few days, crowds similarly targeted strikers in other towns up and down the line—in Leslie, Heber Springs, and Eureka Springs, Arkansas. The actions of these citizen mobs numbering more than 1,500 people effectively ended the strike by expelling the strikers. The national railroad unions finally threw in the towel in December 1923, bringing to an official close one of the longest railroad strikes in American history. While other railway strikes saw greater loss of life, this was the only one ended through a mob uprising.

The strike on the Missouri and North Arkansas Railroad reflects some of the major economic issues that preoccupied the United States in the years following the Great War. During the administration of President Woodrow Wilson, workers had won significant concessions in wages, hours and conditions of labor, and the recognition of unions as their bargaining agent. Federal control over the nation's railroads after the United States entered the war only solidified these gains for railway workers. Labor turmoil returned in 1919 in many industries, while railroads remained under the administration of the federal government. As train lines were returned to private hands in 1920, and after the November election of a probusiness Republican president, Warren G. Harding, railroad companies began to look for ways to make money. A wage cut and resulting strike on the M&NA, a relatively small railroad in an isolated region of the country, presaged the issues that would dominate America's railroads in the 1920s. As for the country as a whole, the strike spelled a loss for labor and a gain for business interests.

The M&NA strike and its violent conclusion tell us much about the fragile economy of the Ozark region following the Great War. Many residents along the railroad had become dependent on the line to ship timber products and fruit and receive manufactured items, fuel, and the US mail in return. Businessmen and community boosters were convinced that the railroad must run at all costs. The strike demonstrates the gulf that lay between these well-heeled community leaders and the laboring classes. The conflict progressed to the point where neither side could have empathy with the other, ending chances for negotiation or compromise. The actions of the mobs were anything but spontaneous. The violence that ended the strike resulted from deliberate planning by railroad officials and their supporters in the community. The political system, from local to state and federal levels, ignored or even justified illegal violence, demonstrating that elected officials prioritized economic interests of the privileged over constitutional rights for all. As the railroad connected citizens with the mainstream of America, the strike would reveal how thin the line could be between civil order and mob rule.

Soon after the strike ended, contemporaries understood the significant nature of the event. Within a year, two books appeared from participant observers, one who favored the strikers and the other who supported the railroad. The Reverend John Kelly Farris arrived in Harrison in early December 1922 to become the pastor of the town's Methodist church (a congregation of the Methodist Episcopal Church, South). He endeavored to maintain a neutral position, for his congregation contained members on both sides of the conflict. Within a month, however, he found his sympathies moving toward the strikers, a position that became galvanized on January 16, 1923, with the hanging of Ed Gregor and the expulsion of the strikers from Harrison. Gregor had been a member of Farris's congregation. Farris began speaking out against the actions of a lawless mob. By the end of the year he lost his pastorate in Harrison and returned to his hometown of Wynne, Arkansas, where he wrote his account, *The Harrison Riot, or The Reign of the Mob on the Missouri and North Arkansas Railroad*. He self-published the book on January 15, 1924, exactly one year after the mob stormed Harrison.

While Farris was writing his book, another clergyman, the Reverend Walter F. Bradley, pastor of Harrison's First Presbyterian church, produced an alternative account opposing the strike. In collaboration with the editor of the *Boone County Headlight*, Jesse Lewis Russell, Bradley expanded on articles that had previously appeared in Russell's newspaper condemning strikers and defending the actions of railroad managers and the mob. Bradley and Russell published *An Industrial War: History of the Missouri and North Arkansas Railroad Strike and a Study of the Tremenduous* [*sic*] *Issues Involved* in November 1923, technically before the strike was even over. Bradley's book, along with Harrison's two newspapers, the *Headlight* and the *Harrison Times*, provided the perspective of those opposing the strike.

As the dust settled from the strike and its violent end, a young professor of economics at Hendrix College in Conway, Arkansas, was shopping for a topic for his doctoral dissertation at Columbia University. Orville Thrasher Gooden chose to write about the walkout by union employees of the M&NA Railroad. Columbia University Press published his dissertation as a book, *The Missouri and North Arkansas Railroad Strike*, in 1926, a mere three years after the Harrison riot. In my work for this book, I examined many of the same primary sources as Gooden, including the works of Farris and Bradley. Gooden had the advantage of interviewing participants on both sides. Sadly, his desire to keep confidentiality led him to refrain from naming personal sources from interviews and correspondence. His treatment of the strike was thorough and remarkably evenhanded. His focus, however, was economic rather than historical. He analyzed issues such as wages, prices, and profitability, and he thrashed out the dynamics of relations between owners/financiers and various government regulators such as the Interstate Commerce Commission (ICC) and the US Railroad Labor Board (RLB).[1] Like Gooden, I have endeavored to understand the perspectives of both sides of the strike. While Gooden's book addresses the economic issues that formed the context of the strike, this account uses the strike to explore how a community could rupture into embittered camps for which defeat or victory seemed to be the only possible resolution. This study also examines how the county, state, and federal governments became handmaidens to the conflict, protecting the railroad and whitewashing the illegal actions taken by citizen mobs to end the strike.

When the M&NA began service on its 360-mile line through the Ozarks in 1909, it opened up one of the most isolated areas of the United States. Settlers mostly from upland Tennessee, Kentucky, Virginia, and North Carolina had arrived in the Ozarks in the three decades preceding the Civil War, appropriating the hunting lands of the Osage Indians for hardscrabble farms. These settlers scratched together a living on small plots of land, taking advantage of river bottoms that cut the uplifted plateau. The Civil War badly divided the population. Arkansas seceded and joined the Confederacy, while Missouri remained in the Union. But the Ozark regions of both states saw residents mixed in their loyalties throughout the war. The rugged terrain and low population density made the area ideal for the activities of guerrillas and marauders loyal to one side or the other, or to no side. The Ozarks came out of the Civil War with a near collapse of civil society, as a place where guns and private justice prevailed, with grudges sufficient to span into succeeding generations.

Yet the late 1800s began to look like a time of great promise for the region. Market towns in county seats began to grow and acquire the veneer of civilization. The University of Arkansas was established in Fayetteville, the largest and most cosmopolitan town in the Arkansas Ozarks. Springfield, Missouri, became a prosperous anchor on the northern side of the Ozarks, with rail connections to St. Louis by 1870 and Kansas City a decade later. Deposits of lead and zinc were found in the mountains in north central Arkansas. Large expanses of virgin hardwood and shortleaf pine promised great rewards if only transportation existed to ship the timber.[2]

The last three decades of the nineteenth century saw a flurry of railroad building throughout the United States. The railroads could make or break a community. Older towns miles away from a line withered as new towns bustled along the road. The construction of a railway and purchase of the rolling stock required enormous capital. Often local investors raised the money for short lines and chartered small companies to run the operation. Longer routes required such resources that big-city financiers and bankers controlled the railroad companies with operations managed from regional offices. When these owners made decisions, expectations of profitability often trumped local concerns.

By the turn of the century, two large railroad operations, the Frisco and the Missouri Pacific, had built lines or bought up smaller routes encircling the Ozark region. The St. Louis and San Francisco Railway Company (commonly known as the Frisco) built a line from St. Louis southwest to Springfield, where the railroad had its headquarters. By the early 1880s the company had laid tracks southwest to Fayetteville and Fort Smith, in western Arkansas, on the way to Dallas and points beyond, though the line never made it west of Texas. The Frisco also bought a line that stretched from Kansas City to Springfield and, by the late 1880s, laid rails east through the Ozark Plateau, before turning southeast to Memphis.

While the Frisco lines traversed the northern and western edges of the Missouri and Arkansas Ozarks, by 1900 an even larger system framed the region on the east and south. From humble origins, Jason "Jay" Gould had become one of the wealthiest men in America through various speculative investments, especially in railroads. From his base in New York City, he envisioned an enormous system that would run through the Midwest and West all the way to the Pacific. Gould died in 1892, but his son George Jay Gould kept acquiring lines and constructing new ones into the early 1900s. The Gould railroad empire had numerous spokes and branches with different names, but eventually it coalesced under the moniker of the Missouri Pacific Railroad Company, with its headquarters in St. Louis. The company's St. Louis, Iron Mountain, and Southern Line ran from St. Louis southwest to Little Rock, and then on to Texarkana and Dallas, with the tracks between the Missouri state line and Little Rock running just a few miles east of where the Ozark hills met the flatlands of the Arkansas Delta. Gould purchased existing rail lines from Memphis to Little Rock and from Little Rock west in the Arkansas River Valley to Fort Smith. Thus by 1900 the Gould system was the largest in Arkansas, with lines running south and east of the Ozark Mountains.

The Missouri and North Arkansas Railroad was chartered in August 1906 with the goal of bisecting the Ozarks from northwest to southeast, through mountainous terrain that lacked a transportation infrastructure. This railroad was twenty-five years in coming. It had begun as a short line with tourism, rather than freight, as the motivating factor. In 1879 and 1880, in a scenic area of the Arkansas Ozarks, a town had rapidly begun to grow around some natural springs. By the time of the 1880 census, Eureka Springs had a population of nearly four thousand people, making it the second-largest town in Arkansas, surpassed only by the capital, Little Rock. Investors smelling the potential for profit arrived with money. Luxury hotels, bathing facilities, and beautiful Victorian homes were constructed with anticipation that the spa town could become a resort of national prominence. All that was missing was a way for tourists to get there.

The leading booster for Eureka Springs was Powell Clayton, Republican governor of Arkansas during Reconstruction and US senator thereafter. This colorful and controversial public figure assembled a group of investors, mostly Republican businessmen from Little Rock and St. Louis, who chartered the Eureka Springs Railway Company in 1882 with capital stock of a half million dollars. Their goal was to build a six-mile railroad from the resort town through the mountains to Beaver, Arkansas. The Frisco had built a thirteen-mile extension off its main route at Seligman, Missouri, a new town created by the arrival of the railroad just north of the Arkansas state line. The

Eureka Springs Railway acquired the thirteen miles of existing track from Beaver to Seligman. After completion of the six-mile connection in January 1883, morning and evening trains carried passengers between Eureka Springs and the Frisco Line at Seligman, with travel time of approximately an hour. The Eureka Springs Railway had its business office in the Sanford Building on Spring Street in Eureka Springs, with its operations and shops clustered around the depot.[3]

In 1890 stockholders of the Eureka Springs Railway voted to extend the line to Harrison, Arkansas, about fifty miles to the east. The project languished, however, until the discovery of zinc and lead in the later 1890s in the region just east of Harrison. With new motivation, Powell Clayton and the largest stockholder, Richard C. Kerens, a wealthy businessman and Republican politician in St. Louis, began raising money to build the extension to Harrison, the seat of Boone County and a commercial hub for northern Arkansas. In May 1899 these investors, including businessmen from Little Rock and St. Louis and some local men in Eureka Springs and Harrison, chartered the St. Louis and North Arkansas Railroad, as the expanded line would be called. From two and a half miles north of Eureka Springs, construction began east through mountainous territory. The route necessitated a tunnel, numerous bridges, high grades, and sharp curves. Subsistence farmers along the route were so overjoyed to have a railway through the area that they often donated the rights-of-way. Citizens in Harrison raised $40,000, some men even mortgaging their homes or businesses to contribute, a sizable effort for a town of 1,500. The main line bypassed Berryville, the primary seat of Carroll County, connecting with a two-mile spur. The line then continued to Green Forest and Alpena, with the last spikes hammered into rails in Harrison on March 22, 1901. Great fanfare met the first passenger train as it rolled into Harrison a few weeks later. Regular service between Harrison and Seligman included a daily passenger train and a daily freight train that also accommodated some passengers. The sixty-six-mile journey took four hours. The railroad transported its first carload of zinc ore north to a smelter in Missouri on April 7, 1901. The future for the line appeared promising.[4]

By the time the railroad reached Harrison, its owners were already discussing further penetration into the Arkansas Ozarks. Construction of the extension began in the summer. From Harrison

Railroad officials and the city band celebrate the arrival of the first passenger train in Harrison, April 15, 1901. *Courtesy of Arkansas State Archives, Photo Collection, G4763.*

the route turned south toward an active zinc field near St. Joe and kept going through mountainous terrain to Marshall, the county seat of Searcy County. Some of the steepest grades for the entire line involved descending and ascending to cross the scenic Buffalo River, north of Marshall. The river was prone to flooding with a big rain, and so the Buffalo crossing necessitated concrete footings and a large iron bridge. The route reached Leslie by September 1903, where the exploitation of vast stands of hardwood timber was just beginning. With daily passenger and freight service to Leslie, construction halted. The company built a depot as the terminus for the line, with an engine shed, a shop building, yard tracks, and a wye to turn locomotives around for the return trip north.[5]

Railroad owners had originally planned to continue south from Leslie out of the Ozarks to Conway, where the line could connect with the Missouri Pacific toward Little Rock. But in 1905, after much consideration, construction resumed with a turn to the east toward the ultimate destination of Helena, an old river port on the Mississippi

River that had rail connections on the Yazoo and Mississippi Valley Railroad to Memphis and New Orleans. It was a fateful decision that would contribute to long-term problems for the railroad. But it made more sense in 1905. At a moment of seemingly infinite promise for railroads, the Helena location offered the prospect of continued expansion of the line through flat terrain to the Gulf of Mexico at Mobile or Pensacola. This dream never came to fruition, for Helena would become the terminus for the M&NA, remaining as such until the railroad's death in 1946.

In May 1906, as construction moved toward Helena, the railroad was reorganized into a new entity that took the name Missouri and North Arkansas Railroad Company. A committee of five investors purchased the property and rights of the St. Louis and North Arkansas for $2 million. Other than Powell Clayton, who was by then living in Washington, DC, the owners were prominent St. Louis businessmen: John Scullin and Richard C. Kerens, who had long been invested in the line; David R. Francis, a former mayor of St. Louis and governor of Missouri; and Robert S. Brookings, a wealthy patron of Washington University and later what would become the Brookings Institution in the nation's capital. This reorganization and infusion of money from financiers in St. Louis signified a shift in the focus of the company from local interests to urban capitalism.[6]

Construction on both ends of the line continued over the next three years. The company upgraded the original section of track between Seligman and Eureka Springs, and laid track to the northern terminus of Joplin. The owners negotiated rights to use the Frisco tracks for the nine miles from Seligman north to Wayne, from where the Frisco turned northeast to Springfield. They laid thirty-one miles of track from Wayne northwest to Neosho. The M&NA acquired trackage rights to run on the Kansas City Southern for the final twenty miles north to Joplin. From Leslie the route ran to the southeast roughly along the Little Red River, crossing it three times, through sparsely inhabited timber-clad mountains to Heber Springs, where the mountains gave way to hills on to Searcy. From Leslie to Heber Springs, a distance of sixty-one miles, some 160 curves made up half of the total mileage. Just four miles east of Searcy, in the small town of Kensett, the M&NA met the Gould company's Iron Mountain Line, through which passengers could connect to Little Rock or St. Louis. From Kensett, the rest of the route went through the flat land of the delta, more or less in a straight line southeast all the way to Helena.

Once the construction crews exited the Ozarks, the rails went down fast. As workers were building the line from Kensett, others moved northwest from Helena. The only hitch was an eight-mile stretch through swampy bottomlands between the White and Cache Rivers. There, much fill had to be brought in and a long drawbridge built over the White River, which still saw steamboat traffic, with another long bridge over the Cache. Despite an elevated track through the swamp, the White and Cache were prone to flooding, which would later frequently shut down the southern end of the line. On March 1, 1909, after this stretch was completed, the route opened for passengers and freight. From end to end, the line stretched 360 miles, with just over 300 of those miles in Arkansas. Passenger trains left Joplin and Helena at around 6:00 a.m. each day, arriving at the other end at around 11:30 p.m.

The arrival of train service brought great change for a relatively remote and undeveloped region. The process of constructing a railroad line injected resources into the area. Local men left their farms, especially in the slow winter months, and worked alongside crews of immigrants from Ireland, Greece, Austria, Bulgaria, and other countries, as well as prisoners leased for minimal pay. Some two thousand men were at work in the section between Leslie and Searcy in 1907 and 1908. To lay crossties and build hundreds of wooden bridges and trestles, the railroad company needed vast quantities of milled timber. The Heber Springs Milling Company got an order for 250,000 board feet of lumber, and nearby Pangburn Lumber Company was commissioned for an additional 200,000 board feet for the section from Leslie to Searcy.[7]

The new train service affected the economy of the Ozarks. Some local subsistence farmers found the decent and regular wages attractive and moved to Harrison, Leslie, or Heber Springs to work for the railroad. Inbound freight cars brought manufactured items, petroleum, canned goods, and other foodstuffs to the market towns up and down the line. But more freight was going out than coming in. The route between Harrison and Marshall ran on the western edge of the zinc and lead fields, and limestone and marble were quarried

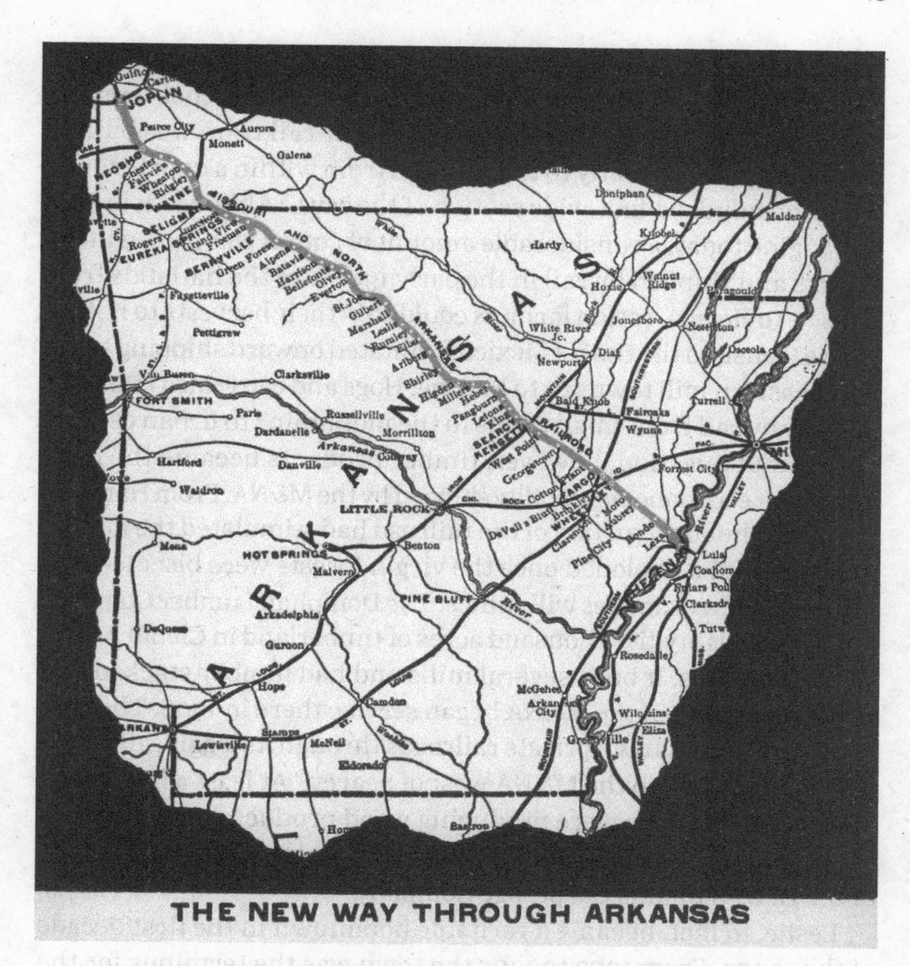

The route of the Missouri and North Arkansas Railroad, and other lines in Arkansas, from a 1912 M&NA timetable. *Courtesy of Steven C. Hawkins.*

and shipped from this area as well. Some farmers began investing in tens of thousands of fruit trees. Several commercial fruit farms opened up along the M&NA northwest of Harrison. Just to the east of Leslie, the Elberta Fruit Farm had 22,500 peach, apple, and pear trees producing by 1914. Searcy County became known for production of strawberries, with locals boasting that one could pick the luscious fruits growing on mountain slopes without bending over. Zack, a small stop just south of the Buffalo River north of Marshall, had Blowing Cave not far from the train stop. The cave was turned into a storage facility for fruit, vegetables, and other perishables; it functioned as a natural refrigerator, with constant cool temperatures, even during the summer heat. A light-rail tram was built to transport goods directly to the railroad from within a quarter-mile-deep and hundred-foot-wide section of the cave.[8] Although it is hard to imagine today, a considerable amount of cotton was grown in the Ozarks and shipped by rail in the early 1900s. In the flatlands from Kensett to Helena, cotton farmers could ship their harvests to Helena, where transit to the Gulf of Mexico facilitated onward shipping to the northeastern mill towns or to Europe. Hogs and cattle also made the journey by rail from small farms in the mountains to urban centers.

Without question, however, timber products became the most important economic commodity shipped by the M&NA. From Harrison to Searcy the construction of the railroad had stimulated the lumber industry, and it exploded once the virgin forests were bisected by a railroad. A few examples will suffice. The Doniphan Lumber Company purchased eighty-five thousand acres of timberland in Cleburne and White Counties. It built several mills and had lumber stacked and ready to ship when the M&NA began service there in 1908. The company even built its own private railroads through its logging districts, which connected to the M&NA west of Searcy.[9] At least a half dozen companies in Leslie were producing wood products soon after the railroad arrived in 1903. But they were dwarfed by the arrival in 1907 of the H. D. Williams Cooperage Company.

Leslie, in fact, became a veritable boomtown in the first decade of the 1900s. From 1903 to 1907 the town was the terminus for the North Arkansas Line, as the M&NA was also called. Leslie joined Eureka Springs as the location of shops to service the railroad and a site for change of crews. Moreover, Leslie became the headquarters for construction down the line after 1906. In the fall of 1907, the H. D. Williams Cooperage Company, which had exhausted the local supply of wood in Poplar Bluff, Missouri, relocated to Leslie. Within a few years, its main site on the edge of Leslie, alongside the M&NA, covered sixty-eight acres and employed 1,200 men. The cooperage leased some eighty-five thousand acres of forest south and west of town and had logging camps using thirteen portable sawmills. The company laid seventeen miles of a small rail line, called the Dinkey, to bring the lumber to Leslie to ship out on the M&NA. The Dinkey employed a Shay-type locomotive that used gears to traverse sharp curves and high grades at low speed. The company claimed to produce at its peak five thousand barrels a day, which made it the largest producer of barrels and staves in the world. It shipped completed barrels and staves ready for assembly, in varying sizes for specific purposes, throughout the country and to Europe. For the next few years, white oak barrels from Leslie aged some of the finest American whiskeys and French wines. The H. D. Williams Cooperage supplied a large percentage of the total freight shipped by the North Arkansas Line.[10]

Besides the economic impact, rail service transformed the area in many ways. Travel through the Ozarks had been notoriously difficult over routes that were more trails than roads. Wagon and automobile journeys over these dirt roads left one rattled to the bone. The M&NA added to regular steam passenger/freight trains smaller motor cars just for passenger service, with interiors finished in mahogany, plush upholstery, and Spanish leather. A gasoline engine turned a generator that provided electric power to move the seventy-passenger car. A brass rail observation deck on the rear allowed passengers to enjoy the extraordinary mountain scenery. The company even purchased a Pullman to offer sleeping car service between Joplin and Helena, complete with a full-meal buffet. Mail delivery became more reliable. The railroad created new towns from whole cloth, such as Shirley, Edgemont, and West Helena, just as the Frisco had birthed Seligman in the 1880s. Other towns, like Berryville, Harrison, Marshall, Heber Springs, and Searcy, all grew rapidly in the years immediately following the railroad's arrival. It appeared that the inhabitants of the Ozarks, so often caricatured as hillbillies, were poised to shed some of their rustic ways as they entered the mainstream of the country's economy and culture.[11]

Soon after the railroad's arrival, some citizens of Harrison began a "community improvement" project to expel the town's small Black population. A hundred Black men, women, and children—7.6 percent of the town's population in 1900—had their homes, a church, and a school in a neighborhood on the east side of downtown, near the railroad tracks. On Saturday, September 30, 1905, a Black man was arrested for breaking into the home of a local white physician. Two days later a group of about twenty white men stormed the jail, where he was being held with another Black man. The mob took the two men, whipped them, and ordered them to leave town. They then rode through the Black neighborhood, burning several homes and shooting out the windows of others. Some eight to ten Black men were tied to trees and whipped, while others were thrown into Crooked Creek, running south of town. Most of Harrison's African American families left within a few days, leaving their possessions behind. Just a few families remained. A few years later, in January 1909, a white mob reassembled and threatened to lynch Charles Stinnett, a Black man found guilty of assaulting an older white woman. On March 24, 1909, Stinnett was hanged at a scaffold erected behind the jail in Harrison. The last of the town's Black residents fled to other locations, with the exception of an elderly woman, a longtime live-in servant of a white family, who remained until her death in 1914. The expulsion of Harrison's African American residents in 1905 and 1909 served as a dress rehearsal for the expulsion of strikers in 1923.[12]

Harrison emerged as the railroad's leading town, with its population more than doubling between 1910 and 1920. The railroad promised to connect the region to the national economy. The only problem was that the North Arkansas Line did not make money. By the time the company had completed the railroad and purchased the rolling stock, investors had put millions of dollars toward the railroad. Yet only in one year, 1907, had the M&NA's income exceeded its expenses, with a slight profit of nearly $44,000. In no years was interest paid on the bonds. To avoid bankruptcy, on April 1, 1912, the company went into receivership, which allowed it to issue new bond certificates. Federal judge Jacob Trieber of Little Rock, of the US District Court for the Eastern District of Arkansas, appointed several of the chief investors in St. Louis as receivers. This process appears irrational by modern standards, whereby courts now appoint receivers without a conflict of interest to oversee a company in financial distress. However, in the early 1900s the rules for railroad receiverships differed from those for other corporations. The federal government accepted the premise that a railroad was too important to the public interest to go bankrupt, with its assets sold off piecemeal to pay creditors. The special railroad receivership allowed for a federal judge to name the chief investors, who were often bankers, as receivers. They would make adjustments to stabilize the company, often by issuing new bonds, receiver's certificates, which brought an infusion of new capital. For any of these changes, the insiders who guided the receiverships had to get approval from the federal judge. This explains Judge Trieber's close relationship with the M&NA while it was in receivership between 1912 and 1922. Receiverships had become common in the early twentieth century, with approximately half the nation's railroads going into receivership for an average period of three to four years. Both the Frisco and the Missouri Pacific had been in receivership in the 1910s. The practice had largely replaced the issuance of new stock as a strategy to finance the industry.[13]

The new general manager, Edward M. Wise, whom the St. Louis investors had hired the year before, believed that the company needed to spend money to make money. After the infusion of new capital in 1912, he bought new and better passenger cars and reorganized the administration of the railroad. In 1913 the general offices were moved from Eureka Springs, where the railroad had begun but which had become a minor stop on a spur off the main line, to Harrison. The M&NA spent $15,000 to build the new brick Kirby Building, on the northeastern corner of the town's main square, to house the offices. The second floor had a fireproof vault and space for forty employees. A new depot just a block to the east was built to match Harrison's prominence as headquarters of the line. The company spent $175,000 to develop the operations center on some sixty acres southeast of town, alongside Crooked Creek. An enormous machine shop there attached to a six-stall roundhouse with an eighty-foot turntable. A coach shop, warehouse, and other buildings completed the complex. Harrison had outbid Leslie, offering cash and land, to induce the railroad to choose the town as headquarters. Leslie had previously functioned as the center point in the line, where crews changed and the shops serviced locomotives. Leslie further lost out as the line was divided into three segments, corresponding to the eight-hour workday (legally mandated for railroad workers in 1917) and a union-negotiated limit of a hundred miles for a crew. The line divided into zones from Joplin to Harrison, Harrison to Heber Springs, and Heber Springs to Helena. Heber Springs thus received an upgrade and expansion of facilities as infrastructure was scaled back in Eureka Springs and Leslie. As a consolation prize, the railroad built beautiful depots of native stone in the two towns. Both depots still stand as of this writing.[14]

The M&NA shops in Harrison. *Courtesy of Ray Hanley.*

Despite the infusion of cash from the issuance of new bond certificates in 1912, the M&NA continued to lose money—more than $100,000 in each of the following five years. The population base of the Ozarks and eastern Arkansas was simply not sufficient to generate profitable passenger traffic. The route was probably the most expensive to operate of all railroads in Arkansas. With the sharp curves and steep grades, average speed was low. And locomotives could pull on average only fifteen loaded freight cars, compared to forty-five on the Frisco and the Missouri Pacific. Landslides and washouts frequently delayed the relatively slow service, earning the M&NA the nickname "May Never Arrive."[15]

In addition to these general challenges, three events conspired to make the M&NA run red ink. One was the construction of a rival railroad through the Ozarks, the White River Line. In the early 1880s, while Jay Gould himself oversaw his railroad empire, the company built an extension of its St. Louis, Iron Mountain, and Southern Line northwest into the Ozarks to Batesville. The nearly thirty-mile spur connected the old port town on the White River to Diaz, just a couple of miles north of Newport. In late 1901, while the M&NA was laying track south from Harrison to Leslie, the Iron Mountain began construction from Batesville of its so-called White River Division. The line was to run from Diaz diagonally northwest through the Ozarks to Branson, Missouri, before meeting the Gould company's Joplin Division of the Missouri Pacific at Carthage. With the Gould company's millions, the construction proceeded quickly, and by early 1906 the line was in operation. Obviously, it would compete directly with the North Arkansas Line, running roughly parallel within forty miles north of the M&NA. At its stop at Bergman, this White River Line was just ten miles east of the M&NA's headquarters in Harrison. Gould's White River Division had several advantages. The shorter, 265-mile line was built to the highest standards. It had heavier bridges, fewer curves, and lower grades than the M&NA, which traversed a more mountainous landscape. Yet, the White River Line constructed six expensive tunnels compared to the M&NA's one. Freight shipping would be quicker and cheaper. The White River also ran closer to the epicenter of the zinc mining district in Yell County, Arkansas, and the small town of Zinc, just fifteen miles southeast of Harrison in Boone County. And, of course, the White River Division was integrated into the larger Gould railroad system. In comparison, the stand-alone M&NA looked like a small, inefficient affair.[16]

If competition with the White River Line was a challenge from the get-go, a couple of events damaged the earning potential for the North Arkansas. A fire in November 1912 consumed most of the H. D. Williams Cooperage in Leslie. It did not return to partial operation for the better part of a year. The company had insurance to rebuild on a smaller scale, but the M&NA had to simply absorb the loss of freight revenue. The H. D. Williams Cooperage Company declared bankruptcy in 1915 and was reorganized the next year as the Export Cooperage Company of Leslie. But it never again produced at the peak levels achieved before the fire.[17]

Meanwhile, on August 5, 1914, the North Arkansas Line experienced more than just economic woes. One of its gasoline passenger cars, completely loaded with some riders even standing, left Joplin on the rails of the Kansas City Southern. About ten miles out of town, as the car entered a long curve at the base of a hill, the driver caught sight of a much larger train approaching. The brakes could not stop either train, both traveling approximately thirty-five miles an hour, and the two trains collided head-on. The locomotive and seven-car passenger train of the Kansas City Southern stayed on the rails and pushed the smaller motor car more than six hundred feet down the tracks. Around half the passengers on the M&NA train, and the entire crew, some forty-three in all, perished. Most died from the impact of the crash, but some were consumed in a raging fire after the motor car's gasoline tank exploded. No one on the Kansas City Southern lost their life. After litigation, the two railroad companies shared equal responsibility for the accident. But the payouts to families of victims, eventually totaling around $190,000, further decimated the M&NA's account books.[18]

On the day before this horrible accident, Germany had invaded Belgium, marking the beginning of fighting in World War I. As the dominoes fell and the great countries of Europe and their empires joined the war, the price of strategic metals skyrocketed. Rush, the village at the center of the zinc mines, became another boomtown, with two thousand inhabitants living in quickly thrown-up shacks, even tents, and several thousand more living in encampments in the surrounding area. About fourteen miles from the M&NA's nearest depot, at Gilbert, Rush was near where the Buffalo River empties into the White River. It was slightly closer to the White River Line's station at Yellville. Even so, the M&NA began to add platforms for the transfer of ore at stations between Marshall and Harrison. General manager Wise, ever ready to spend more money, began talk of extending a spur alongside the Buffalo River from Gilbert to Rush to get a greater share of the zinc shipments. Before any action could be taken, however, the White River Line began construction in early 1916 of its own spur to connect Rush. The M&NA had once again missed a chance, though the boom in zinc and lead would prove short lived. Prices of the two metals plummeted after the end of the war, and Rush became Arkansas's most well-known ghost town.[19]

One investor, the banker Festus J. Wade of St. Louis, led a group of businessmen who opposed Wise and his free-spending ways. Through the spring of 1916, they endeavored to sell the M&NA to a larger railroad company. When these efforts failed, Wade convinced Judge Trieber to name him sole receiver, and he then promptly replaced Wise with a new general manager, Charles Albert Phelan. The thirty-six-year-old Phelan had previously worked for the Illinois Central Railroad. He moved to Harrison with his family from Chicago in July 1916. Wade and Phelan imposed a program of economy. For the last six months of 1916, the railroad operated in the black. After the

United States entered the war, in April 1917, all railroads saw increased traffic. With plenty of zinc and lead ore shipping, the M&NA turned a profit in 1917, the first year since 1907. As men were heading off to war, shortages of manpower, equipment, and supplies (rather than lack of profits) became the new problems.[20]

World War I would be a turning point in the fortunes of labor in America's railroad industry. The later 1800s had seen contentious struggles between workers and the carriers' owners and managers. In major strikes in 1877, 1886, and 1894 angry workers damaged tracks and engines, and in some cases attacked strikebreakers. Armed guards hired by the railroads, aided by police, state militias, and federal troops, put down the strikes, resulting in loss of life and lingering bitterness. While the 1877 strike was more spontaneous than organized, the Knights of Labor attempted in 1886 to unite railroad workers with other laborers for a mass uprising, especially against the Gould rail system in the country's midsection. Missouri, Arkansas, Kansas, and Texas saw the widest scope of the strike, with governors of both Missouri and Arkansas calling for "law-respecting" citizens to rise up to restore order. The failure of the strike broke the Knights of Labor, a first attempt to gather workers of various stripes together into a common organization. In the Pullman strike and boycott of 1894, centered on the company's vast headquarters and manufacturing complex on the south side of Chicago, a new organization, the American Railway Union, attempted to speak for all types of railroad workers. The leader of the union, Eugene V. Debs, called for a nationwide boycott of all trains that carried a Pullman sleeper car. President Grover Cleveland ordered US infantry troops to stop strikers from stalling trains. Debs was arrested. After his release, he transitioned the American Railway Union from an inclusive labor union into a political organization that would give birth to the Socialist Party, which he would lead well into the twentieth century. In these labor conflicts of the 1800s, government at state and federal levels consistently sided with the carriers, a factor that surely helped convince Debs to forsake union organization for politics.[21]

As these two short-lived inclusive unions lost their fights against the big railroad companies, leadership of the railway labor movement fell to an assortment of so-called railroad brotherhoods, each dedicated to workers in specific crafts of the industry. The brotherhoods had originated in the 1800s as guilds that regulated entry qualifications and work quality for specific occupations. Operating like fraternal organizations with much Masonic-style ritualism, they provided social and insurance benefits to members. Traditionalist and conservative in nature, these brotherhoods had stood aloof from the strikes of 1886 and 1894. By 1900 four of the brotherhoods had become dominant: the Brotherhood of Locomotive Engineers, Order of Railway Conductors, Brotherhood of Locomotive Firemen and Enginemen, and Brotherhood of Railroad Trainmen. These "Big Four" represented the most-skilled and highest-paid workers in the running trades. Less organized were the employees who did not work on the moving trains, the shopmen who repaired engines and cars and the maintenance of way workers who took care of the tracks. By 1909 the American Federation of Labor (AFL) had established a Railroad Employees Department to represent organizations of lesser-skilled workers.[22]

With these less militant unions representing railway workers, the federal government began to encourage mediation and arbitration to resolve labor disputes. In 1898 Congress passed the Erdman Act, which established a role for the government to appoint ad hoc boards to mediate between carriers and brotherhoods acting as representatives of employees. The act made it illegal for a railroad involved in interstate commerce to ban or fire workers on account of union membership. Fifteen years later, the Newlands Labor Act of 1913 expanded Erdman to create a permanent board of arbitration/mediation. In the twenty years following the Pullman strike, the brotherhoods gradually began to look like modern unions rather than fraternal clubs. They evolved into some of the most powerful labor organizations in the country, with the federal government enshrining their role in collective bargaining.[23]

The labor-friendly policies of Democratic president Woodrow Wilson only added to the confidence of the railroad brotherhoods. As Wilson campaigned for a second term in 1916 on an openly progressive and prolabor agenda, the Big Four brotherhoods began a push for an eight-hour workday for workers in the running trades, even announcing a strike deadline for Labor Day, September 4. Wilson personally intervened and secured passage of the Adamson Act, which institutionalized the eight-hour day, with pay of the former ten-hour day, for railroad workers who worked aboard the moving trains, a huge precedent for labor in general.[24]

Owners and managers pushed back against these gains for labor. In the early 1900s, the open-shop movement became a label for employers who wanted to make employment contracts with workers as individuals rather than union members. While they were supposed to be blind to union membership after the Erdman Act, in reality these employers often discriminated against union workers in hiring decisions. Many open-shop advocates refused to recognize unions as representing employees when negotiating wages and working conditions. Despite the apparent progressivism of the Erdman and Newlands Labor Acts, participation in arbitration/mediation was voluntary. Railroads could ignore the federally convened boards if they thought they had the upper hand. However, as time went on and the brotherhoods gained influence in the Wilson years, the carriers increasingly accepted the government's role. But even after the Adamson Act took effect, on January 1, 1917, railroad companies refused to accept the eight-hour day and challenged the constitutionality of the new law. The brotherhoods again threatened to strike. President Wilson appealed to both sides to stand down until the US Supreme Court could issue a decision. A five-to-four ruling came down on March 19, 1917, just before the country's entry into war, affirming the act and the principle of federal authority to regulate interstate commerce.[25]

Labor would only build on these gains during the war years. On December 1, 1917, needing greater efficiency in the war economy, the Interstate Commerce Commission recommended to President Wilson that the federal government take over the administration of the country's railroads. Wilson's proclamation doing so went into effect at noon on December 28. He appointed William G. McAdoo, his son-in-law and secretary of the treasury, as head of the new US Railroad Administration (USRA). McAdoo and his agency immediately began a series of reforms to standardize service and equipment, eliminate redundant competition, consolidate some facilities, and reduce shortages affecting the war effort. The measures had more impact on the larger trunk railroads than on small operations like the M&NA. But soon several general policies hit home. The USRA guaranteed railroad companies net incomes equal to their average for the three years prior to June 30, 1917. Given that the M&NA had run a loss over that period, this policy was clearly problematic. Moreover, by the end of April 1918 the government announced a wage increase for railway workers of an average of 16 percent, to be paid beginning on May 25 but retroactive to January 1. These wages on the M&NA were set the same as for larger railroads in areas with a much higher cost of living than the Ozarks. One can imagine that the employees of the M&NA rejoiced. The USRA increased rates for freight by 25 percent, effective June 10, which was expected to help the railroads pay the higher wages.

After six months of government operation, the USRA concluded that small railroads such as the M&NA, unlike the large trunk lines, did not fit the nationalization model. It announced that more than 1,500 short lines were to be returned to private ownership on July 1, 1918. At the time the M&NA reverted to private control, it had not yet paid workers the mandated wage increases. Moreover, the company balked at the recommendation, put forth by the USRA's wage commission in August, that a further wage increase be implemented for certain classes of railroad workers, including shopmen. In its early years the M&NA had proudly proclaimed itself as operating on an open-shop basis. Harrison had a lodge of the Brotherhood of Locomotive Firemen and Enginemen and probably other brotherhoods by 1916. But by the summer of 1918 approximately half of the railroad's 1,200 employees were union members. Between 100 and 120 union shopmen in Harrison responded to the railroad's refusal to raise wages by going on strike, shutting down the entire railroad on September 17, 1918. The US Department of Labor appointed a Little Rock attorney, E. G. Shoffner, to go to Harrison as a commissioner of conciliation to negotiate the demands for wage increases. Officials of the various railroad brotherhoods came to Harrison on behalf of workers. The M&NA's receiver, Festus Wade, however, convinced the USRA to take back control of the railroad, restoring the government subsidy. Employees went back to work on September 24.[26]

This one-week strike foreshadowed the problems that were to come. The labor unrest so troubled general manager Charles Phelan that he resigned and took a USRA position administering a terminal of the Baltimore and Ohio Railroad. The M&NA's superintendent, James S. Reddoch, was promoted to general manager. The flow of government funds allowed for the promised wage increases to the standard national rates. This action satisfied employees, and the following year was relatively quiet. But the company ran a deficit of expenses over income of more than $600,000 in 1919, the largest deficit in the company's history to that time. Much of that deficit resulted from the increased wages. After the end of the war, freight revenues declined with the collapse of the zinc and lead market. The cooperages along the North Arkansas Line also lost orders from breweries and distilleries after the ratification of the Eighteenth Amendment, in January 1919, as the nation prepared for Prohibition to take effect a year later.[27]

As the Great War receded into the past, the federal government began to dismantle the pieces of war socialism that had kept the labor movement relatively pacified. Republicans won a majority in both the House and Senate in the November 1918 elections, which took place during the worst days of the Spanish flu epidemic. The railroad companies prepared to take back gains labor had made during the years of government administration, such as wage increases, standardized work rules, and the recognition of unions. The brotherhoods fought hard for a permanent nationalization of the railroads. In January 1919 the Senate Committee on Interstate and Foreign Commerce began hearings on the railroads question, under its chair, Albert B. Cummins (R-IA). The general counsel for the Brotherhood of Locomotive Engineers, Glenn Plumb, attended the hearings and forcefully presented a proposal that the brotherhoods all endorsed. The so-called Plumb Plan argued that railroads were a public utility that the federal government should fully control. It called for the government to buy out the stock and bonds of owners at a court-determined value of investment. The Plumb Plan brought the brotherhoods into greater coordination than ever, even leading them to found a weekly newspaper, *Labor*, published in Washington, DC, to disseminate propaganda for the nationalization of railroads. To most Americans in 1919, the idea smacked of the sort of bolshevism that government officials at all levels were brutally suppressing, and the Plumb Plan gained little traction outside of union lodges.[28]

Senator Cummins and his partner in the House, Representative John Esch (R-WI), instead drafted bills to return all the nation's railroads to private hands, with a few concessions to unions. The final Esch-Cummins bill, passed as the Transportation Act of 1920, went into effect on March 1, 1920. It expanded the powers of the ICC, encouraged mergers, and created the Railroad Labor Board to hear labor disputes on a voluntary basis. Of the RLB's nine members, three represented labor, three the railroad companies, and three the public interest. The act gave the railroads a six-month guarantee period for further subsidy, if necessary. But it did not outlaw strikes on the interstate railroads, a demand made by many carriers. After President Wilson, in April, made the appointments constituting the RLB, the board initially posed as friendly to labor. Its first order required that authorized representatives of carriers and employees must conference in advance of appearing before the RLB, thus implicitly enshrining unions as speaking for railroad workers. The railroads complained that the order instituted a virtual closed shop. Then, on July 26, 1920, the RLB announced a wage increase to bring railroad wages up to the level of other industries. The increase averaged 26 percent and was retroactive to May 1. Despite these concessions to labor, the sixteen railroad brotherhoods went on record as opposing the Transportation Act.[29]

To prepare for the return to private management on March 1, 1920, the St. Louis directors of the M&NA had met in January in Harrison and voted to bring back Charles Phelan as general manager, with James Reddoch returning to his former job as superintendent. Phelan then resigned his job with the USRA, left his family at their home in Atlantic City, New Jersey, and returned to his old job in Harrison. On March 12 Judge Trieber named him receiver, succeeding Festus Wade, the first time that the company's general manager had held this decision-making power. The thirty-eight-year-old manager/receiver faced formidable challenges. The government had lost $800,000 on the M&NA during its time of control. Besides the ongoing deficits, the payroll was approximately two-thirds higher than it had been in 1917. Phelan was left with a wage rate that might make sense for New Jersey, but not for Harrison, Arkansas. The clock was ticking. He had six months of subsidy, until September 1, to find a way to make the railroad solvent. Phelan had grown up working for the railroads. Born to Irish parents who had first immigrated to Ontario, Canada, and then to Chicago, he had gone to work for the Illinois Central Railroad at the age of sixteen as a messenger boy. He worked his way up the company over eighteen years before taking the job as general manager of the M&NA, moving his family from Chicago to a new house on O'Neal Heights in Harrison in 1916. Yet when confronted by his employees in September 1918, he had bailed. Now, in March 1920, Phelan was back for a second try, this time with the added muscle of receivership.[30]

As the September 1 deadline approached, it became clear to Phelan that the railroad could not survive under its current terms. Eighty cents of every dollar the company earned went toward wages, a figure Phelan thought unsustainable. In speeches and a public letter to newspapers, he declared that the M&NA would likely discontinue services. He announced a hike in passenger and freight rates to take effect October 1. By the end of 1920, the company was still bleeding red ink. After much deliberation, and with the consultation of Judge Trieber, Phelan announced that the railroad would reduce wages by 20 percent effective February 1, 1921, saving the company $25,000 a month. This cut would take wages back to the level of April 1920, preserving the first round of government-mandated increases. Phelan asked union representatives to meet with him on January 20 to negotiate the wage reduction. At this meeting the local representatives of employees refused the proposed pay cut but floated the idea of a reduction in the workforce to save the monthly $25,000. Phelan rejected this proposal. On February 1, the shopmen in Harrison walked off the job, leaving their tools behind them. The strike had begun.[31]

CHAPTER TWO

THE STRIKE BEGINS: FEBRUARY–JULY 1921

WORLD WAR I HAD ended in a revolutionary moment. The Bolshevik Revolution in Russia was constructing a new order. Communists were fighting right-wing gangs in the streets of German cities. In the United States, the labor movement came out of the war flexing big muscles. Unions had the greatest membership in American history, and in 1919 more than 3,500 strikes took place, mobilizing some 22 percent of the workforce. Local law enforcement and business elements throughout the country harassed the most radical labor group, the Industrial Workers of the World (IWW), because of its revolutionary rhetoric. Arkansas's General Assembly in March 1919 passed Act 512, an anarchy law, to prevent the introduction or spread of bolshevism, making it a criminal offense to advocate the overthrow of the government of Arkansas or the United States. Six months later, near Elaine, Arkansas, on the night of September 30, 1919, a group of impoverished Black sharecroppers met in a church to organize an agricultural union. Within a few days, an angry white mob, strengthened by soldiers with machine guns sent by the governor, began shooting at African Americans. Historians are still arguing about the death toll, with estimates ranging from a couple of dozen to several hundred Black residents massacred. In the 1920 presidential election, Eugene V. Debs—former locomotive fireman, founding member of the IWW, and perennial candidate for the Socialist Party—polled nearly a million votes, the Socialist Party's largest vote ever. But that same year American voters turned from the prolabor policies of President Woodrow Wilson's administration and elected the champion of business from Ohio, the Republican Warren G. Harding.[1]

The threats of radical labor and national political trends might seem far removed from the remote and rustic towns along the tracks of the M&NA. In Harrison, where the strike began, railroad workers and management were generally well integrated into the community of nearly four thousand citizens. The employees of the railroad were almost entirely local men of the Ozarks, not immigrants speaking non-English languages or transplants from large northern cities. The Reverend Walter F. Bradley, who vigorously opposed the strike, admitted that union members in Harrison were just a bunch of "home boys," not radical anarchists. In contrast, general manager Charles Albert Phelan, as a Roman Catholic and the son of Irish immigrants, might appear to be an "outsider" in the heavily Protestant and Anglo-Saxon Ozarks, having moved to Arkansas to manage the railroad from somewhere else, just like most other officers of the M&NA. The Brotherhood of Locomotive Engineers, Bradley said, was just another fraternal organization. According to Bradley, 65 percent of M&NA employees were (like their managers) members of Masonic lodges. Others belonged to the Odd Fellows, Woodmen, Shriners, and other fraternal groups. Most strikers, like the officers, owned their homes outright or were buying them. The strikers and the management of the M&NA attended the same Methodist, Baptist, and Presbyterian churches. In 1917, the wives of future strike leader Pete Venable, general manager Phelan, and Jack Murray (who succeeded Phelan in July 1921) attended the same ladies' card group. Venable and Murray were both Knights Templar Masons. But the strike would make the two men bitter enemies. Contemporaries insinuated that Murray's hand guided the mob that lynched Ed C. Gregor on the morning of January 16, 1923. They believed that Gregor only met that tragic fate because Venable was out of town and unavailable. Within weeks of its beginning, the strike began to divide residents of Harrison into adversarial factions of "us" and "them."[2]

The strike began with the shopmen. As the workers who maintained the rolling stock—blacksmiths, machinists, boilermakers, electricians, carmen, and sheet metal workers—shopmen were among the largest contingents of railroad employees. Represented by the Federated Shops Craft, which was part of Samuel Gompers's American Federation of Labor (AFL), the shopmen were particularly assertive locally and nationally. They had initiated the one-week strike on the

Harrison's leading citizens at a costume party in happier times, 1916.
Courtesy of Mike Christeson.

M&NA in September 1918. Almost all the railroad's shopmen worked and lived in Harrison.[3]

After Phelan announced his plan for wage cuts effective February 1, 1921, local union representatives met with management one last time on January 29, requesting that Phelan table any reduction in wages until the matter could come before the Railroad Labor Board (RLB). Phelan refused to suspend the cuts, but he did agree to appeal jointly with the unions for a hearing before the RLB. The leader of the shopmen in Harrison, Tillman Jines, had already traveled to Chicago for a meeting with his union chiefs. Upon hearing of Phelan's position, Jines telegraphed back to Harrison, instructing the 125 shopmen to walk out on February 1. The shopmen put down their tools and left the railroad yard, but leaders of the Big Four and other brotherhood lodges chose to wait for the RLB's ruling before taking any action. On February 8, the RLB set a hearing for February 15 in Chicago, but recommended no changes in pay until it could review the matter. Phelan notified the board on February 9 that he was going through with the pay cuts immediately anyway, on account of the M&NA's inability to pay the higher wages. Meanwhile, the company began advertising in local newspapers for machinists, boilermakers, coppersmiths, blacksmiths, and other jobs paying from forty-nine to seventy-two cents an hour. Within a week of the shopmen's walkout, the M&NA had hired some sixty men to replace them, some workers coming from as far away as Kansas City.

Pete Venable, the local secretary for the Order of Railway Conductors, pointed out that Phelan received the generous salary of $12,000 as general manager and another $3,000 as receiver for the indebted railroad. He also insinuated that Phelan had appropriated additional money when the line was under government control and that he had sold a private car for railroad officials and pocketed those proceeds, too. (He neglected to mention that Phelan's base pay, like that of all other employees, had been reduced by 20 percent in February.) Some two hundred businessmen and two hundred farmers in the area signed petitions protesting Phelan's actions against the shopmen in Harrison.[4]

When Phelan came before the RLB in Chicago on February 15 and 16, he argued that the board had no jurisdiction over the wages matter because the M&NA had been in receivership since 1912. Moreover, federal judge Jacob Trieber had already given his approval for the pay cuts. Phelan claimed, in addition, that the wage reduction was reasonable on account of a lower cost of living along the line, compared to other parts of the United States. Officers for the unions argued, conversely, that the RLB should not even hear Phelan, given his failure to follow the board's directive regarding the wage cut. On February 21 the RLB ruled that the M&NA had indeed acted improperly in reducing wages in advance of a hearing, but that employees should continue to work at the lower pay "under protest" until further negotiations in Harrison could resolve the dispute. In case these talks failed, the RLB set March 5, the day after President Harding's inauguration, as the date for a second hearing in Chicago to establish fair wages for the troubled carrier.[5]

There would be no compromise. Representatives of the shopmen indicated their willingness to return to work at the reduced wages, pending the continued negotiations under direction of the RLB. Phelan, however, claimed that the striking shopmen were no longer employees of the railroad, having been replaced already by new men. At some point in the late-stage negotiations, union representatives suggested to Phelan that employees would accept the 20 percent wage cuts if he would guarantee that no further reductions would follow. This he refused to do. Local labor leaders informed Phelan that all union employees would join the shopmen on strike at 3:00 a.m. on Saturday, February 26. Somewhere between 450 and 600 workers walked out, over half of the company's employees. The last M&NA train rolled into Joplin at 10:50 p.m. on Friday, February 25. The crew was stuck and could not get home. The intransigence of Charles Phelan clearly led to an all-out strike. While unions indicated some willingness to compromise, they failed to fully accept that a railroad could not continue to run while insolvent. And the RLB failed to provide real leadership. All three sides shared some blame for the debacle that would follow.[6]

The national officers of the railroad brotherhoods cooperated closely with one another as the strike began. They established a standing committee to oversee the strike, and eight officers of the various brotherhoods came to Harrison in late February to direct the local representatives. Evidently, the railroad brotherhoods understood that this strike on a small railroad was a bellwether for future attempts to dismantle the gains railway workers had made during the wartime years of government control. As participants in an authorized strike, the union employees of the M&NA would receive benefits, which typically ran from sixty to one hundred dollars a month, considerably less than the wages the men had formerly received. The local officers of the brotherhoods constituted a "coordinating committee" in Harrison, chaired by James E. Queen, the local head of the Order of Railway Conductors. In each town along the line with strikers, such as Joplin, Eureka Springs, Leslie, Heber Springs, Searcy, and Helena, committees directed local strike activities and reported to the coordinating committee in Harrison.[7]

The immediate business for Phelan and the management team was to keep the railroad running. Most strikers resided in Harrison, but about fifty lived in Heber Springs. Leslie and Eureka Springs had a couple dozen each, and other strikers were scattered at points up and down the line. After a few days, some trains began running with nonstriking workers, reinforced by office staff and management officials. Superintendent James S. Reddoch, traffic manager Jack Murray, and chief clerk Frank Mitchell were acting as conductors and engineers, strikers claimed, creating a dangerous situation for the line. The first train from Harrison after the strike began reached Joplin three hours late on February 28. The first train south from Harrison reached Searcy the next day, after forty-eight hours of travel. Managers from the main office manned the locomotive, five freight cars, and two passenger coaches transporting strikebreakers. On March 2, a train finally reached Helena. Meanwhile, Phelan had agents searching for new employees locally and afield, especially in Kansas City and St. Louis. The general manager could be confident that there were plenty of unemployed railway workers to hire as strikebreakers, given that the number of railroad employees nationally had declined from 2.2 million in August 1920 to 1.6 million by March 1921. By Wednesday, March 2, strikebreakers were working in Harrison, Leslie, and Helena. Phelan announced that he had hired a large number of new workers and that regular passenger service would resume the following week.[8]

The arrival of strikebreakers, especially strangers from outside the state, brought discord to a new level. Strikers verbally harassed strikebreakers along the picket lines and in town. Strikers hurled epithets like "scab" and "scaley" even at wives and children of the strikebreakers. Even though the unions instructed strikers to stay off railroad property, someone scrawled "SCABS" on the caboose of an M&NA train in Neosho as it was leaving the station. In Harrison, strikers made the rounds of downtown businesses to threaten a boycott, a frequent tool of labor in the early 1900s, unless merchants and managers refused service to strikebreakers. Some business owners complied out of sympathy with these local men they knew. Others feared the loss of business, worried that strikers who owed them money would walk away from their debts. Strikers "suggested" to strikebreakers that they quit their jobs and return from whence they had come. Rev. Bradley said that several hundred new employees responded to intimidation and left. For example, one machinist who had brought his wife and child from Tennessee refused at first to be bullied. While he was on duty at the shop, strikers showed up at his house and threw a load of firewood through the window, frightening his wife and three-year-old daughter. The whole family thereafter returned to Tennessee. Harrison's mayor, Guy L. Trimble, proclaimed that he would protect all citizens regardless of their position on the strike. But strikebreakers complained that police in Harrison provided them no protection because city officials sympathized with the strikers. On the other hand, Pete Venable charged that M&NA superintendent Reddoch had furnished strikebreakers with 45-caliber Colt pistols and that they carried the weapons unmolested by police officers.[9]

Even the railroad's general manager was not above the use of force. Word got out that train no. 202 was heading north into Harrison carrying a group of strikebreakers. Some strikers met the train at the stop just south of town. Strikers were ordering the strikebreakers off the train as Phelan and some of his guards parked Phelan's large touring car across the road. Phelan pulled out a gun and threatened to use it if strikers did not desist. Phelan would later pay a fine for brandishing a gun in violation of the law.[10]

With the escalating tensions, some eighty business and professional people in Harrison gathered on Saturday night, March 5, in Rotary Hall on the second floor of the Farmers Bank building, on the northeastern corner of the main square. Phelan read a prepared statement in which he threatened to move the offices of the M&NA to another town if local citizens denied lodging and food to the railroad's new employees and if the city failed to provide protection for them. James Queen, the head of the strikers' coordinating committee, was allowed to speak, and he pledged the unions' support for law and order. The meeting created the Harrison Protective League, which resolved to take no position on the strike, but to support the town's police officers in their work to keep order in the community. The assembly pledged to sell goods and services to new employees of the railroad. The meeting raised $500 to pay for additional guards to patrol the town. While the Protective League professed that it did not take sides, its commitment to provide services to strikebreakers suggested otherwise. The choice of the name associated the group with the American Protective League, which had appeared in the months following the US entry into World War I. The American Protective League had organized volunteer detectives who pledged to root out disloyalty, whether that be German speakers or slackers who failed to register for selective service. The choice of the name Protective League by Harrison's leading citizens implied that strikers were somehow less than patriotic Americans.[11]

While the stated goal of the Protective League was to keep order, after the evening of March 16 its real work became the protection of railroad property. A 180-foot bridge over Long Creek about a mile

Labor's opinion about the local response to the M&NA Railroad strike. *Railway Federationist, May 21, 1921.*

east of Alpena—ten miles northwest of Harrison—was consumed by fire. Around the same time a smaller bridge burned at Pindall, to the south. Harrison was now cut off by rail from both directions. Phelan immediately charged that strikers had burned the bridges. Strike leaders in Harrison countered that inadequate service by inexperienced workers had caused engines to drop ash and flames, resulting in the fires. A national union official, Martin C. Carey, noted that wooden bridges had burned around the same time on the Missouri Pacific's White River Line, resulting from sparks emanating from the engine's firebox, but that nobody there had claimed arson. Besides the burned bridges, Phelan claimed that strikers had placed obstructions on tracks, pulled up spikes and ties, cut telegraph lines, and opened switches in the face of oncoming trains. These depredations, Phelan said, made operation of the railroad unsafe for employees, passengers, and freight. He shut down the railroad on March 17, and he stated that it would remain shut until federal or state authorities could provide adequate protection. Phelan communicated this position to the governors of Arkansas and Missouri, the Interstate Commerce Commission (ICC), and Judge Trieber.[12]

The sheriff of Boone County, J. S. "Silby" Johnson, telegraphed Arkansas governor Thomas C. McRae asking him to send a unit of the National Guard to restore order. After some deliberation McRae declined to send troops, saying that the M&NA was in the hands of a federal court, as it was in receivership. He told Johnson that he expected the sheriff to use his own authority to control the lawlessness in his county and protect property. Johnson issued a proclamation allowing landowners along the line to make citizen's arrests if they found any individuals engaging in vandalism. On March 21, the circuit judge of Boone County, James M. Shinn, approved 127 special deputies to police the area. Even three women, Mrs. C. E. Yard, Mrs. Joan Schaefer, and Miss May Ziegler, were appointed as special deputies to assist in protection of railroad property, the first time that women had ever served in such a role in Boone County. By the beginning of April, bloodhounds had arrived from the Tucker state prison farm, accompanied by their keeper. Harrison's Protective League hired five men to patrol railroad property at night. Under the order of a federal judge in Kansas City, US marshals left Joplin for communities along the Missouri portion of the line, all the way to Seligman, to safeguard the property of the M&NA. Mayor Trimble sent telegrams to Governor McRae, Senators Joe T. Robinson (D-AR) and Thaddeus Caraway (D-AR), and Congressman John Tillman (D-AR). The mayor claimed that order prevailed in Harrison and troops were not needed, but he asked the government officials to intercede for some effective mediation to end the strike.[13]

Scuffles in the streets of Harrison and along the railway line became daily occurrences. W. A. Greene, a strikebreaker from Kansas City, fought with a group of strikers after they had insulted his wife. Greene got the worst of it as the strikers broke a rib, gouged out an eye, and bit off part of his ear. In Shirley, a union sympathizer, Lycurgus B. McGlathery, was arrested for assaulting the station agent while drunk. On the other hand, strikers who committed mischief on railroad property faced gunfire from reckless patrols. Guards started shooting at two men they thought were pulling up spikes north of Harrison, before the men disappeared into the darkness. Another patrol fired on men thought to be tampering with switches at the

Capps station, just north of Harrison. The *Harrison Times* advised the public to stay off railroad property, for the patrols might shoot at innocent people they suspected were committing depredations to the railroad.[14]

The courts got into the action. Harrison's municipal court prosecuted railroad officials and strikebreakers. But federal and circuit courts, from the beginning, used their power against strikers and their sympathizers. Judge Trieber sent US marshals to Heber Springs to arrest striker Pete Bettys, charged with attacking J. S. "Will" Ledbetter, a telegraph operator who had taken his place. He was sentenced within a week in federal court in Little Rock. The grand jury in Boone County's circuit court was in session in the last two weeks of March, just after the damage to railroad property began. Judge Shinn instructed jurors that though picketing was a legal activity, strikers could not attempt to induce new employees to leave their job. Such action was a misdemeanor punishable by a heavy penalty. The jury indicted two local strike leaders, Tillman Jines and Ed Ben, for interfering with witnesses and breaching the peace. Marvin Lineberry was indicted for the assault on strikebreaker W. A. Greene. A week later, rabble-rouser Pete Venable and eleven other strikers were arrested for breaching the peace and given bonds of $250 each. Strikers William A. Duncan and Walter Husky were arrested for violating liquor laws.[15]

Besides these strikers, the grand jury issued a summons for six officials of the national railroad brotherhoods who were staying in Harrison to direct the strike. The union representatives were to address the destruction of railroad property. However, the grand jury adjourned on March 31, before the union men had the chance to speak to the charges. W. C. Jenkins, an official from Moline, Illinois, representing the Federated Shop Crafts, was arrested and charged with attempting to bribe Mr. and Mrs. Greene to return to Kansas City instead of appearing as witnesses in court against Lineberry. The local justice system found H. C. O'Neil, who had come to Harrison to represent the Brotherhood of Railway Electricians, guilty of drunken disorderliness. O'Neil took the morning train out of Harrison after he was released from the county jail, leaving the other union representatives to pay his fine. By the first of April, the Boone County grand jury had returned forty-eight indictments, almost all of them against those who supported the strike.[16]

Harrison's Protective League threw itself into action on behalf of Phelan and the railroad. The league's executive committee met on the evening of March 19 to consider expelling the national union officials from Harrison. They called another full meeting of the league two days later, with seventy in attendance. This meeting passed a resolution that condemned the unions' position in calling the strike, as well as "the acts of anarchy and bolshevism." The group commended Judge Shinn for appointing special deputies and called for Sheriff Johnson to deputize as many extra men as necessary. Finally, the league asked for Mayor Trimble's resignation because of his activities on behalf of strikers. Trimble had allegedly been observed in private meetings with strike leaders at his office, and with brotherhood representatives at their headquarters at the Midway Hotel, Harrison's nicest establishment (located at the corner of Sycamore Street and Stephenson Avenue). Trimble's biggest offense, the league said, was misrepresenting affairs in Harrison to Governor McRae. Trimble's claim that order was prevailing in Harrison had influenced McRae's decision not to send troops to the town. Trimble denied favoring the strikers and refused to resign.[17]

Meanwhile, similar meetings to organize citizen patrols took place up and down the line, from the Missouri border to Kensett. Venable alleged that representatives of the railroad traveled north as far as Eureka Springs and south to Heber Springs to organize the opposition to strikers. The southern part of the line, south and east of Kensett, which ran through the flat Arkansas Delta, had seen little trouble, a pattern that would generally hold true for the two-year duration of the strike. In Marshall on the evening of March 18, fifty-four citizens assembled at the courthouse and unanimously condemned the strike and the unions. The assembly blasted the burning of Pindall bridge—in Searcy County no less—as an act of "anarchy and bolshevism." The group called for the county sheriff to add as many deputies as necessary to protect the railroad in Searcy County and for the courts to prosecute the felonious destruction of property.[18]

Phelan called for a mass meeting in Harrison on the afternoon of March 24 to organize patrols for the whole line. His promise was to resume regular service if protection could be guaranteed. Phelan sent a special train from Eureka Springs to Harrison, carrying two hundred people from Green Forest and Alpena and other points north.

One train ran to the burned bridge over Long Creek, where passengers were transferred to a train waiting on the other side to bring them on to Harrison. Another train originated in Shirley, bringing three hundred citizens from the south. Phelan had immediately begun reconstruction of the two burned bridges and apparently had the Pindall bridge rebuilt sufficiently to accommodate a passenger car, if not a freight train. These were clearly free special trains run by the M&NA to bring supporters to Harrison. The owner of the Strand Theater in Leslie, Leon Bland Greenhaw, boarded the train to do business in Harrison. When it was learned he was not there to support the railroad, the conductor put him off the train at Cove, five miles north of Leslie. Although he offered to pay the standard fare, he was ejected in a pouring rain with three pieces of heavy luggage. He had to walk to a farmhouse, where he convinced someone to take him by wagon to Marshall through rain and mud.[19]

The meeting of approximately a thousand people in Harrison's Lyric Theater on March 24 announced twenty-four-hour patrols of the railroad line in Carroll, Boone, and Searcy Counties. The assembly repeated the earlier resolutions against the strike and the "bolshevist" destruction of property and called again for Mayor Trimble's resignation. The meeting allowed for much speechmaking. The *Boone County Headlight* reported that perhaps a score of prominent men from up and down the line spoke, the most long-winded being Judge J. S. Maples and county judge Joe S. Fancher of Berryville, attorney Andrew L. Kinney of Green Forest, attorneys Jackson F. Henley and Stephen W. Woods of Marshall, and attorney John I. Worthington of Harrison. Edmund M. Mays, a thirty-eight-year-old manufacturer and banker in Leslie, gave the keynote address. He asserted that the M&NA was really the property of the people it served, not of the financiers far away in St. Louis, who had never seen any return on their investment. "We need the road and must have it," he said. Mays criticized the citizens of Harrison for stealing the shops from Leslie back in 1913 and then not protecting the new employees when they came during the strike. The good people of Leslie, he said, had taken strikebreakers there into their homes. As a final jab at Harrison, Mays said that the folks of Leslie would never have allowed a bunch of union agitators to set up their headquarters in the town. If it had happened in Leslie, he said, "They'd be out of here before the sun sets tonight and they'd stay out."[20]

The meeting picked up on Mays's suggestion to eject the agitators. It appointed a committee, with Woods as chair and with one man representing each county, tasked with informing the union representatives that they were being held accountable for the destruction of property and that they should leave the state. The committee members walked from the Lyric Theater to the Midway Hotel, where the representatives were staying, only to find out that they were being held by the court under a $500 bond. Sheriff Johnson assured the committee that the men "would be placed where they could commit no more depredations in Arkansas."[21]

By early April, these citizen supporters of the railroad had decided that speechmaking and "resoluting" had gotten them nowhere. The Boone County grand jury adjourned on March 31 and released the union representatives from their summons. The seven officials who were still in Harrison were now free to go, as requested by the citizens' assembly. Instead, they stayed in their rooms at the Midway Hotel. On April 2, a committee of three bankers, James M. Wagley, Walter S. Pettit, and Robert A. Wilson, visited them on behalf of the Protective League and again suggested that they leave, indicating that they faced danger if they stayed in Harrison. The union officials said that the headquarters of both the M&NA and the local unions were in Harrison, so they were staying. Four days later, on Wednesday, April 6, the M&NA ran its special trains again to bring a crowd back to Harrison. Others arrived by car, by wagon, and on foot. This time there were contingents from the Missouri side of the line and as far south as Cotton Plant in the Arkansas Delta. About six hundred from out of town joined several hundred citizens of Harrison as the crowd assembled at the railroad yards about midday. No speechmaking was necessary. They simply selected their leaders and began their march to the Midway Hotel to "visit" the union representatives, with the "invitation" that they immediately depart the state of Arkansas.[22]

Strikers and their union leaders had gotten wind of what was to come when the special trains were observed in the wee hours of April 6 leaving Harrison, heading north and south to pick up the mob. Before noon, leaders summoned strikers to Union Hall on the main square and gave them instructions to stay at home that day, no matter what might happen to the union leaders. It appears that strikers generally followed these instructions. At around 2:00 p.m., a crowd of approximately seven hundred arrived downtown and surrounded the Midway Hotel. The owner/manager of the hotel, George W. O'Neal, expressed concern about the mob outside his establishment, but he allowed a delegation of eleven men to enter the hotel parlor. There, the appointed leader, Jackson Henley of Marshall, told the union leaders that they had to leave Harrison and the state at once. Martin Carey, the representative for the Order of Railway Conductors, resisted on behalf of the union leaders. Henley said that his group would hear no argument and gave the men five minutes to confer. The representatives reluctantly agreed to leave. They immediately packed their bags and left Harrison by automobile, but as they were departing they asked permission to stay overnight in Eureka Springs and drive out of state the next day. The delegation agreed. This was apparently a ruse on the part of the union representatives, for the convoy instead drove directly to Branson, where they could make rail connections. Carroll County sheriff Ed McShane and a group of citizens in Eureka Springs made the rounds of the hotels looking for the union men and two wives, prepared to tell them that "anybody not good enough to stay in Harrison is not good enough for Eureka." McShane said he could have three hundred men in the streets within fifteen minutes to enforce this ultimatum. Fortunately, it was not necessary. Some of the union leaders returned to their homes from Branson, but Carey and L. B. Eddy traveled on to Joplin, from where they planned to keep in touch with strikers in Harrison by phone. Two other brotherhood representatives, W. J. Potts and George W. Anderson, soon joined them in Joplin.[23]

The two sides tried to spin the story of what happened on April 6 in contrary ways. Heads of the railroad brotherhoods sent Governor McRae a telegram alleging that an armed mob had expelled their representatives from Harrison. McRae washed his hands of the matter, indicating that he had no plans to investigate and that the unions had no recourse other than the courts. After a few days in Joplin, Carey, Eddy, and Potts left for Washington, DC. They eventually landed a meeting at the White House with President Harding and Senator Albert B. Cummins (R-IA). The union officials alleged that the mob that had expelled them from Harrison had been heavily armed and that many had been intoxicated. Other union representatives and local leader Tillman Jines told the press that they had observed men

Labor's take on the expulsion of the national railway union officials. *Labor, April 30, 1921.*

in the crowd carrying shotguns and revolvers and drinking whiskey out of fruit jars. Two years later, at the legislative hearings, one striker reported that the special train that had picked up men that morning in Leslie had also acquired a cargo of "white mule," another name for illegal moonshine. Another striker claimed that general manager Phelan and superintendent James Reddoch had taken charge of the mob upon the train's arrival in Harrison and outfitted some men with rifles and ammunition. An 1881 law had made it illegal to carry concealed weapons in Arkansas, with the understanding that the visible carrying of weapons was for acceptable purposes like hunting, not for threatening behavior or criminal activity.[24]

On the other hand, Jackson Henley, chair of the delegation that had met with the union representatives in the parlor of the Midway Hotel, disputed the characterization of the crowd as a drunken mob. Woods said that he had not seen or smelled liquor on any participant, nor had he seen any guns or heard any threats of violence. He denied that his group had made any threat to the men, directly or indirectly. But yet he told the legislators that northern Arkansas was "not conducive to the health, happiness, and prosperity of men of the Carey type," clearly an implied threat.[25]

The citizens who expelled the officials of the railroad brotherhoods had the deluded idea that the strike might end, or that at least the property violence would cease, after these outsiders were gone. They were wrong. On April 12, Harrison's Protective League, which now claimed three hundred members, called three local strike leaders—James Queen, Tillman Jines, and Pete Venable—to appear. Attorney and league member John Worthington read a prepared address, gave the strikers a copy, allowed no discussion, and then dismissed them. He gave them notice that the league would not allow the railroad to be junked and that all interference with its operation must cease. Instead, attacks against railroad property and harassment of strikebreakers not only continued but extended farther up and down the line. Two more bridges were burned in the month of April. Jack Murray, the railroad's traffic manager, issued a public statement declaring that telegraph wires had been grounded, spikes pulled, switches thrown, blue vitriol placed in water tanks, and emery dust inserted in bearings and other parts of engines, all causing expensive damage. By April 25, the court of Boone County had paid out $2,192.50 to nearly a hundred men for their services in guarding the track and property of the M&NA. Jesse Lewis Russell, editor of the *Boone County Headlight* and a founding member of Harrison's Protective League, said that the town's citizens were spending an additional $500 a week to protect the railroad.[26]

The justice system continued its assault on the unions. Sheriff Johnson arrested two new men employed by the M&NA as coppersmiths on suspicion that they were spies giving information to enemies of the railroad. They were tried under the charge of conspiracy, then fined and released. In federal court in Little Rock, Judge Trieber was still hearing cases in late April of strikers accused of harassing strikebreakers. He sentenced one, Claude Binkley, a union machinist of Harrison, to six months in jail. Binkley's crime had been to curse and verbally threaten strikebreakers and the citizens of Harrison in general.[27]

As they received the accusations of espionage, verbal abuse, and property violence, strikers gained the sympathy of workers on other lines where the M&NA made connections. Several union ticket agents of other railroads refused to allow nonunion agents of the M&NA to sell tickets in joint offices where the lines intersected. The M&NA

was forced to set up boxcars on its own right-of-way to sell tickets at Neosho and Seligman in Missouri, and at Kensett, Wheatley, and Helena in Arkansas. These union agents also allegedly bad-mouthed the M&NA, discouraging prospective passengers from riding on a road they deemed dangerous and inefficient.[28]

Union officials and local strike leaders engaged in a relentless propaganda campaign. The editors of *Labor* sent several thousand copies of its account of the April 6 mob action from Washington, DC, to Harrison to counter the version promoted in local newspapers. W. C. Jenkins, the representative of the shopmen, picked up a pen after his return home to Illinois and castigated the M&NA for its shoddy service and safety record, publishing his account in the *Railway Federationist*, the official paper of the AFL's Railroad Employees Department. Passengers should not put their lives in the hands of the inexperienced casual laborers—"roughnecks and river rats" as he called them—who now ran the M&NA's trains. Jenkins said that by mid-May the company's employees were already complaining that they had not received wages for six weeks. He described a collision that had occurred on April 27, when the M&NA's train no. 20 had disregarded signals and rammed the Rock Island no. 46 at the crossing at Wheatley, causing the M&NA engine and sixteen cars to turn over. Traffic on both lines was delayed by four hours. The *Railway Federationist* also published a report submitted to the Bureau of Locomotive Inspection in Washington, DC, that cataloged a list of several dozen safety issues in April alone. Violations of basic operation ranged from inoperative brakes, leaking pipes, and defective air gauges to loose and missing bolts. Improperly maintained ash pans and fireboxes that dropped coal and hot cinders, the paper asserted, likely explained the burned bridges—instead of intentional arson, as alleged by the railroad. Pickets along the line reported that conditions were so dire that traffic manager Murray rode almost every train.[29]

The railroad experienced a public relations disaster in early June, when its general manager and two prominent supporters were prosecuted for shooting up the town during a drunken spree. Allegedly, in the early morning hours, Charles Phelan was drinking white mule with Walter L. Snapp, an orchardist and leading member of the Protective League (Snapp was also on the payroll as a "special agent" of the M&NA). At around 1:30 a.m. on Friday, June 3, the men took a walk around the downtown square going from Phelan's office to a local establishment, Wilson's Restaurant, firing guns along the way. They saw the lights on in the office of Dr. Charles M. Routh, and the two visited him for a while. Routh and Snapp were two of the eleven men who had entered the Midway Hotel on April 6 to expel the union officials, when Snapp was alleged to have been brandishing a pistol. Snapp and Phelan collected Routh, and the three men continued carousing through downtown Harrison. Some strikers on picket duty summoned a constable, John Toney, and a deputy marshal, Jake Reed. Others walked to the county jail and complained to the deputy sheriff on duty, who apparently consulted with Sheriff Johnson and Judge Shinn. The officers talked to the drunken men but did not detain or disarm them. Later, strikers and other bystanders reported seeing the three men riding in Snapp's car, shooting as they drove east across the railroad tracks and toward Eagle Heights, a neighborhood where many strikers lived. There more gunshots followed. The three men continued driving around town, shooting, until around 6:25 a.m. The whole population of Harrison must have heard the gunfire. As if this were not enough, on the following day, a Saturday when the streets were full of people, a drunk Phelan wandered around downtown after the supper hour, merrily greeting people, even strikers. Some of the Protective League leaders and Phelan's management team, including Murray and the M&NA lawyer J. Sam Rowland, tried to get him off the streets. Finally, about midnight, superintendent Reddoch got Phelan in his car and drove him away.[30]

Two weeks later, on Saturday, June 18, Phelan, Snapp, and Routh appeared before Mayor Trimble in municipal court, charged with brandishing weapons and disturbing the peace. Given that no officer of the law had arrested the men, city attorney Oscar W. Hudgins prosecuted the case based on affidavits from strikers and testimony from some other witnesses to the events who had no connection to the railroad. Phelan and Snapp acted as if they considered the trial a joke and made no effort to cross-examine witnesses or present any defense. In the presentation of the evidence, Dr. Routh came off as more of a peacemaker than a Wild West gunslinger, so Trimble acquitted him. But the mayor found Phelan and Snapp guilty and fined each man fifty dollars for the weapons charge per Arkansas's

1881 gun law, and seventy-five dollars for disturbance of the peace. The two defendants announced their intention to appeal to Judge Shinn's circuit court.[31]

Meanwhile, allegations of sabotage along the railroad continued. Reports surfaced of a shipment from Carthage, Missouri, via the White River Line, of a large quantity of emery dust to Tillman Jines. Someone found a bomb in a coal chute and more blue vitriol in water tanks at Harrison. The *Railway Federationist* on July 9 alleged that pickets in Harrison had observed Dr. Routh and Ben Rowland, a local automobile dealer, prowling near the shop yards and under the nearby railroad bridge over Crooked Creek, around midnight. The next day a bomb was discovered and wires cut, and the company blamed it all on strikers. Routh held Pete Venable responsible for the article, sued him in circuit court for $50,000 for defamation of character, and forced Venable at gunpoint to sign a retraction. Venable denied any responsibility for the article and secured an injunction from chancery court to keep the retraction from being published, arguing that he had signed the statement under duress.[32] By summer, Venable had clearly emerged as the most radical of the strike leaders, even though he officially held the lesser office of local secretary of the Order of Railway Conductors.

Faced with continuing bad publicity, an intractable standoff with the strikers, and an inability to meet payroll, Phelan experienced a meltdown of sorts. He left Harrison on Friday, July 8, and on the next day he mailed from St. Louis letters of resignation as general manager and receiver to Judge Trieber and heads of various departments of the railroad. Venable asserted that the transcripts of Phelan's trial in municipal court had been submitted to Judge Trieber and that the company had removed Phelan as general manager. In any case, a representative of the investors in St. Louis, Charles Gilbert, traveled to Little Rock to confer with Trieber as to who should succeed Phelan. Superintendent Reddoch appeared the most likely candidate, given that he had previously served as general manager for a year and a half. Instead, he resigned his position with the M&NA, nursing a broken arm. Reddoch may have been passed over for the top job because in April he had admitted that inexperienced strikebreakers had left switches open and improperly maintained engines. He said that management of the Frisco and Kansas City Southern had complained that the M&NA engines had dropped fire on the segments of the line owned by these two railroads. Somehow, the brotherhoods' newspaper, *Labor*, got hold of Reddoch's statements and published them. Trieber and Gilbert on July 18 named Jack Murray, the railroad's traffic manager, as both general manager and receiver. Acting for Trieber, who went away on vacation, federal judge Frank A. Youmans of Fort Smith told Murray that if the railroad could not meet its July 15 payroll by July 20, it would be shut down. Representatives from communities up and down the line met with Murray at Rotary Hall in Harrison and asked the railroad to continue service from Kensett, or at least Leslie, to meet the Frisco Line at Seligman. To do so, Murray said, the citizens would need to raise $150,000. When this did not happen and the M&NA could not make its payment, Murray and J. Sam Rowland petitioned Judge Youmans to close the line. On July 23 Youmans ordered the M&NA to suspend operations effective July 31. The railroad's employees began leaving Harrison and other towns along the line to look for work elsewhere.[33]

It appears that the strike destroyed Phelan both professionally and personally. Shortly before he resigned, he sent his family out of Harrison to the tranquil forests near Sault Ste. Marie, Ontario. From St. Louis, where Phelan mailed his resignation letters, he traveled to Detroit, presumably on his way to join his wife and five children. He was never heard from again. Mrs. Ellen Phelan had brought her family to Chicago by September. Two years later, a widely circulated press release indicated that she was running a boardinghouse there, abandoned by her husband. Mrs. Phelan said that Festus J. Wade, the chief St. Louis financier of the M&NA (who had hired Phelan in 1916 and again in 1920), had offered to send Phelan to a sanitarium if he could be found. Her husband had given no signs, she said, of being "mentally unstrung." What happened to Charles Phelan remains a mystery.[34]

Phelan was both a perpetrator and a victim in this war between business and labor in 1921. His stubborn unwillingness to compromise with union demands certainly led to the failure to preserve his job and to operate the railroad. Some compromise, a smaller pay cut perhaps or an agreement to hire back striking shopmen, would likely have kept union men working. Instead, on June 20 Phelan expanded the 20 percent pay cut to 25 percent, further ruining any chance of getting strikers back to work.

The national representatives from the union brotherhoods who camped in Harrison from late February to April 6 discouraged compromise on the side of labor. But they clearly understood that rail companies across the nation were seeking to reduce the wages inflated from the government controls during the Great War. In mid-April, shortly after the mob expelled the union officials from Harrison, the RLB held hearings with several railroads asking for wage reductions, following the lead of the M&NA. At this time, presidential appointments for expiring positions of the RLB moved the needle on the board toward a procarrier position. President Harding appointed Walter McMenimen for one of the labor seats, despite protests from the railroad brotherhoods. In his other appointment, Harding chose Ben Hooper, the former governor of Tennessee, for a public seat designated as nonbiased. Hooper's strong support for the railroad companies quickly became obvious; at one point he even publicly called for the banning of strikes on the nation's railroads. By June 1921, the RLB approved wage cuts across the railroad industry nationwide averaging 12.5 percent, effective July 1. This reduction had no impact on the M&NA, given that Phelan had already cut wages by 25 percent. A year later, with Ben Hooper as chair, the RLB would approve another 12 percent wage cut, thereby bringing on the two-month-long national shopmen's strike, the largest railroad strike since the Pullman strike of 1894.[35] The union officials clearly wished to take a stand with the M&NA in 1921 for the sake of the bigger picture, and they failed.

The most tragic consequence of the 1921 strike was the way it disrupted communities along the M&NA line. Just like the Civil War had done when it fractured this same area sixty years before, the strike split Ozark residents into warring factions in just a few months' time. Each side lost empathy for the other. The "home boys" employed by the railroad became "bolsheviks" and "anarchists" in the minds of the railroad's supporters. The crowd that assembled in Harrison on April 6 became a mob intent on actions that were clearly illegal. While Mayor Trimble clearly favored the strikers, the county and state justice system, as well as the federal court, either supported or acquiesced to the mob.

The *North Arkansas Star* of Berryville, on June 17, 1921, editorialized that what Harrison needed was "a good strong camp of the Ku Klux Klan." "The best medicine for idle strikers," the editor said, was "a few masked men with a good bull whip." He was not alone in this thinking. Within just a few weeks, two recruiters arrived in Little Rock to organize the Ku Klux Klan in Arkansas. By the following summer, there were Klan chapters along the M&NA line in Helena, Wheatley, Cotton Plant, Searcy, Heber Springs, Leslie, Marshall, Harrison, Berryville, and Eureka Springs in Arkansas, and Neosho and Joplin in Missouri.[36] The April 6 mob action would foreshadow, like a dress rehearsal, a more violent blowout, organized and manned by Klansmen, that targeted not just union officials from out of state, but local strikers and sympathizers. This mob violence marked the de facto end of the strike in January 1923.

CHAPTER 3

NO TRAINS RUN: AUGUST 1921–MAY 1922

AS THE M&NA'S LAST trains rolled through the Ozarks, communities along the line went into deep mourning. The final scheduled passenger train left Harrison on Sunday, July 31, at 3:35 p.m. Around three hundred people, including numerous strikers, gathered at the depot on Stephenson Avenue to say farewell. Someone had hung black crepe over the doors of the office, and crews draped black banners and ribbons on the train. Over the next week the railroad moved all its rolling stock from up and down the line to store in the yards in Harrison. As the last of the freight cars pulled out of Joplin on August 4 bound for Harrison, railroad men for the other lines came out of their offices to watch and then returned to work.[1]

In the nine months of the railroad's suspension, residents threw themselves into a flurry of activity to improve their existing surface roads to connecting points on other rail lines, a laborious and expensive task. They also made efforts to find a buyer for the M&NA. As these efforts failed, the investors in St. Louis and the new general manager, Jack Murray, reached out to the federal government in hopes of a loan sufficient to get the trains running again. Meanwhile, the strikers loitered on the streets of Harrison, Leslie, and other towns along the line.

Since the railroad's arrival in the first decade of the century, a large portion of the area had become dependent on the M&NA for essential services. The suspension of the M&NA's service had little impact on residents of the 60-mile Missouri segment of the line, given that about half of the M&NA route there ran on tracks of other railroads, the Frisco and Kansas City Southern. Similarly, in the 70 miles from Kensett to Helena, three other railroad lines traversed the flat delta, providing access for freight and passenger traffic. It was the

210-mile section in the Arkansas Ozarks with no other rail connections, between the Missouri state line and Searcy, that would be most damaged by the suspension of the M&NA.

The railroad had previously brought daily mail to communities up and down the line, with postmen then taking bundles of mail by automobile, and even wagon, to small post offices in rural areas. New arrangements were necessary immediately to receive and send mail. Within days Harrison began receiving its mail by way of Bergman on the White River Line. While the ten miles of dirt road were steep and rocky, Harrison was lucky to be at the closest point to another rail line of all the towns along the M&NA between Seligman and Searcy. Trucks took mail from Harrison north to Alpena and south to Everton and Pindall. Mail carriers took the post from Pindall on treacherous roads west to Jasper to serve the entirety of Newton County. Eureka Springs was also relatively well positioned. By 1921 the resort town had one of the only hard surface roads in the Ozarks, connecting it to the Frisco's rail line at Seligman. The ride took just an hour, with one-way taxi fare of $2.25. Citizens of Eureka Springs received daily mail just as they had with rail service, and in fact got their morning papers even earlier than before. From Eureka, mail traveled by truck to Berryville and Green Forest, with the day's mail getting to the end of the route by 1:00 p.m.[2]

Other communities were not so fortunate. Clinton and Shirley, in Van Buren County, began getting mail by way of the Missouri Pacific connection in Morrilton, fifty-two miles to the southeast. Previously, Porter Johnson had carried mail from Shirley's M&NA depot to Clinton, but after August 1 he began a long day's journey from Shirley to Clinton to Morrilton and back. Besides carrying the mail, he could accommodate two passengers riding along. Heber Springs began receiving mail trucked in over rugged roads from Searcy, but it arrived four hours later than before. By the end of the year, businessmen in Heber Springs were petitioning the US Post Office Department to bring their mail from Conway, forty-two miles to the south, because the roads were better. Marshall and Leslie, for their part, began getting mail from the Sylamore station on the White River Line, approximately forty miles away on terrible roads.[3]

Immediately after the suspension of the railroad, county judges in the Arkansas Ozarks began ambitious work programs to improve the roads. Besides the hard surface road between Eureka Springs and Seligman, some towns like Harrison had a few streets that had been paved. There were some "all-weather" roads of gravel. But the majority of Ozark roads were little better than dirt trails, rocky and steep, and in wet or icy weather practically impassable. The roads certainly were not suitable for heavy hauling. The whole area serviced by the M&NA became a road construction zone in the late summer and fall of 1921. Heber Springs had rough mountainous roads in all directions. White County to the east and Faulkner County to the south quickly began competing in their construction efforts, grading and improving the roads to connect Heber Springs to Searcy or, alternatively, Conway. By October, White County had completed the road west to the Cleburne County line, and by the end of the year Faulkner County was constructing a hard top road from Conway north to the boundary with Cleburne County. Newton County, which had depended on Harrison as its shipping point, began improvement of a road to connect with the Missouri Pacific a hundred miles to the south, at Russellville. A four-mile stretch of the Marshall–Sylamore Road was completely impassable, and work began in August to make it accessible to truck and wagon. The Harrison Rotary Club members volunteered fifteen to twenty trucks to haul gravel to improve the Bergman Road. Even the state got involved. When the Arkansas Highway Department learned in December that it would receive twelve tractors from the US Department of War, officials announced that they would be loaned to counties previously served by the M&NA. An unusually dry fall aided the efforts to improve the roads.[4]

Automobile and wagon traffic plied the improving roads. Taxis ran regularly between Harrison and Bergman, and Eureka Springs and Seligman. Jitney service, unlicensed vehicles that offered regular rideshare transportation, connected travelers from the smaller communities to market towns and the nearest rail connections. Trucks and wagons carried out agricultural produce and some lighter timber products and brought in essentials supplies. Merchants in the towns had been given two weeks of advance notice before the railroad shut down, so they had stockpiled as much merchandise as was possible. Nonetheless, there was much rejoicing when the first shipment of ice arrived in Marshall in the hot August weather, having been shipped down the White River Line from the ice plant in Cotter, and then trucked the forty miles from the Sylamore station. To serve soda fountain drinks to tourists, Eureka Springs had its ice transported from Rogers, thirty miles to the west. By the end of the year, Sylamore, six miles north of Mountain View in Stone County, was handling goods going to a large area of Stone, Van Buren, and Searcy Counties. On one day in December, 1,300 pounds of sugar and 1,000 pounds of coffee were unloaded there to haul to stores across the Ozarks. Wagons pulled by a team of horses often hauled heavier cargo. On a single day in April 1922, someone observed 200 wagons loaded with chickens from the southern parts of Searcy County pass through St. Joe on their way to Harrison, the collecting point, from where the poultry was trucked to meet the train in Bergman. Eggs, milk, and cream were transported out of Boone and Carroll Counties, but at less of a profit than before. Livestock, previously shipped on the M&NA, had to be driven overland, in scenes reminiscent of earlier days, to the nearest rail point. Farmers complained that the drives expended a large portion of the body weight of the animals and thus profits. They gave up sending calves for the veal market, for they could not survive the journey. After the cotton harvest in Searcy County in January 1922, a string of 75 wagons hauled 226 bales of cotton from Marshall to meet the train in Sylamore. As a sign of how badly people needed work, 167 showed up when an advertisement asked for teams and wagons to haul the cotton.[5]

As folks figured out how to manage without a railroad, community leaders looked for a person or company to buy the North Arkansas Line and get it running again. The Arkansas Railroad Commission solicited buyers to no avail. In August 1921, a group of Harrison businessmen corresponded with the head of the Missouri Pacific Railroad, Benjamin Franklin Bush, to inquire about a spur to connect the town to Bergman. Bush unequivocally said no. When the vice president of the Frisco Line, T. A. Hamilton, visited Harrison by automobile in late August, a round of rumors spread that the line might take over the M&NA. This, too, came to nothing. Some prominent business leaders in Harrison floated the idea of raising a half million dollars to purchase the north end of the tracks and sufficient rolling stock to get the railroad running to Missouri. Leslie's Export Cooperage, the reconstituted H. D. Williams Cooperage after the great fire of 1912, tried unsuccessfully in September to lease a section of the M&NA tracks between Leslie and Kensett to carry freight and passengers to the Missouri Pacific. Around the same time in Helena, a committee of prominent citizens conferred with E. C. Nelson, the manager of the Chicago Mill and Lumber Company there, about a way to move company lumber trains on the M&NA tracks from Cotton Plant to Helena. Again, the plan failed.[6]

The most ambitious, and ludicrous, plan was an attempt to convince Henry Ford to purchase the M&NA. The idea apparently originated in late August within the Joplin Chamber of Commerce. The Rotary Club of Harrison led the efforts there. By September 6, a delegation of nine men representing towns up and down the line, from Joplin to Helena, left for Detroit, seeking a meeting with the automobile magnate. Robert A. Wilson of the Protective League represented Harrison. The banker William C. Johnson and the wood manufacturer/banker Edmund M. Mays represented Heber Springs and Leslie, respectively. Ford was away in Washington, DC, but his representative and private secretary, Ernest G. Liebold, met with the group. He listened attentively to their proposal, gave them a tour of the Ford plant, and assured them he would bring the matter to Ford's attention. They returned to Missouri and Arkansas to await Ford's decision. It never came.[7]

Even though residents tried to make alternative arrangements to ship products and get supplies, residents in the Arkansas Ozarks experienced tremendous economic suffering in the last half of 1921 and first half of 1922. Orchardists had planted tens of thousands of apple, peach, and pear trees after the railroad penetrated Carroll, Boone, and Searcy Counties. Strawberries had become a cash crop in Searcy County, an area so rugged that it offered few opportunities for commercial agriculture. The uncertainty about transporting crops to market by truck or wagon over jarring roads (especially something as fragile as strawberries) created much stress for fruit farmers. Some fruit and berries, in the more remote areas, were left to rot in the fields. Dairy and poultry products continued to bounce along the bumpy roads, but at less of a profit than before. One dairy farmer in Zack, Wallace A. Rogers, began turning his milk into cheese and selling it to stores in the area because of the challenges of transporting raw milk.[8]

The greatest suffering came for those whose livelihood depended on the timber industry. The economies of Searcy, Van Buren, and

Cleburne Counties had largely shifted to timber and wood products after the M&NA laid tracks through the area. The product was simply too heavy and bulky to ship profitably by wagon or truck over the poor roads. Through the nine months the railroad was inactive, hundreds of thousands of dollars' worth of lumber and wood products sat decaying on the rail switches alongside the main tracks of the M&NA. Farmers who supplemented their meager incomes in the winter months by cutting ties for the railroad or selling wood to the mills lost this opportunity.[9]

Timber and the train had accounted for Leslie's boom from just a tiny village to the largest town in Searcy County, with nearly two thousand people. With the multiple wood manufacturers there, the town was probably the hardest hit by the railroad's suspension. The companies shut down completely, their existing inventory of wood products stacked up alongside the tracks in Leslie. Many of the hundreds of employees in Leslie and the forests to the south and west began to leave, looking for work elsewhere. The Export Cooperage Company allowed workers in company housing in Leslie to live rent free through the winter and until service on the railroad began again in May, but by the beginning of 1922 they had exhausted credit at stores, and their families were facing starvation. The principal of the Leslie schools, Irene Jones, observed that children were dropping out of school because they lacked shoes, clothing, and supplies. Others were coming to school clearly malnourished and inadequately clothed. Students went home at lunchtime, she discovered, and returned pretending that they had eaten. Some families lived for two weeks eating nothing but dry corn bread, with perhaps a bit of molasses. She began a donation drive for clothing and food. She convinced the Red Cross to fund a program to feed about thirty-five to forty students breakfast and lunch in a basement room at the school. Teachers and high school girls did the cooking. Local grocers and farmers donated food and gallons of fresh milk daily, and farmers brought meat, potatoes, and other vegetables they had raised or grown at home. Irene Jones continued feeding the students in Leslie from January through May.[10]

Besides farmers and workers in wood, others felt the bite from the railroad's suspension. Inflation hit all products that had to be shipped into the area, from fuels such as gasoline and coal, to staple foods like coffee, sugar, and flour, to manufactured products. Three businesses in Harrison went bankrupt, and businessmen up and down the line lost their life savings. St. Joe storekeepers said that their business declined by half during the nine months the railroad did not run. Merchants who could afford to extend credit for staples did so to their own peril. Business revenue dropped by half in Pangburn, a small town in White County founded when the M&NA came through the area. Insurance companies stopped writing policies for residents of the town, deeming them an undesirable risk. The *Leslie News* closed its doors, and its editor, Merton Smith, moved to Harrison to work for the *Boone County Headlight*. While inflation and unemployment went up, property values were going down. A Harrison real estate agent said that already by September 1921 the value of farmland in the area had dropped 25 to 40 percent, and that even with the diminished price for land it was hard to find prospective buyers. In Van Buren and Cleburne Counties, which had become wholly dependent on timber exploitation, property values had depreciated by 40 to 75 percent. An outward migration began, especially in Edgemont, Shirley, and Elba; others lacked the resources to move. Pangburn and Leslie would never regain the population they lost with the suspension of the railroad. Many of those who remained found themselves unable to pay their taxes. In their winter term, grand juries of Searcy, Van Buren, and Cleburne Counties petitioned Governor Thomas C. McRae to extend the deadline for tax payment to July 1922. The governor complied with the request.[11]

As people experienced the economic fallout from the suspension of the railroad, their animosity toward strikers in Eureka Springs, Leslie, Pangburn, Heber Springs, Harrison, and other towns only grew. Some strikers worked on farms or found other jobs in their neighborhoods. Some left the area to find work. The *Harrison Daily Times* reported that a third of the town's strikers departed on September 6, many of them bound for California, where jobs were awaiting them. But the largest number stayed and drew their union benefits. They loitered in groups on street corners or in parks, perhaps did some picketing, and registered daily at Union Hall on the courthouse square. Strikers received benefits ranging from $30 to $150 a month, depending on the brotherhood in which they held membership. Dispatchers made the most, shopmen and maintenance of way men the least. Most strikers received from $60 to $100 a month. The Maintenance of Way Brotherhood assessed all its members nationwide an extra fifty cents a month to increase the strike benefit for the M&NA strikers. A few fights erupted and threats were uttered between strikers and strikebreakers who remained in Harrison, but generally the bickering died down and the damage to railroad property ceased during the nine months the trains did not run.[12]

By late September, when it became clear that no one wished to buy the M&NA, the investors began planning for a way to get the trains running again. From October until the railroad resumed service in May, a complicated and drawn-out series of negotiations followed, involving the St. Louis owners, the railroad administration in Harrison, politicians, the Interstate Commerce Commission (ICC), the Railroad Labor Board (RLB), national union officials, and local leaders of the strikers. The leader of the St. Louis investors, Festus J. Wade, met in late September in Washington with both Arkansas senators, Joe T. Robinson and Thaddeus Caraway, and the two representatives whose districts lay in the path of the M&NA, William Oldfield and John Tillman. The elected officials encouraged Wade to approach the ICC about a way to get the railroad afloat. Wade asked the ICC for $3.5 million: $3 million to pay off the remaining receiver's certificates and other debts, and an additional half million for the necessary rehabilitation of the railroad's property.

The next step was to approach the unions with an offer. Wade invited local representatives from the Big Four brotherhoods to meet with him and general manager Murray in St. Louis on October 10. James E. Queen, the head of the local strikers' committee, led the delegation, which was brought to St. Louis at Wade's personal expense. At this meeting, Murray and Wade presented the strikers with a written proposal, of which the key provision was that unions accept a 25 percent wage reduction from the present national scale approved by the RLB. This proposal, of course, asked the unions to accept a larger wage cut than the reduction that had started the strike. However, Wade and Murray made a major concession. They specified that the wage rate would be reviewed yearly, and that any profit generated in excess of expenses would go toward raises for all employees. This process would continue until wages were restored to the national scale. Wade pledged that owners would not receive one cent until the government loan was paid off and wage levels met the national scale.

Compared to the hard-nosed position taken by former general manager Charles Albert Phelan, the offer showed a desire to have union labor. From the perspective of history, it seems like a fair offer.[13]

Wade traveled to Chicago the following day to present the plan to national union officials there. The local representatives were to return to Harrison and then caucus with committees of strikers in towns up and down the line. Strikers had convinced Wade to request that the Protective Leagues in Harrison and elsewhere guarantee safe travel for the union representatives to consult with committees of strikers along the M&NA. Evidently, these union men feared violence if they traveled through communities that had suffered mightily on account of the strike. It appears that after Queen and other strike leaders caucused with the strikers in Missouri and Arkansas, most of the rank and file favored resuming work at the lower wages, while leaders of the local strike committees wanted to remain on strike. Queen emerged as the spokesman for compromise, while others followed the lead of Pete Venable, who wanted nothing less than victory. The negotiations came to a standstill, and finally, by the beginning of December, the unions rejected Wade's offer. It is not clear whether it was the union officials in Chicago or the strikers themselves, or both, who chose to continue the strike.[14]

Murray and Wade moved to implement their plan to resume railroad service with or without the strikers. Wade returned to Washington, where he met with President Warren G. Harding and the ICC to sort out the details of the $3.5 million government loan. The plan now involved a redivision of the percentage of freight payments with other railroads for their joint hauls. Murray asked the RLB for a hearing to pitch the proposal, essentially the same plan of October 10 that the unions had rejected. Union officials and local strike leaders petitioned the RLB to keep this hearing from taking place. They said that in the meetings of October 10 and 11 in St. Louis and Chicago, the railroad company had presented an ultimatum, not engaged in negotiations as required by the Transportation Act of 1920 and the RLB. Strikers argued that, moreover, the M&NA already stood in contempt by failing to comply with the board's original recommendation of February 8, 1921. Lastly, union officials said that the RLB lacked jurisdiction over a railroad that existed only on paper, a carrier that did not run on tracks. Despite these efforts by labor, the RLB set a hearing for February 15, 1922.[15]

Hopes elevated for the resumption of railroad service as news of the plan passed through the towns along the line. The American Legion organized a mass meeting of five hundred citizens in Heber Springs and sent petitions supporting the proposal to the ICC, the RLB, Governor McRae, federal judge Jacob Trieber, Wade, and others. Similar meetings took place in Eureka Springs, Helena, Harrison, Leslie, Cotton Plant, Kensett, Marshall, and Shirley. A hundred businessmen in Joplin signed a petition of support for Wade's plan. Governor McRae communicated his support to the ICC.[16]

During the first three months of 1922, various levels of the federal government helped the M&NA in its plans to resume operation. The ICC held two and a half days of hearings on January 16–18 to redistribute the freight payments. Besides Murray, Wade, and Charles Gilbert attending for the M&NA, representatives were there from the Missouri Pacific, Frisco, Kansas City Southern, Missouri-Kansas-Texas, Illinois Central, Santa Fe, and Yazoo and Mississippi Valley lines. The M&NA officials proposed a 25 percent increase in the share the carrier would receive. Senator Robinson, Congressman Tillman, and Jack Murray made presentations in favor of the redistribution. The representatives from the other lines, as one would expect, opposed the plan. Wade offered an example of the proposed change: if an item cost $1.20 to ship from Harrison to San Francisco, the M&NA would previously have gotten twenty cents and the trunk line one dollar. But if the proposal was approved, the M&NA would receive forty cents and the longer carrier eighty cents. After much deliberation, the ICC approved the plan. Wade announced that the increased percentage would bring approximately $300,000 in additional earnings for the company.[17]

To facilitate the plan, Murray, Wade, and Judge Trieber made arrangements for the Missouri and North Arkansas Rail*road* to be reconstituted as a new company, the Missouri and North Arkansas Rail*way*. As part of the railroad receivership system, the ICC allowed railroads in financial distress to be reorganized as a new company with the assets sold in whole by the owners to themselves. This way the railroad would stay intact, instead of having its assets sold piecemeal. Trieber announced that the property of the old company would be sold at auction, with the lowest bid set at $3 million. Bidders would be required to post a forfeit of $20,000, an obvious attempt to discourage other prospective buyers. Clearly the arrangement set things up for the reconstituted M&NA to purchase itself. Judge Trieber set the date for the sale: April 10 at 3:00 p.m., at the south door of the Boone County Courthouse in Harrison.[18]

A final piece to come into place for the railroad was a positive decision from the RLB. Murray went to Chicago for a one-day hearing before the board on February 15. As expected, he proposed the plan for the 25 percent wage cut that unions had rejected two months earlier. If unions would accept the offer and strikers return to work, Murray said, the M&NA would become a closed-shop operation, a major concession on the part of management.

Wade had already explained to the ICC that "a man could support a family in the middle of Arkansas at one third of what is necessary in New York or Washington." Murray presented the board with an array of supporting materials, such as sworn statements about the lower cost of living in the railroad's service area and petitions by local citizens in favor of the railroad's plan. Three days after the meeting, the RLB issued decision 724, which granted the request for the wage reduction and rejected all the arguments posed by the unions. The board directed representatives of the railroad and strikers to meet by March 1 to "properly and fairly apply this decision"—in other words, to get back to work. Clearly, the RLB, now a year into President Harding's administration and under Ben Hooper as chair, took a different posture than it had when the strike had begun, three weeks before the Republican president was inaugurated.[19]

As directed by the RLB, Murray attempted to meet with strikers to discuss their return to work. The strikers continually stalled until the March 1 deadline had passed—another chance missed. The more radical strike leaders, Pete Venable and Tillman Jines, immediately went on a public relations campaign to discredit the ICC's deal with the railroad. Officials of the railroad brotherhoods in Chicago filed protests against the loan. They sent a flurry of letters and telegrams asking why the government would prop up a defunct railroad so that it could wage war against labor. The ICC's $3.5 million loan, they said, allowed the railroad's owners to pay themselves back what they had lent the company as holders of the receiver's certificates and moreover keep from losing their original investment if the line was scrapped. While the strikers presented a united front to the M&NA

and the public, others like James Queen believed they should take the offer of reduced wages and go back to work. Unhappy with the hard-line position that won out, Queen resigned as chair of the strikers' coordinating committee, although he remained on the committee as the leader of the conductors.[20]

In March and April, Murray and Wade moved ahead with plans to get the railroad running. Much work was to be done. Wade traveled back and forth between St. Louis and Washington to establish the details of the fifteen-year loan at 6 percent interest. His bank, the Mercantile Trust Company of St. Louis, managed the receipt and disbursements of the government funds. Wade summoned Murray to St. Louis to work out the details of the sale and restoration of the railroad's operation on an open-shop basis. Murray announced the expectation that the line would resume service again in May. He assured the nervous strawberry growers of Searcy County that the railroad would be able to ship their berries. He estimated that two hundred refrigerated cars would be committed for the strawberry crop. Orders for shipping began pouring in at the M&NA's office on the Harrison square. A rush of optimism swept the area. The pay reduction promised to save the company $310,000 annually, in addition to the $300,000 in earnings garnered through the freight payment redistribution. It looked like the M&NA might finally begin to turn a profit.

The businessmen of Harrison rejoiced and began to plan for better days. Harrison's Rotary Club unanimously elected Murray as an active member in recognition of his efforts in getting the railroad running again, and sent Wade a telegram of appreciation for his services. While all this activity was going on, there were municipal elections in Harrison. Retired businessman Jasper L. Clute ran against incumbent mayor Guy Trimble, who had championed the strikers. The Rotary Club, under the presidency of J. Sam Rowland, attorney for the M&NA, unanimously endorsed Clute as the "law and order candidate." The election was focused on the strike. Clute won narrowly on April 4, 1922. Venable said that the day after Clute's election, Walter L. Snapp and several other railroad supporters visited Clute to tell him what was expected of him. He rejected their directions in absolute terms. They then asked him to resign, which he refused to do. The Protective League threatened him throughout the rest of the year. The heavy-handed tactics of the railroad supporters backfired, pushing the mayor they had elected into the arms of the strikers.[21]

The sale of the Missouri and North Arkansas Railroad to the Missouri and North Arkansas Railway took place as planned on April 10. A crowd of five hundred people showed up at the courthouse to observe. The atmosphere was festive; stores held special sales to mark the occasion. Charles Gilbert came from St. Louis to place the bid on behalf of the reconstituted M&NA. Jack Murray, as the receiver, presided over the quick ceremony. The new company bought the old company for $3 million and, as expected, was the only bidder. The owners were the former investors of St. Louis who held the receiver's certificates, as well as stockholders, the largest being G. M. Pyle, who owned 29,991 shares. Murray, five other members of the railroad's management team in Harrison, and local lawyer John Worthington were also made owners, with one share each. Murray left immediately for Little Rock to report the sale to Judge Trieber.[22]

During the rest of April, Murray and the management staff in Harrison busied themselves preparing for the railroad to operate again in May. He and chief engineer Harry Armstrong traveled the length of the line to evaluate its condition. They found it in better shape than they had expected and announced that repair work would be minimal. They inspected the rolling stock parked in the Harrison yards and at a few other points on the line: 640 freight cars, 22 passenger cars, and 24 engines. The other urgent need was at least 700 workers to get the railroad running. Murray made one last overture to the strikers by calling their leaders to his office on the afternoon of April 25. He asked the group whether they were willing to accept decision 724 of the RLB, which offered them employment at the 25 percent wage reduction. William J. Harrelson of the Brotherhood of Locomotive Engineers was now the leader of the group, although James Queen was present as the representative for conductors. After some deliberation, the strike leaders unanimously rejected Murray's offer, saying that they did not consider it to be a living wage. Murray immediately directed his department heads to hire nonunion labor. Among the new employees was twenty-four-year-old Edith Keener, a recent graduate of the University of Arkansas who was hired to manage payroll and time sheets for M&NA employees. Murray announced that Miss Keener might be the only woman in Arkansas to hold such a post. The April 25 meeting of Murray and the six union representatives was the last formal conversation between management and strikers.[23]

Citizens of Harrison were thrilled to hear the sounds of locomotives switching in the rail yards as engineers prepared them for the reopening of the line. By the first week of May, the carrier was transporting some freight between Leslie and Seligman. Hundreds of carloads of staves, barrelheads, and other hardwood products were sitting in Leslie ready to ship out. The first train going south reached Heber Springs on the morning of May 5. At the sound of the train whistle, an impromptu crowd ran to the depot to greet the train, which held eighteen carloads of fertilizer. Merchants left their stores, schools dismissed, and women presented bouquets to the train crews, including a Mr. Green, who was Murray's personal representative. Towns up and down the line planned festivities, complete with bands playing music and speechmaking by politicians, to mark the reinauguration of railroad service. Regular passenger and freight trains ran between Seligman and Leslie on May 8. By May 15, service extended from Neosho to Kensett. By early June, the M&NA trains ran the entire length of the line, from Joplin to Helena. Mail service had switched back to the railroad. The M&NA managed to ship a hundred carloads of strawberries, the last of the year's crop. Business picked up in towns along the line. The timber products companies began hiring again in Leslie, and in Van Buren and Cleburne Counties. Heber Springs acquired a new stave mill, and a new barbershop and a meat market began serving customers. After being shuttered for nearly a year, the Morrow Hotel reopened, expecting tourists to return to the town's seven springs.[24]

In the nine months that the line did not operate, the M&NA benefited while the strikers lost ground. The company had avoided selling the railroad for scrap, which would have brought investors only pennies on the dollar, probably much less than their outstanding debt. The railroad lost less money with the trains idle than running. The sweetheart deal the company received from the ICC was everything that Wade and Murray had asked for—a government bailout loan with a recalculation of freight haulage payments to the M&NA's advantage. Strikers were losing the public relations war. For nine months they continued to collect their benefits while timber products workers lost their jobs, shopkeepers' business declined, farmers worried how they would get their crops to market, and consumers paid more for most products and were inconvenienced in travel. Strikers had multiple chances to compromise and come back to work. Each time—in October, in February, and in April—the union leaders rejected the company's offer, even in defiance of orders from the RLB. Strikers had only one card left to play in their game with the railroad: violence.

CHAPTER 4

CONFLICT DEEPENS: JUNE–DECEMBER 1922

IN EARLY JUNE 1922, the prospects appeared positive for the M&NA, and the railroad's supporters were euphoric. The line was running a regular schedule of passengers and freight. The company had secured the $3.5 million loan and substantially increased its profits on joint hauls. It employed almost a thousand nonunion workers, whose wages were paid at the 25 percent reduced rate. Now that the railroad was up and running again, general manager Jack Murray and the investors had little incentive to negotiate with the unions. Strikers, on the other hand, had nothing to celebrate. They had no leverage to apply except threats to take down the railroad entirely.

The nationwide shopmen's strike in July demonstrated the Railroad Labor Board's (RLB) more hostile posture toward unions and gave strikers no reason to believe that any support would come from the federal government. As the M&NA and the strikers dug into their positions, most residents resolved to support the railroad. The organization of the Ku Klux Klan in towns up and down the line in the last half of 1922 lent antistrike efforts a degree of organization and ideology lacking before. In addition, primary and general elections for county and state offices in August and October, and even the federal election in November, added a level of political mobilization to the conflict, similar to Harrison's municipal elections the preceding April. As the strike moved along in its second year, any peaceful resolution between the two sides seemed increasingly impossible.

The giddy elation of having railroad service again on the M&NA line did not last long. Sabotage against railroad property began almost immediately. On May 18 a switch was thrown near Searcy, and a small bridge burned near Pindall on May 30. At Leslie, conductor Marion Atterberry got into a fight with a striker, Grover Leslie, as Atterberry tried to board a train to begin his shift. The two were separated after five minutes of "extremely rough fighting," apparently with Leslie getting the worst of it. In early June in Heber Springs, two strikers were arrested and charged with assault against a strikebreaker, following an altercation in the city park. Murray accused strikers of throwing stones at trainmen, causing injuries to employees. Someone unleashed gunfire on a caboose as it approached the tunnel east of Eureka Springs. Emery dust was found in the delicate parts of several locomotives. Troublemakers cut air hoses at Harrison and Kensett in Arkansas, and at Seligman and Wayne in Missouri. On the evening of June 8, a bomb exploded in Harrison near the Riverside Hotel, where several strikebreakers were boarding, causing no injuries and little damage. As this violence continued, the Brotherhood of Railroad Trainmen, meeting in Toronto, voted to increase monthly benefits for strikers on the M&NA and the Alabama, Birmingham, and Atlantic Railroad from $60 to $100, with an additional $200 of back pay. Prospects for any settlement looked increasingly dire.[1]

In letters to newspapers along the line, Murray said that the railroad really belonged not to a group of investors in St. Louis but to the people it served. In a veiled call for vigilante actions, Murray appealed to the public to take responsibility for saving the railroad. Harrison's Protective League met on Tuesday, June 6, to strategize a response to the renewed violence. The league voted to put merchants on record as favoring the open shop, which in the 1920s meant a refusal to negotiate with unions. Just as strikers and their sympathizers the year before had boycotted certain businesses that assisted strikebreakers, the league promoted a boycott of businesses that chose not to display a card that said, "We are for open shop." The league also planned for a mass meeting on the following Saturday, with citizens from the entire service area of the railroad. Several thousand citizens gathered on the courthouse lawn in Harrison on June 10, standing for three hours of speechmaking. Many strikers were in the audience but made no attempt to speak or gesture. Attorney J. Sam Rowland spoke for the M&NA, explaining that strikers had refused to come back to work at the wages approved by the RLB. John J. Johnson, a Harrison physician and leader in Harrison's Protective League, chaired the meeting. He read a list of the alleged depredations that had occurred since the railroad had resumed service, and he said that there was agitation for "extreme measures to end the strike." Johnson encouraged the crowd to boycott businesses that sympathized with the strikers and told them not to employ strikers or members of their family. Circuit judge James M. Shinn assured the crowd he would prosecute anyone who interfered with the operation of the railroad. The Reverend W. T. Martin of Harrison's Methodist church proclaimed that the community's ministerial alliance did not take sides between labor and capital, but would support any movement to continue operation of the railroad. Dr. Johnson said if there was to be mob violence or bloodshed it would be the fault of the strikers, not the people of Harrison. Strike leader Pete Venable later said that speakers at the meeting advocated hanging or shooting strikers or running them out of the state.[2]

The Protective League's call for a boycott further divided the community. The group established committees to deliver the open-shop cards to everyone engaged in business, asking them to display the cards and to refuse service to strikers. Some merchants who had been selling to strikers on credit were reluctant to post the cards, but risked losing business of railroad supporters if they did not comply. Businesses touted their support of the railroad in newspaper advertisements, such as those for the Parker's Open-Shop Cleaning Service or Holt's Confectionary, which sold "open-shop bread." Within a few weeks, businesses in Harrison had taken sides. Strikers printed and distributed a flyer decrying the actions of the Harrison Protective League, accusing it of orchestrating the loss of jobs of two locals—young saleswoman Roxie Toney and dry goods clerk Joe Lineberry—because of their relationships with strikers. One banker fired a janitor, Bud Eoff, because of his support for the strike. By the summer of 1922, not only Martin at the Methodist church but also the Reverend Walter F. Bradley of the Presbyterian church had thrown in his lot with the railroad. Many strikers stopped attending church, feeling that the churches had chosen the other side. The fraternal lodges, women's clubs, American Legion, and even some families and friendships were reported divided between pro-strike and pro-railroad factions. Schoolchildren in Harrison squabbled over the strike on the playground. The mayor of Heber Springs,

Marcus E. Vinson, said that strikers would not allow their children to play with children of strikebreakers. Dr. Henry Vance Kirby, more than sixty years later, recalled that his family was shunned because his father sympathized with the strikers. They pulled their shades at dark and would only leave the house for church and school. The strike even disrupted social relationships. One railroad supporter, Sam Dennis, explained that the strike ended his friendship with Newton J. Grove, a conductor on the M&NA. The two men formerly met up in Harrison hotels for cold drinks and cigars. After the strike began, Grove would only grunt when the two passed on the street. Dennis asked Grove why he would not speak, and Grove said, "the boys would get me in the Lodge Hall and skin the hell out of me."[3]

The troubles intensified over the summer, not just in Harrison, but up and down the line. Later in June, three bridges burned over five days: at Lexa (just north of Helena), at Freeman (near Berryville), and between Fairview and Wheaton in Missouri. While most of the earlier sabotage had occurred in the Arkansas Ozarks, the new damage was on the northern and southern ends of the line. The forty-foot span destroyed near Fairview created a particular frenzy because suspects were apprehended and charged with the crime. Former Fairview station agent John Armstrong and Arthur "Will" Skelton were quickly arrested and taken to a park where angry men had assembled. Two officers from Neosho arrived, "rescued" the accused men from the crowd, and took them to jail in Neosho without bail, perhaps for their own safety. The cases against Armstrong and Skelton would later be dismissed because of lack of evidence. Officers arrested other alleged perpetrators in Missouri for placing blue vitriol in water pumps at Ridgely and Stark City. Citizens of Wheaton, Fairview, Ridgely, and Stark City organized their own Protective League in a meeting that overflowed the tent where they met. The Missouri citizens declared the strikers' violence as "Bolshevism in its ugliest form." The local newspaper reported that sentiments there were at such a pitch that "we believe it would be unpleasant for the person or persons who commit further depredations." Similarly, after the burning of the Pindall bridge in Arkansas, a newspaper reported that "Marshall citizens are in such a state of mind that a 'hanging bee' may happen if perpetrators are found."[4]

Boone County authorities uncovered what they claimed was a plot by strikers to bring weapons, ammunition, and other instruments of destruction into the area. On June 26 Sheriff J. S. "Silby" Johnson arrested three men as they made their way home toward Harrison, carrying in their automobile two thousand rounds of shotgun, buckshot, and pistol shells. Two of the men, Norman Stevens and J. O. "Rufus" Barnett, were strikers, and the third, James S. Selby, was a merchant known to be sympathetic to the strikers. The three men were returning from Springfield, where they had purchased ammunition from a wholesale hardware distributor. Selby insisted he was bringing the 150 pounds of ammunition to sell at his store. A salesman in the Springfield establishment, John Swindler, was aware of the tension in Harrison and phoned the Boone County sheriff's office. After apprehending the men, Sheriff Johnson also arrested Pete Venable, charging him as a coconspirator in a plot to murder employees of the railroad. The evidence presented against Venable was testimony from a neighbor, Mrs. Doyle Woodruff, that she had seen an unusually large number of men going in and out of Venable's house on the day of the purchase of the ammunition. Judge Shinn approved a warrant to search Venable's home. No weapons or ammunition were found, but officers did find a box buried in his garden that contained two boxes of dynamite caps, a roll of fuse, and a quantity of emery dust. Venable claimed that he had the caps and fuse in connection with an interest he had in some mining property. The emery dust, he said, was to use with his automobile and to sharpen his lawn mower.[5]

Some context helps explain the indictments for a conspiracy to commit murder. On June 22, just four days before the arrests, a mob of strikers near Herrin, Illinois, had tortured and murdered eighteen strikebreakers at a strip coal mine. The killing followed the shooting of two strikers the night before, as they approached the mine demanding the dismissal of the strikebreakers. The Herrin massacre captured headlines in newspapers from coast to coast. In Harrison, it may have prompted authorities to arrest and indict men on the grounds that they "might commit a crime." Venable filed a motion on July 20 in Judge Shinn's court to quash the search warrant, saying it was issued without grounds. Nonetheless, he was brought to trial in October, before the other two men. A jury in Judge Shinn's court found Venable guilty and fined him $100, a small consequence for conspiracy to commit murder. Venable's lawyers, Elbridge G. Mitchell, Sam Williams, and Oscar W. Hudgins, immediately appealed the case to the Arkansas Supreme Court, arguing that no evidence linked

Venable to a crime. They noted that the prosecuting attorney, Karl Greenhaw, had referenced the Herrin massacre in his closing arguments, comments that were prejudicial and inflammatory to a jury. The state high court agreed to hear the case, but in the following January it upheld the circuit court's decision. Barnett and Stevens were also found guilty of conspiracy in October 1922. And in early January 1923, the Boone County circuit court tried Selby for possessing pistol cartridges. He was found guilty and fined $200.[6]

Rumors abounded through the summer and fall of 1922 that strikers possessed two machine guns. They were indicted in the courts of Boone Count for crimes ranging from breaching the peace to gaming to carrying a pistol—even as strikebreakers carried arms in the streets unmolested by officers. Venable said that the M&NA furnished strikebreakers with 45-caliber Colt pistols upon hire. He alleged that J. Sam Rowland had issued guns to railroad guards that he had received from the Arkansas state militia.[7]

Increasingly, the conflict was personified by the key leaders on each side, James Theodore "Pete" Venable and John Collins "Jack" Murray. Born in Texas in 1881, Venable was short in stature, with piercing blue eyes and dark brown hair. As early as 1910 Venable had worked for the M&NA as a conductor, moving from Eureka Springs after the headquarters shifted to Harrison. As secretary of the local Order of Railway Conductors, he managed the payment of strike benefits for members of this brotherhood. He lacked any greater official capacity as leader of the strike, and he did not serve on the coordinating committee of the local brotherhoods. But both supporters of the railroad and some strikers viewed Venable, a man of fiery temperament, as the leader of the radical faction, willing to use depredations to defeat the railroad. The county judicial system went after him from the beginning of the strike until he and his wife fled Arkansas in 1923.

Jack Murray, like Venable, had a long history with the M&NA. Born in Chicago in 1884, he had grown up in Cincinnati and begun work with railroads, graduating from office boy to file clerk. In 1911 he came to Eureka Springs to become the chief traffic clerk for the M&NA, and he moved to Harrison with the other office staff in 1916. Unlike his predecessor as general manager, Charles Albert Phelan, Murray was an affable fellow, with a wry smile, who gained much support from the community. He and Venable had much in common, both small men in their late thirties who were Presbyterians and Knights Templars. They would have known each other since 1911. They and their wives were neighbors, living just a block apart on the north side of downtown Harrison. Neither couple had children. Before the strike, their wives attended the same ladies' card club. But the strike made Pete Venable and Jack Murray mortal enemies. Murray complained that he and his wife received countless insults. He had become calloused to the point that insults did not affect him, he said. It was not the same, however, for his wife, Helen. Venable charged that Murray orchestrated the conspiracy for a mob to end the strike, including a plan to take Venable's life.[8]

During the last week of June, Murray organized a special booster train to showcase the railroad. He gave free passage to 125 Little Rock businessmen and newspapermen on seven cars, including sleeping accommodations. Reporters gushed about the first-class appointments, food, and drink on the line. The only criticism concerned a fight with mosquitoes on the departure night in Helena, but by the next morning they were feted with a breakfast in Cotton Plant of chicken, rolls, bacon, and eggs. In Searcy the guests received a tour of Galloway College. At lunch in Heber Springs, the group feasted by the springs on a fifty-pound catfish caught that morning in the Little Red River. Marshall honored the passengers with flags and bunting and a song by a chorus of more than a hundred voices. The train got to Harrison late because some passengers feared they would be molested by strikers, and so Murray personally piloted the train slowly and carefully. Despite the late arrival, the group was met by two hundred people at the Harrison station and fed an evening meal at 11:30 p.m. by the Mothers Club. They retired for the night's rest well after midnight, in the M&NA yards under armed guard. After a sumptuous breakfast the next morning, the expedition was rolling again. The guests received baskets of peaches and berries at Berryville, then a tour of the springs at Eureka Springs. Everywhere along the line, people greeted the group with flags, bunting, cheers, and signs declaring, "We are for the M.&N. A. and Murray's management." The reporter for the *Arkansas Democrat* suggested that the whole area would vote for Murray if he ran for governor. The four hundred strikers obviously had a different opinion.[9]

Another factor adding to support for the railroad in the summer of 1922 was the arrival of the Ku Klux Klan. Two recruiters, brothers Lloyd and Allen Brown, traveled to Little Rock from Houston, Texas, in July 1921 to organize the Klan in Arkansas. Little Rock became the alpha chapter of the Klan, securing its charter by October as Klan no. 1 of the Realm of Arkansas. By the end of the year around a dozen towns in the state had Klan chapters. Eventually more than 150 Klans were chartered in Arkansas. Helena had Klan no. 3, Cotton Plant's Klan was organized by March 1922, and Searcy's Klan no. 40 was organized that spring. It appears that the Klan arrived in southwest Missouri by way of Klan recruiters from Oklahoma. Joplin had the first public activity of the Klan in Missouri, with an organizational meeting in March 1921 in the rooftop garden of the Connor Hotel. By October, Joplin's Klan no. 3 of the Realm of Missouri and Nebraska was rumored to have a thousand members. Farther southwest on the M&NA, Neosho's Klan no. 7 existed by early 1922.[10]

While the Klan was established by spring 1922 along the M&NA in Missouri to the northwest and in the flatlands of Arkansas from Searcy to Helena, the Invisible Empire arrived in the railroad towns of the Arkansas Ozarks during the summer and fall of 1922, just after the M&NA had begun running again. The Harrison City Council, at its monthly meeting on June 5, 1922, passed by a four-to-two vote an ordinance "prohibiting secret societies parading in mask and meeting in mask" within the city limits, an indication that the Klan was already organizing in the town. The Berryville newspaper reported about a Klan visitation in mid-July to the town's Methodist church, where robed Klansmen solemnly processed in and presented the pastor with a letter of commendation and $22.95 in cash. The editor, William J. Douglas, believed it to be the first public appearance of the Ku Klux Klan in northwest Arkansas. When the Berryville Klan received its charter in late August, Douglas gushed that now the town was "in line with other progressive places over the country." Around the same time, men in Marshall were organizing what would become Klan no. 88, rumored to have as many as 250 members. In Harrison in late August, a large cheering crowd attended an informational meeting about the Klan. The meeting opened with a band concert, a prayer by the Methodist church's Rev. Martin, and the singing of "America." By early October, Harrison's Klan no. 101

had received its charter. At an evening Klonkave later in the month in a field outside of town, 80 new Klansmen were "naturalized" into the organization. Eureka Springs had its Klan by November, for it was sending resolutions to the Klan's national newspaper, the *Searchlight*. Heber Springs was just a bit later, getting its charter as Klan no. 126 on December 18, 1922. It usually took from one to three months after a chapter was organized for the paperwork to be approved by the Imperial Palace in Atlanta, and for a handsome charter to be printed and delivered to the chapter. Leslie also had a Klan, its number and date of organization unknown. It existed, however, by January 1923, when Klansmen in robes and hoods were said to be beating strikers with horsewhips in the streets of downtown.[11]

IMPERIAL PALACE, INVISIBLE EMPIRE

Knights of the Ku Klux Klan

(INCORPORATED)

To All Who Read and Respect These Lines, Greeting:

Whereas, The Imperial Wizard hath received a petition from the following named citizens of the Invisible Empire,

... et al, praying for themselves and others and their successors to be instituted a Klan of the Order under the name and number of

PAT CLEBURNE Klan No. 126, Realm of ARKANSAS, and same to be located at HEBER SPRINGS, in the County of ..., State of ARKANSAS, United States of America, and they having given assurance of their fidelity to the order and their competency to render the service required, and their ready willingness to take upon themselves and their successors the responsibilities thereof, and their serious determined purpose, to rightly use and not abuse the powers, privileges and prerogatives conferred on them as such, and the pledge to be faithful and true to the Imperial Authority of the Order, and to all things so construed to and required of them.

Now Know Ye, that I, the Imperial Wizard, Emperor of the Invisible Empire, Knights of the Ku Klux Klan, on this the Eighteenth day of the Twelfth Month of the Year of Our Lord Nineteen Hundred and Twenty-two, and on the ... day of the ... week of the ... Month of the Year of the Klan, LVI and in the ... Cycle of the third Reign of our Reincarnation, by Authority possessed by me, do issue this

Charter

to the aforesaid petitioners, their associates and successors, under the name and number aforesaid from the day and date hereon, and same is effective from the date of its acceptance by said Klan as certified below by its Exalted Cyclops.

By His Majesty,—

CERTIFICATE OF ACCEPTANCE

The Heber Springs Klan charter. *Courtesy of Cleburne County Historical Society.*

While the "when" of the Klan's arrival along the North Arkansas Line is known, the "who" of the Klan remains a bit more enigmatic. As it was a secret society where members in public settings wore robes and masks, the identity of specific Klansmen was generally unknown. However, it is clear what sort of men joined the Klan. Two Arkansas Klans broke the rules and failed to destroy their membership records after the chapters ceased to exist. Historians have analyzed the membership of Bentonville's Klan no. 69, in the Ozark hills of northwest Arkansas, and Monticello's Klan no. 108, in the flatlands of the delta in the southeastern corner of the state. The profiles of Klan members in these upland and lowland towns were almost identical. Klansmen overwhelmingly represented the communities' political, economic, and social elites. County and city officials, businessmen, and professionals such as lawyers, physicians, teachers, newspapermen, and clergymen dominated the Klan lists. Farmers were also common, but these were not peasants on small plots of land; they were prosperous, large-scale agriculturalists. Bentonville, being a railroad town, had eleven Klan members who worked for the railroad, but the largest number of these were conductors, engineers, and station agents, not rank and file. Klansmen in Bentonville and Monticello had many social connections. They worshipped together at Baptist, Methodist, Christian (Disciples of Christ), and Presbyterian churches. They were members of the same Masonic lodges and other fraternal organizations. Arkansas newspapers frequently noted that Klans contained the community's leading men: as the *Lonoke Democrat* put it, "the very cream of our citizenship."[12]

In other words, Klansmen appear to be the same sort of people who formed the Protective Leagues to oppose the strike in towns along the M&NA. Identities are known of some Klansmen in Heber Springs and Harrison, and they played leading roles in opposing the strike in these two communities. The charter for Klan no. 126 of Heber Springs lists the chapter's thirteen officers: the county judge, the mayor, two attorneys, two merchants, a physician, two druggists, a real estate agent, the pastor of the town's First Baptist church, the president of one of the town's banks, and the vice president of the other. Several of these Klansmen would lead the vigilante action against strikers in January 1923. The exalted cyclops of Harrison's Klan no. 101 was the Reverend Walter F. Bradley, pastor of the Presbyterian church and member of the Protective League. Bradley lectured publicly on behalf of the Klan in communities surrounding Harrison. Succeeding Bradley as exalted cyclops was Walter L. Snapp, who operated an eighty-acre apple orchard six miles southeast of town and had previously served as vice president of the Protective League. It was Snapp, alongside M&NA general manager Phelan and Dr. Charles M. Routh, who had shot up the town in a drunken spree one night in June 1921. During the strike Snapp received pay as a "special agent" for the M&NA, until the line shut down on July 31, 1921. Venable charged that this part of Snapp's "job" involved traveling to neighboring areas to rouse the public against the strike. Boone County sheriff Silby Johnson was also a Klansman, as was cattle farmer Robert "Bob" Shaddox, elected to replace Johnson in October. Decades later, one Harrison old-timer, Dr. Henry Vance Kirby, recalled watching Klansmen arrive for their regular evening Klonkaves in Shaddox's pasture on the outskirts of town. Vance, who was fourteen in 1922, said that Klansmen were the leading men of Harrison. He said that his father, Leander B. Kirby, who operated a drugstore in downtown Harrison, showed him a letter he had received from the Klan, directing him to join the organization, pay dues, and do guard duty. If he refused, the Klan threatened to boycott his store. After Leander Kirby declined to join the local Klan, Shaddox told the proprietor he would not go into his drugstore to buy even a pencil. Shaddox's boycott continued for ten years, Dr. Kirby said. Other Klansmen who were "outed" by the Harrison newspaper and who actively opposed the strike included dentist Troy Coffman, merchant Luther "Clay" Holt, and M&NA attorney J. Sam Rowland.[13]

The arrival of Klaverns of the Ku Klux Klan in 1922 in the towns along the North Arkansas Line provided organization and communication for the opposition to the railroad strike. In addition, the Klan lent a degree of ideological conviction to the antistrike movement. When men were naturalized as members of the Ku Klux Klan, they swore an oath of allegiance to the Invisible Empire and its tenets. The 1920s Klan professed white supremacy, prejudice against Catholics and Jews, and opposition to immigration, and it crusaded against moonshiners, bootleggers, and other purveyors of vice. As with fascism, Klan ideology derived power from its negativity, by haranguing groups it opposed. Less well known than its nativism was the Klan's opposition to radical labor. The Klan professed to support a "closer relationship between capital and labor" and suggested that the Klavern could provide a place where both sides could get to know each other. However, as has been demonstrated, Klan chapters were middle-class men's clubs. They rarely admitted blue-collar workers.

Two of the twelve Klan tenets were pointedly antilabor. One principle called for "the prevention of fires and destruction of property by lawless elements," while another opposed "unwarranted strikes by foreign labor agitators." This language was code for the personification of radical labor and socialism, the Industrial Workers of the World (IWW). In January 1922, after a gusher had prompted an oil and gas boom near El Dorado in south Arkansas, the local Klan went on the attack against eight IWW members who had come to organize the roughnecks who had poured into the area seeking work. One IWW leader was tarred and feathered, and the others were placed on a train and told never to return. Klan lecturers in Arkansas, such as Ben Bogard and Basil Newton, railed in their speeches against the IWW and "Bolsheviki" elements, calling them anti-American and anti-Christian.

While it is impossible to know what exactly took place inside the wall of secrecy that enclosed the Klans in the towns along the M&NA, several utterances make clear how they categorized strikers as labor radicals comparable to the IWW. This position reflected either dishonesty or ignorance, for the railroad brotherhoods had a reputation as some of the most conservative and traditional unions of the nation's labor movement. At a public Klan lecture in Harrison in August on the subject of Americanism, the speaker made a veiled attack on the NAACP and declared the Klan's opposition to "Jesuits, Jews, I.W.W.'s, bootleggers, and purveyors of vice." In November 1922 in Eureka Springs, the Klan adopted a set of resolutions condemning "Bolshevism, Socialism, IWWism," and other revolutionary movements, and declared that "this Klan pledges its wholehearted support to national headquarters of the Ku Klux Klan and to all fellow Klansmen in ridding our beloved republic of the curse of these elements of disorder." Jasper's Klan in October advertised its main cause as the "destruction of bolshevism." On July 2, Harrison's exalted cyclops, Rev. Walter Bradley, gave a special sermon to his Presbyterian congregation on the topic of Americanism. Fellow Klansman Rev. Martin dismissed services at the Methodist church and brought his congregation to hear

The Reverend Walter F. Bradley. *Boone County Herald, March 29, 1923.*

Bradley's sermon. The exalted cyclops attributed the problems with radical labor to foreign immigration, which, he said, was changing the Anglo-Saxon nature of the United States. Samuel Gompers, the head of the American Federation of Labor (AFL), Bradley noted, was a foreign-born Jew. Organized labor had sworn allegiance to the "Red Flag of Anarchy, or a black Flag of Rebellion." Bradley questioned whether "Organized Labor has a right to claim privileges or protection under our Constitution when it has apparently sworn fealty to a different one of its own." This demonization of labor radicals by the Klan, and Bradley's questioning of whether the Constitution even protected their rights, prepared the way for the violent attack against strikers that would follow in January 1923 in Harrison, Leslie, Heber Springs, and Eureka Springs.[14]

The nationwide shopmen's strike in July 1922 further discredited railroad employees in the eyes of much of the public. The issue at stake was essentially the same that had prompted the strike on the M&NA.

The RLB approved a reduction in wages averaging 12 percent for railway shopmen. The reduction did not apply to other occupations, such as conductors, engineers, and brakemen. The cut would take effect on July 1. Strike ballots went out to union members throughout the railroad industry. Shopmen and maintenance of way workers voted to strike, while the brotherhoods representing other occupations of railway work broke ranks and voted against the strike. On July 1 some four hundred thousand shopmen and maintenance of way workers walked off the job, one hundred thousand of them in Chicago alone. The RLB, under chair Ben Hooper, declared the strike illegal by a five-to-two vote. With the board's antilabor drift, strikers were protesting the RLB as much as they were the carriers. Railroads immediately began replacing striking employees with strikebreakers. Some cuts and slowdowns in service occurred, but the trains did not stop running. Strikers did some sabotage of trains and tracks, like that on the M&NA, and there was periodic violence as company guards fired on strikers in some locations. In Arkansas, violent exchanges occurred along the Missouri Pacific lines in Hoxie, Van Buren, and Little Rock.[15]

The strike ended after a federal judge in northern Illinois, James H. Wilkerson, the same judge who would later sentence Al Capone, issued an injunction on September 1 prohibiting assemblage in the vicinity of railroad property, picketing, and intimidation of railway workers. The injunction even forbade unions from providing financial support or directing the strike using any means of communication, whether telephones, telegrams, mail, or even word of mouth. Wilkerson acted under the direction of President Warren G. Harding and US attorney general Harry M. Daugherty. Daugherty especially had staked out the position of public hostility toward the strike and unions, announcing that he would use all power at his disposal to prevent unions from destroying the open shop. The secretary of war, John W. Weeks, threatened to send the US Army against strikers in Texas if the governor there would not use the Texas Rangers and National Guard troops at his disposal. With these measures and the so-called Daugherty injunction in hand, the strike began to fall apart in September, a victory for the railroad companies.[16]

The shopmen's strike, the largest railroad labor action since the Pullman strike of 1894, had little direct impact on the M&NA, for none of the one thousand employees of the line in 1922 were members of unions. The strike did inconvenience some of its joint hauls. In late July the freight service temporarily shut down because of a shortage of coal, causing a scare that the region's peach crop might rot in the orchards. But by the middle of August, Jack Murray announced that he had secured a large consignment of coal, and all was good for prompt service. The editor of Berryville's *North Arkansas Star* opined that the addition of four hundred thousand strikers getting benefits might more quickly exhaust union funds and end the M&NA strike. But that did not happen. Murray did admit that the M&NA picked up some freight business, perhaps a hundred extra cars, caused by congestion on the Frisco Line. The failure of the shopmen's strike and the clear anti-union posture of the RLB and the Harding administration provided moral support for the M&NA's fight against strikers in Arkansas and Missouri.[17]

On the day the shopmen's strike began, July 1, chancery judge Ben F. McMahan of Harrison, in response to a petition by Murray and other officials of the M&NA, issued a temporary injunction restraining strikers from picketing, very similar to the Daugherty injunction that would follow in September. Local strike officials in Harrison initially directed strikers to ignore the injunction, claiming that silent picketing off the property of the railroad broke no law. However, within a few days, it was reported that strikers were observing the order. The editor of Berryville's newspaper crowed that the injunction had cooled strikers' enthusiasm for mischief through the prospect of a few weeks in jail in Arkansas's July heat. Two weeks later, federal judge Jacob Trieber issued a similar but permanent injunction against picketing, directed toward striking shopmen of the Missouri Pacific and Rock Island lines in Little Rock. A Kansas City federal judge in late July issued an injunction against picketing for the Missouri portion of the M&NA line. Murray kept petitioning McMahan to make his injunction permanent, and he did so finally after a hearing on December 8. The permanent injunction applied to all parts of the line within the state of Arkansas. McMahan ruled that when strikers refused the wages offered by the company under the RLB's decision, their relationship to the railroad ceased, so any hindrance thereafter to the operation of the railroad constituted a violation of the law.[18]

Elections in the summer and fall of 1922 further polarized communities along the North Arkansas Line. The Fourteenth Judicial District spanned the most acrimonious area of the M&NA line—Boone, Searcy, Van Buren, and Cleburne Counties—along with Newton County to the west and Marion County to the east. In Harrison, both circuit judge James Shinn and prosecuting attorney Karl Greenhaw had served in their roles since January 1, 1919. They had prosecuted strikers with a heavy hand since the strike began in 1921. Shinn and Greenhaw ran for reelection on a platform of law and order, a euphemism understood to mean support for the railroad. Greenhaw faced three other candidates in the August Democratic primary: Neill Reed, a young lawyer from Cleburne County who would become the "kladd" in charge of initiations of the Heber Springs Klan; Virgil Willis, a young lawyer from Bergman who would take a strong anti-Klan stance; and J. C. "Charlie" Smith, a Jasper lawyer whom Greenhaw accused of being in the strikers' bandwagon. In his campaign, Greenhaw made clear his support for management of the M&NA on an open-shop basis. He further declared that strikers had "refused to comply with the decision of the Labor Board and have no right to interfere in any way with the loyal men who are trying to operate this road and save our country from the ruin the strikers were willing to force on it." Greenhaw handily defeated his three opponents, with Smith coming in second. He had no opponent in the October general election. Judge Shinn, on the other hand, was unopposed in the Democratic primary, but Republicans nominated William Franklin "Frank" Reeves, a Marshall lawyer, to run against him in October. It was the first time in eight years that Republicans had bothered to nominate a candidate for the office, but they apparently thought that Shinn was vulnerable because of his support for the railroad. Reeves would later edit the *Eagle*, an anti-Klan newspaper in Marshall. Shinn was reelected with 1,500 votes over Reeves, who carried only Searcy and Newton Counties, which traditionally favored Republicans.[19]

Two other elections centered in Harrison became even more conflicted. Eighty-one-year-old George J. Crump, who had been a shareholder in the railroad from its early days in the 1890s, ran for the state Senate seat representing Boone, Newton, and Marion Counties. Crump's law partner (and Venable's attorney) Oscar Hudgins and his son, George Crump Jr., were accused of leading the prostrike faction within the local Democratic Party. Crump's opponent in the

Democratic primary was Roy W. Milum, a Harrison businessman and railroad supporter. The race became dirty, with Milum accusing Crump, his son, and his son-in-law (former mayor Guy L. Trimble) of trying to blackmail him. Crump accused Milum of debauching a married woman to the point of prosecutable white slavery. Besides the personal attacks, it was clear that the Democratic primary election was a referendum on the strike. Milum defeated Crump by a vote of 1,274 to 1,116. He later won overwhelmingly over his Republican opponent, G. W. Floyd, in October.[20]

A last election that divided supporters of the strike and the railroad was the contest for sheriff of Boone County. Sheriff Silby Johnson had chosen not to run. The sitting representative for Boone County to the Arkansas General Assembly, Lewis Dowell, announced his candidacy for sheriff early. In his campaign, he gave little attention to his two opponents in the Democratic primary, sawmill laborer James M. Bell and livestock dealer Jeptha C. Lee. He focused instead on attacking Shinn and Greenhaw. Dowell and Greenhaw exchanged a series of public letters in local newspapers, with Dowell claiming that Greenhaw and Shinn were in bed with the railroad, while Greenhaw charged that Dowell was in league with the Crumps and Hudgins on behalf of the strikers. After Dowell defeated his two opponents in August, local Republicans nominated Bob Shaddox, the cattle farmer who hosted cross-burning Klonkaves on his pasture west of Harrison. Shaddox was a member of Bradley's Presbyterian church and could be considered the Klan's alternative to Dowell. In a county where Democrats usually outpolled Republicans by four hundred or five hundred votes, Shaddox squeaked by Dowell in the October election, defeating him by fifteen votes and thereby becoming the only Republican to win an elected office that year. Pete Venable charged the Klan with pushing through its anointed candidates in the August and October elections, wiping out Republican and Democratic Party distinctions in order to elect officials who would protect the M&NA. As soon as the October election was over, Venable said, rumors began circulating that strikers would be driven out in January, after the new officials were sworn into office. "Little did we then realize," Venable said, "that these rumors would ever come true."[21]

Meanwhile, the damage to railroad property only accelerated during the last half of 1922. A rash of apparent sabotage occurred in late August, beginning with the burning of a bridge two miles north of Eureka Springs. The bridge burned quickly just after two freight trains crossed it, shortly before midnight on August 19. That same night, just north of Harrison, someone used copper wire to bind together the telegraph lines of the M&NA and Western Union, as well as Southwestern Bell's telephone lines, which used the same poles. The damage put all three communication lines temporarily out of commission. A technician for the telephone company climbed the pole to repair the lines, but someone shot at him, causing the pole to break and him to fall into the tall weeds below. On his way back to Harrison, the technician came across a six-foot-long iron bar placed on the track, with the rails greased in a hundred feet in each direction. He was able to remove the bar just ten minutes before the next train came through. Later in the month, saboteurs burned a bridge near Cotton Plant and attempted to blow up a nearby water tank with dynamite. A quantity of blue vitriol was found in a water tank at Freeman, between Berryville and the tunnel.[22]

In early September extremely dry conditions and a shortage of grass and hay caused cattle farmers in northern Arkansas to ship their herds to market via the M&NA en masse. Citizens of the area joined railroad employees in guarding all bridges between Harrison and Seligman. After the shipments were complete, the armed guards withdrew, and the sabotage/depredations began again. A bridge was burned near Gilbert, another west of Searcy, and a third one between Kensett and Georgetown. Tracks were greased in multiple places up and down the line. Air hoses were cut on trains in Heber Springs, and a water tank was doped with vitriol at Freeman. A bomb was found on the tracks near Cotton Plant. In October and November, another bridge burned, this one near Wheaton, Missouri. Water tanks were contaminated with substances ranging from copper sulfate or sulfuric acid to pine rosin and emery dust in Neosho and Stark City, Missouri. In De View and Aubrey, deep in the Arkansas Delta between Wheatley and Helena, emery dust gummed up train machinery. As before, railroad employees found air hoses cut and tracks greased in multiple locations.[23]

The violence was not exclusively directed at property. At a dance outside Harrison on Friday night, October 27, the striking brakeman Norman Stevens got into a fight with J. F. Clifton, a fireman for the railroad. The brawl began when Stevens called Clifton a "scab."

Stevens beat Clifton unconscious but not before receiving several cuts, including a serious knife slash to his abdomen. Clifton recovered at home, but Stevens was rushed by ambulance to the hospital in Eureka Springs. Such clashes between strikers and strikebreakers were said to have motivated a change made by the M&NA earlier in the fall. In late September the M&NA had announced that Kensett would become the division for crews on all passenger and freight runs, instead of Heber Springs. The change moved strikebreakers to Kensett, away from the strikers congregating in the streets of Heber Springs, and it caused a spurt of demand for housing in Kensett, as several families relocated there.[24]

The enmity was at a boiling point at the end of the year, when the Reverend John Kelly Farris became pastor of Harrison's Methodist church, the largest church in town. He replaced W. T. Martin, who was a vocal supporter of the railroad and the Klan. Martin was transferred to a parish in Hartford, Arkansas, near Fort Smith. Farris, along with his wife, Lenah, and nineteen-year-old daughter, Annie Lee, arrived in Harrison on Saturday, December 2, and he preached his first sermon the next morning. The Farrises came from their home in Wynne, Arkansas, via the White River Line to Bergman and then by taxi to Harrison. Some members of his congregation interpreted his travel on the rival railroad as a statement of opposition to the M&NA, but the arrival of the family's household goods on the M&NA temporarily put this perception to rest. Farris deliberately refrained from taking sides, finding his congregation divided fairly evenly between those who supported the railroad and those who were loyal to the strikers. Prominent supporters of the strikers such as former mayor Trimble and attorneys George Crump Sr. and Elbridge G. Mitchell were members, as was James E. Queen, the local leader of the Order of Railway Conductors. But the congregation also included the M&NA lawyers J. Sam Rowland and J. Loyd Shouse, as well as Clay Holt, Sam Dennis, and Troy Coffman, who would play a key role in putting down the strike. Judge Shinn and prosecuting attorney Greenhaw were also members.[25]

Farris immediately set about getting to know the town and its inhabitants. He walked every street and called on six hundred of the eight hundred homes in Harrison, skillfully avoiding conversation about the strike or the railroad. On one of his visits, he knocked on the door of Pete Venable. Mrs. Venable was not at home, and the reverend had the misfortune of arriving at the very hour that a meeting of the strikers' committee was scheduled to begin. As others arrived, Farris made his exit, but lookouts reported his presence at a "secret session" with strike leaders, further supporting the rumor that the new preacher opposed the railroad. Farris also visited Jack Murray in his office on the square. Murray initially presented a friendly disposition, but upon further conversation he made clear that the price of his favor would be for Farris to take the side of the railroad in the conflict.[26]

A vivid impression Farris received on his first day in Harrison was seeing in the windows of almost all the town's stores and businesses eight-by-ten-inch cards with the printed words, "For Open Shop, Show Your Card." The few shops that did not display the card received the patronage of strikers, Farris learned. What the strikers could not purchase in these stores they had to buy in neighboring towns or via mail order. Farris believed that the boycott system, more than any other factor, forced the residents to take sides and aggravated the enmity between them.[27]

As Farris settled into his role, ministering to strikers and strikebreakers alike, the alleged depredations continued. Murray seemed to think that the strikers' real goal was to destroy the railroad. A dispatch from Harrison published in late November in *Labor* led with the question, "How much longer will the Missouri & North Arkansas Railroad continue to operate?" The article predicted that strikers could hold out longer than the railroad. The Frisco Line announced that it would no longer deliver past Seligman into Arkansas, depriving the M&NA of substantial revenue. Murray was already cutting some of his staff of strikebreakers in the running trades, maintenance of way, and shops in Harrison.[28]

Soon after the article appeared, at Fargo, southeast of Cotton Plant in Monroe County, seventy-eight bales of cotton worth $10,000 were burned while being transferred from the M&NA to the Cotton Belt line. The car, valued at a further $3,000, was destroyed as well. While they were at it, the vandals put emery dust in the machinery of both lines. It appears that the radical wing of the strikers, led by Venable, saw permanently shutting down the railroad as their only way to "win." Apparently, the radical strikers hoped that then someone else would buy the tracks and rolling stock, hire back the strikers, and resume

The Reverend John Kelly Farris. *Farris, The Harrison Riot, 1924.*

operation on a closed-shop basis. Venable had independently reached out to some wealthy oilmen in Tulsa to buy the railroad and extend the western end from Seligman to the booming Oklahoma oil town and the eastern end to Memphis, potentially more profitable hubs than Joplin and Helena. Venable said he even met in St. Louis with a Tulsa man, C. C. Briggs, who had come there to discuss the possible purchase with the M&NA's owners. Nothing came of the proposed deal. Nonetheless, the prospect of the sale of the railroad may have motivated an increase in sabotage by strikers.[29]

By December, Murray's patience had come to an end. He drafted a letter "To the Public," which he posted at all M&NA stations and sent to newspapers in towns up and down the line, denouncing the depredations he alleged were being committed against railroad property. He declared that while the railroad generated an income that exceeded its expenses, it was not bringing a profit for its owners. The line was operated, he said, "solely for the benefit of the public." Then he put the ball in *their* court, saying, "what steps may be necessary to protect the operation of the railroad is a question for the people themselves to decide, as they have the greatest interests in its operation." The statement created a sensation in Harrison and other towns, being perceived as a call to arms for residents along the line. A week later, Murray sent a telegram to the RLB in Chicago cataloging the alleged depredations that had occurred along the M&NA line. At the public meeting in Harrison on June 10, some had already called for strikers to be driven from the state. Through his actions in December, Murray laid the groundwork for the assembling of a mob that would do just that.[30]

The last half of 1922 had seen freight and passengers moving again on the North Arkansas Line. With the strikebreakers gaining experience and working at lower wages, the company had no incentive to bargain with strikers. The Harding administration and the RLB, in their response to the shopmen's strike, signaled their support for railroad owners, not workers. And with the arrival of the Ku Klux Klan and the victory of local government officials who publicly favored the present management of the M&NA, strikers had no cards to play but destruction. The strikers had lost by the end of 1922; they just did not seem to know it.

CHAPTER 5

THE HARRISON RIOT OF JANUARY 1923

AFTER NEARLY TWO YEARS of turmoil, a riot brought the strike to a crashing climax in January 1923. Within twenty-four hours of the rabble's takeover of Harrison on Monday, January 15, a striker was lynched and two sympathizers were publicly stripped and beaten. Others were illegally searched, detained, and forced to abandon their homes and leave town, all with the cooperation of the local "justice" system. Newspapers across the country described the Harrison uprising in vivid detail on their front pages. Parts of the story remain uncertain, obscured by contradictory testimony. What is clear is that the railroad owners and management worked with the community's business and professional leaders to assemble a mob to end the strike on the M&NA.

According to the railroad's general manager, Jack Murray, nine bridges were burned or dynamited along the M&NA line in the first two weeks of 1923, bringing the total number of bridges destroyed in whole or part since the beginning of the strike to twenty-three. On January 6, near Moro, about halfway between Wheatley and Helena, someone placed twelve sticks of dynamite on the south end of a bridge, but the damage was not sufficient to stop the trains. Three days later, a 238-foot-long bridge was destroyed by fire near the Eureka Springs tunnel. That same day, another bridge was found burning seven miles west of Searcy, but the crew from an approaching freight train managed to extinguish the blaze. Four bridges were damaged on Wednesday, January 10. Half of a 131-foot-long bridge was consumed by fire in the early hours near Everton, twelve miles

Burning bridge near Everton. *Enid (OK) Daily News, January 23, 1923.*

south of Harrison. Later a burning bridge just north of Leslie was saved through the efforts of a farmer living nearby. Another bridge was dynamited that day south of Wheatley, and a bridge at Zack, in Searcy County, was damaged by fire. The following day, two bridges in White County burned. One fire was put out by neighboring farmers, but the other, a long bridge near Letona, was nearly destroyed. In addition to the bridges, someone meddled with a switch north of the Harrison depot and placed an axle on the tracks near Bellefonte, causing cars in each case to derail.[1]

On Thursday, January 11, Jack Murray issued another news release declaring that the strikers were trying to shut down the railroad permanently. Murray claimed that evidence of coal oil was found at or near three of the four bridges burned on the previous day. He suspended passenger and freight service between Eureka Springs and Leslie until the company could make necessary repairs. Again, he appealed to the public to act, saying that the value of their own property was at stake if the railroad stopped service entirely. Governor Thomas C. McRae responded by posting a state reward of $300 for the arrest and conviction of anyone burning a bridge of the M&NA.[2]

Strikers maintained that fires along the line resulted from poorly maintained locomotives that dropped hot ash and sparks on the tracks. On one occasion of a burning bridge near Pindall, Pete Venable said that Murray had admitted to Harrison's mayor, Jasper L. Clute, that an ash pan dropping fire had caused the blaze, but then Murray went on to issue a $5,000 reward for the arrest and conviction of the striker who burned the bridge. Venable claimed that the two long bridges that burned in January at Letona and Everton were constructed of highly flammable pine without tin-top fire decking or gravel between the rails, as was customary for railroad bridges. Moreover, Venable said, Arkansas in the fall and winter of 1922 had seen its longest dry spell in forty years. Additional people who gave testimony to the legislative committee that investigated the strike claimed to have witnessed M&NA locomotives spewing fire and hot ash as they traveled or pulled into stations. These witnesses included passengers, landowners along the line, and employees for other railroads that connected to the M&NA. W. O. VanPelt, an agent for the Kansas City Southern, which owned the tracks the M&NA used between Neosho and Joplin, testified that he had complained to the M&NA in July and August 1922 about the fire hazard caused by its faulty engines, which endangered employees of his railroad and the public. Another Kansas City Southern employee, H. E. Littleton, presented the legislative committee with a list of fires along the M&NA that, in his opinion, had been caused by faulty ash pans, combined with rotted timbers, compounded by dry weather. The legislators even received a report from the Bureau of Locomotive Inspection of the Interstate Commerce Commission (ICC), which listed deficiencies of the M&NA's locomotives. The ICC's inspector, A. G. Peck, said that previous inspections had already brought to the attention of M&NA officials the problem of improperly maintained ash pans causing fires along the line.[3]

Another explanation that surfaced during the legislative hearings was that railroad management deliberately burned bridges in January to provide a pretext for the mob action that followed. This theory of false flag operations came to the legislative committee through the testimony of one man and notarized statements of two others who claimed to have been hired by the company to burn its own bridges. Appearing before the committee in Little Rock was John

Devaney, an English drifter who had lost an eye on a battlefield in France and who had come to the United States in 1922. Corroborating his testimony was a notarized affidavit from two professional boxers, Moses Rosen and Henry Raynor, which was mailed from St. Louis to Mayor Clute, who shared it with the legislative committee.

These sources claimed that a man named Sullivan, representing the M&NA, had hired Rosen and Raynor and two other men at an employment bureau in Kansas City on January 4, ostensibly to guard the railroad's property. The four traveled to Dallas by train, where Devaney joined the group, and then to Little Rock. Sullivan gave the men each a Colt 45 pistol in the smoking room of the Little Rock depot as they waited an hour to change trains. They took the Missouri Pacific train to Kensett, and then the five men traveled in a car belonging to Mr. Vining, the M&NA agent in Heber Springs, to Everton. There two of the men went with Sullivan to burn a bridge. Devaney alleged that Sullivan paid each man fifty dollars for their efforts. Devaney said that he and two men stayed in the Harrison area about six days doing guard work on the railroad by night, with orders from Sullivan to shoot any strikers on sight. Their work was easy, Devaney said, mostly killing time, sitting around a fire and smoking. At some point, Sullivan took Rosen and Raynor to Heber Springs, where they met up with Vining and a deputy sheriff, Mr. Robbins. The affidavit claimed that Vining filled a can with gasoline at the depot and then the five men drove east past Pangburn and burned the Letona bridge. They returned to Heber Springs, sleeping at the Horton House Hotel. Sullivan gave Rosen and Raynor each a check for fifty dollars, which they cashed the next day at a bank in Heber Springs. The affidavit alleged that over the next few days, Vining, Robbins, and the two hired men burned four more bridges. They intended to burn a fifth one but were scared away before the fire got started.

This account may be an elaborate fiction; if so, it was peppered with plausible details provided by someone who knew the area and people. Fred E. Vining indeed worked as the railroad's agent in Heber Springs, and Oscar B. Robbins was a leader of the mob that would violently put down the strike in that town. It would have been easy enough to check with the Horton House, the Heber Springs bank, or the Kansas City employment office to corroborate the story, but it appears nobody bothered to do so. An unnamed person did, however, visit Eugenia

Nager, the notary in St. Louis who witnessed the Rosen-Raynor affidavit. Murray presented a notarized statement by Nager declaring that John Devaney had brought the document and she had signed it without having seen Rosen or Raynor. It is curious that Murray could get Nager to make such an admission, which would have presumably cost her license as a notary. One wonders how much money may have changed hands to secure such a confession. Without doubt, some strikers had committed sabotage against railroad property, but how these bridges burned in January 1923 remains uncertain.[4]

While Murray denied that the M&NA had any relationship with a Mr. Sullivan and claimed that the whole story was a fabrication, shortly after the bridges burned local authorities arrested several strikers and charged them with arson. The sheriff of Carroll County, Ed McShane, arrested Omar N. Pritchett, a striking brakeman from Harrison, for burning the long bridge near the Eureka Springs tunnel. The "evidence" leading to Pritchett's arrest was a statement from a witness in Eureka Springs who claimed he saw Pritchett with another striker, Melvin McCurdy, in a car with a gas can visible in the back seat. Ertie Weston, a farmer who lived north of Eureka Springs, testified that two men who identified themselves as McCurdy and Pritchett had stopped at his home looking for whiskey, and that they said they intended that evening to burn one of the railroad's biggest bridges. Pritchett denied having ever met the farmer who made this statement. A third piece of circumstantial evidence was a set of footprints found near the burned bridge. Sheriff McShane and Murray had together investigated the scene of the arson and said they found footprints of two men, one who was wearing approximately size-eight shoes with new rubber heels. Sheriff McShane said that Pritchett when arrested was wearing shoes of the same size and kind. McCurdy was nowhere to be found. After Pritchett's arrest, McShane kept him overnight at Murray's home in Harrison, and then he was taken to the Berryville jail on a $20,000 bond. Pritchett, described as a quiet, slim, soft-spoken, gentle man, said he was twice taken from his cell by "parties interested in the railroad" and questioned with such force he had a broken rib and a gash on the back of his hand. He claimed someone struck him across his temple with the butt end of a gun, which caused him to lose vision in one eye. In his trial it came out that his visitors were Walter L. Snapp and Sam Dennis, prominent supporters of the railroad. Pritchett's lawyers petitioned the governor and the circuit judge that he be removed from Carroll County for his own safety and that his trial have a change of venue. As a result, he was taken to a jail in Bentonville and held there until his trial commenced at the courthouse in Huntsville, in Madison County, in March.[5]

Similarly, in White County, George Welcher was arrested for the burning of the Letona bridge on the accusation of a single witness and some circumstantial evidence. Welcher, a striking conductor, was the secretary of the strikers' organization in Searcy. Verne Dodge, a twenty-year-old mentally handicapped man, accused Welcher and C. H. "Straight Air" Smith, the head of the Searcy strikers, of going with him and another man he did not know to burn the bridge. Ten days later, H. T. Jones was also arrested and charged with the crime. Officers searched Welcher's vehicle and said they found emery dust, a pair of overalls with holes apparently eaten by acid, and letters exchanged between Welcher, Smith, and Pete Venable. Welcher's trial was scheduled for early February in Searcy.[6]

Perhaps the most contentious case concerned charges filed in Harrison against three strikers, Verlin D. "Red" Orr, Albert Stevens, and Luther Wise. Orr and Stevens were arrested on Thursday, the morning after the Everton bridge burned south of Harrison. Jack Halter, the assistant superintendent for the M&NA, swore a statement that he had seen Stevens getting in a Ford coupe in downtown Harrison with a five-gallon oil can at about 9:00 p.m. It is unclear what evidence prompted the arrest of Orr. His wife, Josephine, provided an alibi under oath, swearing that on the previous evening Orr had been home in bed at 8:40 p.m., when she returned from a movie. Former sheriff J. S. "Silby" Johnson investigated the scene at the bridge and found tire tracks in the mud, which he said he knew were like those on Wise's car. Wise was arrested on Friday by sheriff Robert "Bob" Shaddox, deputy sheriff Bryan Holt, and Walter Snapp, who it appears was acting as a deputy. Orr, Wise, and Stevens were each detained under a $10,000 bond. Moreover, Wise was fined $250 for wearing weapons found on him upon his arrest. George W. O'Neal, a prosperous real estate investor who owned the Midway Hotel, posted the bond for Stevens's release.[7]

After the arrest of Stevens and Orr on Thursday, Sheriff Shaddox got permission from circuit judge James M. Shinn to bring the men to his house while they tried to make bail. A crowd of perhaps fifty strikers, some of them armed, gathered around Shaddox's home to "protect the boys" from a lynching. Some of the strikers claimed to have been deputized by Mayor Clute, allowing them to lawfully carry weapons. Deputy sheriff Holt tried unsuccessfully to get the men to disband, fearing that they would try to take the prisoners away. He later reported some names to the Boone County grand jury, which indicted the men for carrying pistols and disturbing the peace. Shaddox's wife was alarmed by the angry crowd outside her door, and Judge Shinn instructed the sheriff to bring the men back to the county jail. Over the next two days, crowds milled around the county jail, as well as the jail in Berryville (where Pritchett was being held at the time), and rumors abounded that lynching of the accused bridge burners was imminent.[8]

As Judge Shinn convened the grand jury for its regularly scheduled session the next day, men still thronged the courthouse lawn. Shinn gave a lengthy speech on Friday with instructions for the jury. He reminded the jury that anyone who burned a railroad bridge or had knowledge of such plans was guilty of a felony offense. He criticized those who on the previous evening had roamed the streets of Harrison claiming to be officers and deputy sheriffs. Mayor Clute had informed him that there were only two city marshals, Mr. William Parr and the night watchman. Sheriff Shaddox had only one deputy, Holt. Shinn told the jury that any man without a commission as an officer of the law who carried a pistol violated the law, whether that person was a striker or a "Ku Kluxer." Shinn turned to Sheriff Shaddox, whom he must have known was a Klansman, and instructed him to disallow any assemblies while the court was in session: "I don't want the strikers to assemble in their meetings and I do not want the Ku Kluxers to have their meetings." Shinn announced that he would fine everyone who congregated in the streets in numbers greater than four. He called on the sheriff and mayor, who were both present, to assist in enforcing this directive. Clearly, Shinn was trying to defuse the crisis and avoid the collapse of civil order. Unfortunately, he lacked the resolve to follow through with his own rulings.[9]

After the arrest of the strikers and Murray's call to the public on Thursday, January 11, citizens in towns up and down the line sprang into action. On Friday, attendees at a mass meeting in Eureka

Springs pledged to protect the railroad's property and asked the US Department of Justice to send deputy marshals. One spokesperson said, "It looks as though anything may happen at any time." A citizens' meeting in Heber Springs raised a $300 reward for the apprehension of those committing depredations against the railroad. On Saturday evening in Kensett, a group of citizens, assisted by employees of the M&NA, rounded up suspects in the burning of the Letona bridge and brought them to the sheriff of White County. At a mass meeting in Searcy, citizens pledged to support the railroad and raise money to protect White County's five bridges along the line. The editor of the *Marshall Mountain Wave*, William Wenrick, ominously suggested in an editorial on Friday that it was time "to decorate a few telegraph poles" with radical strikers. A mass meeting there on Sunday, presided over by Marshall's mayor, Stephen W. Woods, organized the mob for its trip to Harrison the next day.[10]

It appears, then, that by the weekend, plans were already drawn up to assemble a mob. Walter Snapp, George McKinney, Tom Jones, and J. C. "Bud" Baker allegedly went up and down the line giving notice for people to assemble in Harrison on Monday morning, January 15. Murray made a third appeal to the public on Saturday, January 13, saying that the survival of the railroad depended on whatever "protective measures" the public would take. He announced hope that the strike might be ended on Sunday by a meeting of the sixteen railroad brotherhoods in Chicago, which had been called to discuss the M&NA strike and another action taking place on the Alabama, Birmingham, and Atlantic Railroad. Four strike leaders—Pete Venable, Tillman Jines, Edward B. Sebourn, and John W. Crews—had left Harrison on Friday for the meeting in Chicago. Venable said he was invited because of his discussions two weeks before with the Tulsa investors about their possible purchase of the M&NA. While at the meeting in Chicago, Venable said, he learned that plans were already in place for a mob to descend on Harrison. Edward J. Manion, the president of the Order of Railway Telegraphers, which had its headquarters in St. Louis, told Venable that Festus J. Wade had called him (Manion) to his office on Tuesday, January 9, to tell him that a mob was coming to Harrison and would clear out the strikers and hang Venable, James Queen, and Tillman Jines. If Venable's account is true, then plans for a mob action preceded the burning of the three big bridges earlier in the week. Venable alleged that Wade and the St. Louis owners controlled affairs behind the scenes, while railroad officers in Harrison were responsible for the specific plans for the riot. Wade warned Manion, Venable said, that if he had any friends in Harrison, he should get them out before the mob arrived.[11]

The Reverend John Kelly Farris preached twice that Sunday morning, January 14, at the Methodist church, to large and attentive audiences. He said he saw no hint of what was to come the next day. But by Sunday evening, either by telephone or telegraph, word came to Harrison that the brotherhoods in Chicago had voted to continue the strike. The railroad had already dispatched a special train to Leslie to bring citizens from the south to Harrison the next morning. The train was later said to have been ordered and paid for by Noah "Gus" Sawyer (secretary-treasurer of the Export Cooperage Company in Leslie and also mayor of the city), apparently to skirt ICC rules preventing the railroad from providing it for free. Venable alleged that by 10:30 p.m. on Sunday, Murray had called Snapp, who summoned Judge Shinn, Sheriff Shaddox, and prosecuting attorney Karl Greenhaw. The five men, Venable said, met in the railroad's office on the northeast corner of the courthouse square and finalized plans for the following day's activities. Guards were placed around the courthouse lawn and on roads leading out of town to prevent strikers and sympathizers from escaping. Rumors quickly spread on Sunday night in strikers' neighborhoods that a mob was on its way to Harrison. By midnight some strikers began fleeing through field and thicket, avoiding roads, toward the White River Line. Train crews there stopped and picked up some of the desperate strikers directly on the tracks.[12]

On Monday morning, January 15, men armed with shotguns, rifles, and revolvers began pouring into Harrison's central square. They came on foot and by automobile from Harrison and the surrounding countryside, from Newton County to the southwest, and points north on the railroad from Alpena, Green Forest, Berryville, and Eureka Springs. The special train from the south arrived with some three hundred passengers just past noon. It had left Leslie at 6:00 a.m. and picked up men along the way from Marshall, Gilbert, Pindall, St. Joe, Everton, and elsewhere. The trip from Leslie to Harrison was normally a four-hour ride, but the train arrived two hours late. The locomotive had failed, and the company had to send another from Harrison to finish the trip. Newspapers reported that citizens came from 150 miles in each direction to Harrison that day, which would mean that some came from as far away as Joplin to the north and Georgetown, in the east Arkansas Delta, to the south. As the passengers stepped off the train at the depot, a block from the main square, men received a white ribbon to pin to their chests. Dr. Charles M. Routh had gone into a store on the square and bought two bolts of ribbon, lengths of which were passed out to the crowd in order to tell friend from foe. With the train's arrival, the crowd had swelled. Upward of a thousand people now clogged the streets of downtown Harrison.[13]

A mob of such size could mean chaos, but planning had taken place in advance. According to Murray, guards had been posted at every railroad bridge in thirteen Arkansas counties, and in Newton and Barry Counties in Missouri, to prevent strikers from retaliating. Even before the train arrived, the crowd had selected representatives from Boone, Carroll, and Newton Counties for a citizens committee of twelve men to manage the event. A voice vote then determined the remainder of the committee by county, and someone called out Sam Dennis, a traveling salesman from Valley Springs, nine miles southeast of Harrison, as the chair. Besides Dennis, the committee included Luther "Clay" Holt, a Harrison grocer; Troy Coffman, a dentist in Harrison; Tom Morris, the former sheriff of Carroll County, who owned a canning factory and grocery store in Berryville; George Bazore, owner of a flour mill in Berryville; Ab B. Arbaugh, an attorney in Jasper; Lawrence W. Clark, a timberman in Jasper; J. Wilburn Moore, a Jasper banker; Stephen W. Woods, the mayor of Marshall and an attorney; and Jackson F. Henley and William T. Mills, both also Marshall attorneys. The Reverend Walter F. Bradley's account, used by others such as Orville Thrasher Gooden and Jesse Lewis Russell later, says that William J. Douglas, the editor of Berryville's *North Arkansas Star*, was the twelfth member of the committee. However, in Douglas's testimony before the legislative committee, he explained that he was in the crowd on Monday and did not join the committee until later, replacing Tom Morris when the latter became ill and went home to Berryville. Several men who appeared before the citizens committee said that Walter Snapp was a member and in fact that he, rather than Dennis, seemed to be in charge. Bradley's account, published ten months after the fact, was apparently shielding Snapp, his successor as exalted cyclops of the Harrison Klan, for he would have known of Snapp's role in the riot.

The appointed leaders went into Clay Holt's store, on the east side of the square, to get out of the January weather, but then someone suggested they use the meeting room of the Harrison Rotary Club. This hall was on the second floor of the Hooper Building (above the Farmers Bank), on the northeast corner of the square, kitty-corner from the M&NA's office, which was above the Citizens Bank. James Shinn had occupied the space as his law office before he became circuit judge in 1919. Soon after the citizens committee took up quarters there, the women of Harrison brought them a lunch. The group would hold session in the room for the following five days, January 15–19.[14]

As a first item of business, Stephen Woods suggested that the committee send a representative to the Boone County circuit court, then in session. He was appointed to do this task. He quickly went across the street to the courthouse, where he informed Judge Shinn, prosecuting attorney Greenhaw, and the grand jury that the citizens committee had been constituted as an independent body to investigate any property damage to the railroad. Woods promised the court that the committee planned a "peaceful investigation without any violation of the law." Greenhaw later testified at the legislative hearings that the citizens committee had no sanction or relationship with the circuit court and that the court had not issued any search or arrest warrants for the committee's work. But he praised the committee as composed of the best citizens, who were trying to assist officers of the law.[15]

While the committee members enjoyed their lunch in Rotary Hall, outside on the square other men were forming squads under company leaders. The squads left for the homes of strikers and sympathizers to bring them to the committee for interrogation and to search for evidence of sabotage. Some searches and detentions had already begun earlier in the day, an indication that the plans had been made in advance of the arrival of the crowd. Between 8:30 and 9:00 a.m. on Monday, for example, some Harrison men had taken strike leader James Queen into custody near town and questioned him. He was released shortly before the special train arrived, probably because he agreed to testify in the Orr-Wise case. Later that day another squad went to Queen's home seven miles from Harrison but found that he had escaped. Also during the morning hours, Bud Baker and George McKinney led a group of Harrison men who took strikers Charles DeGoche and Norman Stevens into custody, punched them with their guns, and detained them in an automobile near the depot. They were looking for Norman's brother Albert Stevens who was out on bail pending his court case the following Wednesday. DeGoche's wife, Emma, mistakenly believed that the justice system was still functioning and telephoned Judge Shinn and the city marshal, William Parr, to report her husband's rough treatment and illegal detention. When she went to the depot with a Mrs. Clark to check on her husband, McKinney and an M&NA conductor, Lysias B. Chilton, grabbed the two women. Emma DeGoche said that Chilton twisted her arm, kicked her knees, and called her vile names. They searched her, ripping all the buttons off her coat, and pushed her across the train tracks as they released her.[16]

As the squads fanned out across Harrison in the afternoon, the atmosphere became more unrestrained. The crowd remaining in the courthouse square set about to remove any strikers or sympathizers not wearing the white ribbon. Some who were reluctant to leave, Rev. Bradley said, "had the request emphasized by the toe of a rude boot." McKinney was named as a squad leader and provided with a list of names of about a dozen men to bring to the committee. His squad went first to the home of Pete Venable. As Venable was then returning by train from Chicago, his wife, Jennie, explained that he was not at home. They searched the premises from top to bottom. Mrs. Venable said that McKinney's group even tore up the tile in her bathroom floor to search the cistern underneath. They looked inside the basement furnace, which was roaring with a fire. McKinney's men broke the door off her car and cut her phone line. Many men, she said, trailed through her house, pointing guns at her. She named eighteen men specifically, including railroad employees, physicians, and the local undertaker, Doyle B. Woodruff, who lived across the street. McKinney said that some of the men criticized him for being too polite in his interactions with Mrs. Venable. After the ordeal, she was afraid to stay in her home and spent that night with a friend. When she came back to her house the next morning, she found that the mob had returned, broken down the front door, shattered windows (scattering glass over her floors), torn paper off the walls, and thrown clothes out of closets and drawers. Her husband's correspondence, his union records, and a stash of money were gone.[17]

As Jennie Venable surveyed the disarray of her home, at about 2:00 p.m. on Monday, she heard gunshots from a few blocks away. McKinney's squad had gone from her home to that of another striker, Ed C. Gregor, at 214 West Ridge Avenue, just a block and a half northwest of the square. Gregor, a former machinist and boilermaker, had been in charge of the railroad's water supply before the strike. But since early September 1922, he had been employed by the Ozark Power and Water Company, on the Powersite Dam on the White River, near Branson, Missouri. Gregor and his wife, Josie, were members of Farris's Methodist church but had not been attending because of the stand taken toward the strike by Farris's predecessor, the Reverend W. T. Martin. Gregor had worked for the M&NA for more than a decade. Farris described Josie Gregor as a "small, refined woman." The couple had a married daughter, Violet, who lived in Illinois; a son, Orville, who was in 1923 a cadet at the US Naval Academy in Annapolis, Maryland; and a six-year-old daughter, Bonnie Belle. Ed Gregor was a Royal Arch Mason and proudly wore his Master Mason's ring. He and another Harrison man, Albert Raash, had returned the previous Friday from Missouri, as the dam project had just completed. Neither man was in Arkansas when the bridges were burned during the previous two weeks.[18]

On Saturday and Monday morning Ed Gregor did some odd jobs for George Minicus, a baker who was a member of the Harrison City Council and a strike sympathizer. When Gregor came home for lunch he intended to stay in the house, for word had passed quickly about the arrival of the special train and the rabble assembling on the square. Josie, along with some other strikers' wives, walked to the square and surveyed the noisy mob. She observed some men in the crowd wrestling with others, strikers and sympathizers, who were not wearing the white ribbons. She watched a citizen shoot at the feet of one man, Tom Phifer, and then hit him over the head with a gun. Josie returned home and described the scene to her husband. He convinced her to go back and observe while he stayed home with Bonnie Belle. Josie Gregor had just come to the post office, on the northeast corner of the square, when she heard shooting. She asked a man: "Which house?"

The answer came: "The green house on the hill." She yelled: "That's my house and my baby is there." She ran home to find a hundred or more men surrounding her house, guns raised, yelling at her husband, who was standing in the kitchen.[19]

The crowd had approached Gregor's home, and one man went onto the porch, calling him to come out. Gregor yelled in response that he would give the men two minutes to get away from his house or he would shoot their "damn hearts out." A few moments later, Gregor stepped out the back door and fired twice from his double-barreled shotgun. Immediately, the mob responded with a volley of gunfire. Sheriff Shaddox heard it from the courthouse two blocks away, where circuit court was in session. Rev. Farris heard the gunfire from his home south of downtown. Speaking sixty years later, Dr. Henry Vance Kirby remembered hearing the shots from his grammar school. Even George McKinney admitted, "the shooting became promiscuous." When Farris visited Mrs. Gregor the following day, he saw the inside walls on the south and west sides riddled with bullets. He said, "a zinc water bucket and a smaller tin vessel sitting on a table in the rear hall were so perforated with bullets they looked like colanders." The glass doors of the kitchen were shattered. Another shot went through a wall and hit a mattress, scattering cotton over the floors. Two bullets fired from the front yard went directly through the house and hit a strikebreaker, G. W. Blakemore, in the backyard. Ed Gregor and Bonnie Belle miraculously were not injured. It was at this point that Josie Gregor arrived, yelling hysterically that her daughter was in the house and imploring the mob to hold their fire. She went in the back door and found her husband standing in the kitchen, stunned but cursing the "God damn cowardly sons of bitches." Silby Johnson, acting as a special deputy to Sheriff Shaddox, came to the back door to call for Gregor to surrender. Mrs. Gregor pleaded with her husband to go. Johnson assured the couple that he would personally take Gregor to the citizens committee and make sure that no harm came to him. Gregor got his coat, and Johnson walked him to the square. This was the last time that Josie Gregor would see her husband alive.[20]

Josie Gregor stayed behind as the mob rushed in to search her house. McKinney had gone on to apprehend another striker, so leading the search of the Gregor home was Delania E. "Pegleg" Decker, a one-legged hotel owner and photographer from Leslie. Others crowded in,

The Gregor home at 214 West Ridge Avenue, view from the east.
Farris, The Harrison Riot, 1924.

including Dr. Charles Routh, Lysias Chilton, and Dr. Vinet Ruble, a Harrison dentist. Men had entered the basement from a coal door to the backyard and were searching there. They took Gregor's recently fired shotgun and what they claimed was ten pounds of emery dust. Meanwhile, Johnson said, Gregor was "cussing and raising Cain" as he was marched around the square toward Rotary Hall. At around 3:00 p.m. he came before the citizens committee, which found his answers "vindictive and insulting." After about twenty minutes of questioning, the committee put Gregor in the so-called bullpen, a small room to the rear of Rotary Hall, where other prisoners were being held for further questioning. From the window of the bullpen Gregor could see the epicenter of the mob at the intersection of Rush Avenue and Vine Street, and beyond it the square, where squads of armed citizens drilled.[21]

As Gregor went before the committee Monday afternoon and languished in the bullpen, the squads continued to search for strikers and sympathizers. They went toward the home of Albert Stevens, out on bail for the burning of the Everton bridge. Stevens saw the mob coming and ran to the home of a friendly neighbor woman. As the mob raided his home and confiscated ammunition as "evidence," the neighbor hid Stevens between a mattress and featherbed. When the mob later came there, demanding Stevens, Venable, and Tillman Jines, she protested that she knew nothing about them. They searched

Ed C. Gregor. *Labor, February 3, 1923.*

her house but failed to find the well-hidden Stevens. After they left, she shaved Albert close, dabbed him with rouge and powder, and dressed him in one of her gowns, along with hat, veil, and necklace. He was described as a small man with thin features, and the ruse worked. In a hired service car, Albert Stevens managed to get past the guards on the Bergman Road and escape. By 6:00 p.m. the vigilantes ordered the Jones Taxi Company not to send any more cars out of Harrison. Stevens's wife and daughter left Harrison the following week, and their home remained vacant throughout the year.[22]

From the Stevens home, the mob went to the residence of Tillman Jines, apparently unaware that he was at that time with Venable on a train returning from Chicago. Mrs. Fay Jines collected her children from school and then, afraid to go home, went to a friend's house, perched on a hill from which she had a view of her home. At about 4:30 p.m. she saw the mob, which by then had swelled to around 150 men, coming to her house. She recognized several leaders, including Routh, Woodruff, and McKinney. The crowd was distracted when a striker, Ben Turney, ran from the home of his father-in-law, James A. Hughey, and the men took after Turney, shooting as they went. They returned to the Hughey home, kicked open the door, took the screens off the windows, and took away the old man and his son John Hughey. The group then mobbed the Jines home. Fay and her children stayed that night at her friend's home, all sleeping in the middle of the house to guard against gunfire. When she went to her home the next day, she found that it had been ransacked, beveled glass doors shattered, dishes tossed and broken, curtains pulled down, mattresses dragged off beds, and papers scattered over the floors.[23]

In such a manner, the mob went from house to house looking for strikers, detaining those that they found, searching homes, and bringing the strikers and any "evidence" confiscated to the committee in Rotary Hall. Ralph Rea later remembered how, as a thirteen-year-old boy, he had watched as strikers were brought to the northeast corner of the square. He recalled witnessing a few cases of stubborn strikers who received "some persuasive boots in their behinds" and watching as one man was mauled on the head with a pistol. Several strikers who tried to escape were captured at roadblocks leading out of town, and the guards brought them to the committee for interrogation. This process would continue for the next four days. Many of the strikers lived in Eagle Heights, a neighborhood on a hill east of the railroad tracks, not far from the M&NA shops just to the south. By the end of the week, the Eagle Heights area was dark, with most homes empty.

Outside of Rotary Hall, the mob guarded a group of strikers and sympathizers waiting to be brought past the armed guard at the door and ushered before the citizens committee. The twelve men asked strikers about their knowledge of alleged depredations that had occurred to the railroad. According to the committee's secretary, Ab Arbaugh, if the strikers confessed any particulars, this information was shared with the grand jury. The committee asked strikers to pledge their loyalty to the railroad and renounce their strike benefits. If they did not, strikers were "requested" to leave the area served by the railroad, for their safety could not be guaranteed if they remained. In later testimony before the legislative committee, members of the Harrison citizens committee, to a man, insisted that they never ordered strikers to leave or used violence. Some strikers, however, testified that committee members slapped, punched, and hit them with guns, and threatened violence if they did not leave Harrison. In any case, with the committee supported by an armed mob outside and by guards carrying guns in the very same room, the message was clear. Most of the two hundred to three hundred strikers in Harrison would be gone by the end of the week. Those who resisted in any way or gave impolite answers were sent to the bullpen to the rear of the hall. By late Monday, the bullpen was crowded.[24]

The squads also brought before the committee strike sympathizers who had never even worked for the railroad. A group came for George O'Neal at his home next to the Midway Hotel. O'Neal asked the men whether they had a summons or warrant for his arrest. When they said no, he informed them that they would be liable for prosecution for such an action. They did not seem worried. O'Neal called the city marshal, William Parr, to accompany him to Rotary Hall. Parr said that Walter Snapp and Clay Holt, however, pushed him aside and told him to leave. They would forcibly bring Parr back two days later. The committee harangued O'Neal for being friendly with strikers. O'Neal said the main reason he was questioned was his payment of Albert Stevens's bond the previous week. After the committee insisted that he help find Stevens, they let O'Neal go.[25]

As darkness approached, someone brought a quantity of cordwood to the northeast corner of the square. Members of the mob went into nearby Union Hall, above Clay Holt's grocery store on the east side of Vine Street, and began to carry out furnishings, paraphernalia including the lodge seal, and stacks of records and correspondence to fuel a bonfire in the middle of the intersection. Some chairs were kept for seating, while others went to the top of the raging fire. Rev. Farris noted that when strikers burned bridges it was called arson, but when the mob burned union property it was called a bonfire. Sheriff Shaddox was on hand, providing guard duty to the prisoners in the bullpen.[26]

The Mothers Club of Harrison brought dinner for the citizens committee and sandwiches and coffee for the prisoners. The committee continued to deliberate until 7:00 or 8:00 p.m. on Monday. At some point that evening, the group determined to oust Mayor Clute, two

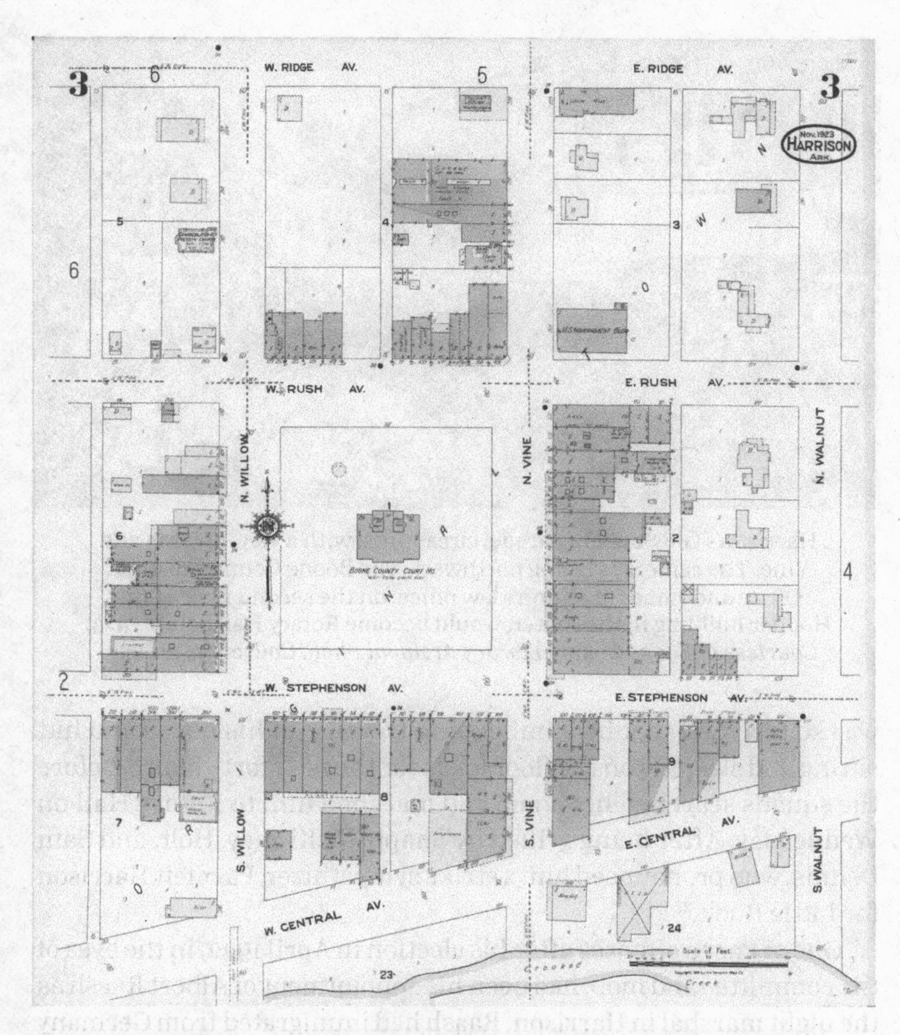

Sanborn insurance map of Harrison, November 1923. On the northeast corner, at the intersection of Rush and Vine, is Rotary Hall, above a bank. The M&NA office sits above another bank on the southeast corner. Directly south of the M&NA office is Ralph D. Cline's furniture store and funeral parlor, and south of that is Clay Holt's grocery story, with Union Hall on the second floor. The Gregor home is visible at the corner of West Ridge and North Willow. *Courtesy of the Library of Congress.*

members of the city council who sympathized with the strikers, and city marshal Parr, and to demand that Parr leave town. The committee proposed holding a special election to replace the four officials. Parr, who had been sent home earlier in the day by the committee,

Harrison's Old Soldiers Parade, circa 1910s, with a view of Rush and Vine. The camera is facing northwest. The Boone County Abstract Office and James M. Shinn's law office, on the second floor of the Hooper Building in the center, would become Rotary Hall before 1923. *Courtesy of Boone County Library Archival Photo Collection, no. 299.*

was so terrified that he climbed into the attic of his house and hid, sitting and sleeping on the floor joists for the next forty hours, before the squads searched his home and marched him to Rotary Hall on Wednesday. After being grilled by Snapp, McKinney, Holt, and Sam Dennis, who pronounced him a strike sympathizer, Parr left Harrison for Little Rock.[27]

One of Parr's offenses after his election in April 1922, in the eyes of the committee and mob, had been his appointment of Albert Raash as the night marshal in Harrison. Raash had immigrated from Germany at age twenty in 1895. He must have spoken with an accent and never bothered to acquire US citizenship. Rev. Bradley said that this brought him the disfavor of the American Legion, a group closely linked in Arkansas to the Ku Klux Klan. Even worse, Bradley said, Raash was rumored to be a member of the Industrial Workers of the World (IWW). He had given up his job as night watchman to go with Ed Gregor to work on the dam project in Missouri during the fall. The two men had just returned to Harrison the previous Friday and could not have been involved in the recent burning of bridges. Nonetheless, between 9:00 and 10:00 p.m. that Monday, as Raash and his wife and

View from Rotary Hall of the mob at the intersection of Rush and Vine. The US Government Building (post office) is to the left, across Rush Avenue from the M&NA headquarters. *St. Louis Post-Dispatch, January 23, 1923.*

children were sitting in their home reading, a group of armed men burst through the door without knocking. They ordered Raash to get his shoes and come with them. He asked twice why they wanted him, given that he had no connection with the strike. They would not answer. Three men grabbed him by the collar and threw him out the door, taking him to the edge of town, punching and kicking him as they went. They tore off his clothes and kept hitting him on the head whenever he tried to speak, eventually knocking him unconscious. They finally let him return home clad in his underwear, ordering him to leave Harrison by the time the sun set the next evening. Raash said his eye was nearly swollen shut, and he could not sleep that night for the pain. The squad came for him the next morning and brought him before the committee. After three hours he was released. He immediately made for the woods to get out of town.[28]

While the squad terrorized Raash, several members of the committee lingered in Rotary Hall, talking about the day's events. Guards continued an all-night vigil. Some out-of-town members of the mob adjourned to hotels. Other slept in homes of welcoming Harrison residents. Some men continued to congregate through the night around the fire on the corner of the square. Rev. Farris said he could hear the tumult from his home, which was close to downtown. His sleep was disturbed by the passing of many cars through the night. Some strikers, meanwhile, headed to the forests outside of town, fearing to sleep in their own homes. Women carried food out to their husbands. It would be a long night. Fortunately, it was relatively warm for January, probably not getting to the point of freezing. A group of eleven refugees came across the farm of Harry S. Ransom, who fed them and let them warm themselves by his fire. Afterward, on Wednesday morning, armed patrols arrived from Harrison, sent by the mob to hunt fleeing strikers. In Ransom's words, "they ordered me to git, and I got." He hid out in the woods himself, until coming out later in the week looking a pitiful sight.[29]

The last members of the citizens committee left Rotary Hall at about 11:00 p.m. on Monday. Sheriff Shaddox, deputy sheriff Bryan Holt, and some others who were guarding eight men in the bullpen (Ed Gregor among them) allowed the prisoners to come into the larger room to sit and lie down on the floor or a table. Two prisoners, James Ralph Curnutt and John Hughey, testified to the legislative committee that sometime around 2:00 or 3:00 a.m., Walter Snapp, who they thought was the committee's chairman, came into the room, called Sheriff Shaddox to the side, and engaged in a whispered conversation. A bit later George McKinney arrived and did the same. Then, at about 4:30 a.m., Shaddox woke two prisoners, Norman Stevens and Charles DeGoche, and told them he was removing them to the county jail. He left with the two men, taking two guards with him. Two other guards were brought into the hall to take their place. Another striker in the bullpen, Henry Grady Crutchfield, suggested that in doing so, Shaddox deliberately abandoned Gregor to the mob. Crutchfield said that at that moment Gregor commented, "There will be some monkey business now." Curnutt and Hughey testified that about thirty minutes later, three men wearing black masks burst into the room and motioned for Ed Gregor to come forward. The two guards yelled for the men to stop. Gregor reached for his coat, which was sitting on a table, but one of the men jerked it out of his hands and threw it on the floor, saying that Gregor would not need it. They pushed Gregor out of the room at the point of their pistols. One prisoner, Walter Suskey, said that he recognized one of the masked men and tried to speak to him, but the prisoners were not allowed to talk. From the window, Hughey said, they could see a crowd of perhaps two hundred people gathered around the bonfire, as eight men drove away with Gregor in two Ford cars, one larger and one smaller.[30]

Pegleg Decker of Leslie, who had been in the mob that searched Gregor's home earlier, was alleged to have boasted to several men gathered in front of the People's Mercantile in Leslie, once he returned home, about being with the group at Rotary Hall. A Leslie man, James Taylor, testified before the legislative committee that Decker said he was present as Gregor was taken down the stairs and away to the railroad bridge over Crooked Creek, on the south side of Harrison, about a half mile away. Taylor said Decker even repeated some of Gregor's last words before he was lowered from the trestle and hanged to his death: "I know every one of you, and if you don't kill me, I'll get you." Taylor testified that when Decker told this story, he wore pinned to his coat a piece of the rope used to lynch Ed Gregor. Decker himself later appeared before the legislative committee and denied Taylor's allegations that he was in the group that took Gregor. He admitted he had seen Gregor's body lying on the ground near the bridge in the care of the undertaker. He said the piece of rope alleged to have been pinned to his coat was just a piece of binder twine tied around a button on another man's coat, which he had taken by accident as he left in haste to catch the special train. This story strains credibility, given that he was then wearing the same coat with the stray piece of twine after his return to Leslie some days later. One Leslie woman, Alda Treece, remembered years later seeing several men who returned from Harrison wearing pieces of rope on their lapels. One wonders who, if not Decker, took the photograph of Gregor's body hanging from the bridge early Tuesday morning, given that Decker was a photographer by profession.[31]

Some sixty years later, Henry Vance Kirby, a longtime Harrison physician, recalled hearing an alternative version of the hanging of Ed Gregor. One of his patients, who spoke as if he had been present at the trestle, suggested that Gregor's killing was more accidental than intentional. According to this story, Gregor's captors tied a noose around his neck to scare him into talking. When he refused, they hung him over the edge momentarily. Gregor gave the Masonic distress signal, but nobody answered. When the men pulled him back up, they found he was dead. In this telling, the men dropped Gregor back down then and left him hanging.[32]

A railroad guard stationed near the bridge, whom authorities never named, said that he had seen two automobiles drive underneath the bridge at around 5:00 a.m., but that it was too dark to tell how many

Delania E. "Pegleg" Decker. *Courtesy of Diana Dunn.*

were in the cars. After a few minutes they drove away. The guard said he heard some groans coming from the bridge, then silence. As soon as it became light enough to see, he found Gregor's body suspended from the bridge. Whoever put the rope around Gregor's neck lacked skill in making a hangman's knot, and as a result the noose had slipped above his chin, leaving burn marks on his face. Similar marks were evident on his wrists, indicating that Gregor had struggled to free himself when his arms were tied. Someone reported the hanging to Sheriff Shaddox, who informed Judge Shinn. The latter instructed the sheriff to assemble a coroner's jury to investigate Gregor's death, which returned the verdict later in the day that Gregor died from strangulation at the hand of unknown parties.[33]

Soon after Gregor's hanging, the mob moved on to the home of George O'Neal. At around 6:45 a.m. on Tuesday, he was awakened when nearly a hundred armed men congregated in front of his house. His son answered the door. The men pushed him back, entered the house, and dragged O'Neal out of bed in his nightclothes. His wife, Eva, was making biscuits as the men mobbed her home, and she threw dough in their faces. Two men restrained her while others took George into the street, where they began hitting him with straps. George McKinney held O'Neal's head between his legs while Tom Jones and J. A. Story held his hands. O'Neal could not see the man who applied the strap from behind. Rev. Farris identified the person as a clergyman from a neighboring town. It was almost certainly the Reverend Dillard Monroe Carter, the Baptist preacher in Leslie. The beating continued until blood ran from O'Neal's naked back. He later testified to the legislative committee that as he was whipped one member of the mob said, "We've just come back from one serious affair and if you contend with this bunch you may get the same thing." O'Neal had been asleep when Gregor was hanged, but he realized later the man was talking about the lynching that had happened an hour and a half before. The mob let O'Neal go, telling him to get dressed and appear before the citizens committee.[34]

The committee reconvened in Rotary Hall at about 7:30 a.m. on Tuesday, January 16, sending the prisoners back to the bullpen. From the window there they could see on the street below the undertaker pull up in an automobile containing a body that was wearing shoes and clothes they recognized as belonging to Ed Gregor. Nearby, in front of the undertaker's establishment, four hundred or five hundred people gathered around the car to view Gregor's body. The committee moved on to its new business. When O'Neal was brought in, the questioning centered on the whereabouts of Albert Stevens. According to O'Neal, Snapp appeared to be in charge. When O'Neal agreed to help locate Stevens to meet his arraignment in circuit court the following day, the committee allowed him to leave. Rev. Farris was also "advised" to visit the committee before ministering as pastor to Mrs. Gregor. Sam Dennis assured Farris that the committee regretted Gregor's death and would have guarded him more carefully had it suspected there was such a chance of violence.[35]

Feeling unsafe in her home Monday night, Josie Gregor (along with Bonnie Belle) had spent the night across the street at the home

The hanging of Ed C. Gregor. *Courtesy of Cleburne County Historical Society.*

of Mayor Clute and his wife. Josie had just returned home Tuesday morning when Jennie Venable and Josephine Trimble, the wife of the former mayor, came to tell her about the death of her husband. When Farris arrived at the Gregor home, he found Josie understandably distraught, upset that she had convinced her husband to surrender after the couple had been promised that no harm would come to him. Several neighbor women, some churchwomen, and undertaker Ralph D. Cline had arrived to assist. Cline and his older brother George, who was a strike sympathizer on Harrison's city council, operated a furniture store/funeral parlor on the east side of the downtown square. They competed with Doyle Woodruff, the pro-railroad undertaker/furniture merchant on the opposite side of the square. Ralph Cline apologized to Josie Gregor for wearing a white ribbon, for he had to wear it, he said. Farris prayed with Mrs. Gregor and discussed arrangements for the disposition of her husband's body. She could not bear the thought of him being buried in Harrison, so she decided to take his remains for burial in Fremont, Missouri, near where the couple had married in 1900. The committee told Farris that Mrs. Gregor must stay at home and her husband's body remain at the funeral home, and that Farris should pick out the casket. Farris wrote telegrams to Gregor's son in Maryland and daughter in Illinois, indicating that their father was dead but that they must not return home. Farris arranged for Watkins's taxi service to take them to Bergman to meet the train that would take Josie, Bonnie Belle, and Ed's body to its final rest in Missouri. Early on Wednesday morning, January 17, Farris and Josie retrieved the body at Cline's funeral parlor, making their way through the mob that still thronged the streets. When Farris got the casket loaded onto the train and Josie and Bonnie Belle safely in their seats in Bergman, Farris said goodbye. The train rolled off at 10:00 a.m.[36]

So, who actually killed Ed Gregor? Walter Snapp, George McKinney, and Sheriff Shaddox appear to have been party to a plan to get the sheriff out of Rotary Hall before three men took Gregor away to his death. The men wore black masks. Members of the Ku Klux Klan were known to wear black masks, instead of the normal white hoods, when they engaged in violent raids. David C. Stephenson, the former grand dragon of the Indiana Klan, said that head Klansman, Imperial Wizard Hiram Evans, had authorized the wearing of black masks when engaged in whipping or killing expeditions. In the most famous murders committed by the Klan, the capture and execution of two white men in Mer Rouge, Louisiana, the Klan executioners wore black masks. Newspapers throughout the country in January 1923 covered the grand jury hearing of Klan leaders in the Mer Rouge case, just as Klansmen in the Arkansas towns along the M&NA planned their mob action. A black hood was even presented in court as evidence in the Mer Rouge trial on January 10, 1923. Snapp, who was already or would soon become the exalted cyclops of the Harrison Klan, appears to have been the person in charge of both the mob and the committee. Several people interrogated by the committee indicated that he was in charge. The railroad brotherhoods' newspaper, *Labor*, on February 3, named Snapp as the principal organizer of the thousand-member mob two weeks before.[37]

Rev. Farris described the scene as he approached the northeast corner of the square to appear before the committee on Tuesday morning. A crowd of men warmed themselves around the fire in the middle of the intersection of Rush and Vine. Nearby was a stand that the "captain of the mob" would mount as a signal that he was to give orders to the armed vigilantes. Farris did not name the captain, but most likely it was Snapp, who seems to have alternated between inside and outside Rotary Hall. A month after the Harrison riot, Pete Venable wrote to Roger Nash Baldwin, the head of the American Civil Liberties Union (ACLU), saying that he had no doubt that Snapp had been the leader of the mob that hanged Gregor. Venable was sure that Snapp, McKinney, and Shaddox were behind the plot. Snapp may have been one of the masked men who took Gregor away. Venable alleged he had "positive proof" that two of the three men were Marion Atterberry, a strikebreaker/conductor from Leslie, and Doyle Woodruff, the undertaker who had approached Gregor's house the day before. Woodruff held membership in Harrison's Masonic lodge. Farris indicated that at least one of Gregor's Masonic brothers was at the bridge when he was hanged.[38]

The lynching of Ed Gregor and beatings of Albert Raash and George O'Neal constituted the most flagrant violence of the Harrison riot. As with political or social violence in general, terror was public, selective, and symbolic. Gregor was a striker, but he had played no role in the recent bridge burnings that were the supposed justification for a militant action. An illegal search of his home brought forth a can of emery dust, but this would not be exceptional for a person who was a machinist by trade. He was lynched because he dared to resist the mob, and perhaps because Tillman Jines and Pete Venable were unavailable. Raash and O'Neal had no connection to the strike, other than friendship and sympathy for strikers. Raash—an immigrant noncitizen who had slept in the same bunkhouse as Gregor—was an easy target for the mob, for who would stand up for him? O'Neal's whipping demonstrated that not even wealth or social status mattered if one chose the wrong side. Word about the lynching and beatings quickly passed around Harrison. The mob had undermined the authority of Harrison's city government and demonstrated the acquiescence, or even support, of county officials. John Hughey later testified that when he was before the citizens committee on Monday afternoon, someone said, "we are going to have to hang three or four union men to make them talk."[39] A few cases of personal violence constituted a sufficient message to anyone who might, like Ed Gregor, consider resistance.

CHAPTER 6

MOB RULE IN HARRISON: JANUARY 16–31, 1923

As the sun rose on Tuesday morning, January 16, after the hanging of Ed C. Gregor and the flogging of George W. O'Neal, downtown Harrison had the appearance of an armed camp. Some three hundred men carrying shotguns, rifles, and pistols milled about the streets. Strikers and sympathizers were nowhere in sight. Men were boiling coffee and cooking on fires around the courthouse square. Almost all shops and offices were closed, but hotels and cafés were doing a thriving business. The worst of the violence was over. The citizens committee resumed meeting at around 7:30 a.m., with the squads ready to do its bidding. Through the rest of the week and month, the mob leaders consolidated their control, in conjunction with Boone County officials: circuit judge James M. Shinn, prosecuting attorney Karl Greenhaw, sheriff Robert "Bob" Shaddox, and the Boone County grand jury. Their near-total expulsion of strikers and several sympathizers would effectually end the strike.[1]

Soon after Judge Shinn learned about Gregor's murder, he worried that the mob had grown out of control. Shortly after 8:00 a.m., he called Greenhaw and Mayor Jasper L. Clute into his office and prepared a telegram to Governor Thomas C. McRae requesting troops be sent to Harrison to restore order. It read: "Situation beyond control of local authorities in this county. One man hanged. We need help to control situation. Send militia company at earliest moment." Shinn also telephoned the governor's office in case the telegram was delayed. He was told that the governor normally arrived at 9:00 a.m., so Shinn called back at 9:05. The judge described to McRae the violence that had occurred and the bitter division between strikers and supporters of the railroad. What was needed, he said, were impartial, unbiased troops. McRae balked at the request, saying that he constitutionally was unable to send a militia when the Arkansas General Assembly was in session. The forty-fourth session of the state legislature had convened on Monday, January 8. Judge Shinn was peeved at McRae's response, so he ordered Sheriff Shaddox to swear in fifty men as special deputies. This was quickly done, for Shaddox merely gave the names of Harrison men who were already part of the mob. Two of the special deputies included George McKinney and Doyle B. Woodruff, who it appears had been part of the conspiracy to hang Gregor. Like foxes guarding the chicken house, the special deputies were patrolling the streets and the M&NA shops by 10:00 a.m. on Tuesday.[2]

McRae referred the request for state militiamen to the General Assembly. In his speech to the legislature on opening day the week before, the governor had declared that no real business or progress was possible in the state without railroads. On Tuesday morning he made clear his desire for permission to send armed forces to Harrison to restore order. In the early afternoon the House and Senate deliberated for thirty minutes and approved the use of troops at the governor's discretion. Under McRae's direction, then, Company H of the Arkansas National Guard, a machine gun battalion of seventy-five men, prepared to go to Harrison. Members were assembled at the armory and readied by Captain Harry Smith. M&NA general manager Jack Murray prepared a special train to meet the company in Kensett and bring the troops on to Harrison. With their doughboy tin hats, uniforms, packs, and weapons, the men were reminiscent of 1917. McRae telegraphed to Harrison that troops would be on their way. Sheriff Shaddox sent a telegram back, saying, "Situation well in hand. Don't need militia. Stop them. Notify Murray not to send train for troops." Mayor Clute, however, telegraphed the governor again, reiterating a request for troops. At 9:00 p.m., just as the soldiers were ready to depart on the Missouri Pacific to catch the M&NA train at Kensett, McRae rescinded the order.[3]

Shaddox clearly misrepresented the situation in Harrison, for the town was anything but quiet. All during the day, the special deputies and the rest of the mob patrolled the streets, bringing strikers before the committee and searching their homes. When a squad came to question one sympathizer, John Branham, on the south side of Harrison, his teenage daughter met the band at the front door. With a revolver in each hand, she warned the men not to approach the house. When they kept coming, she fired two shots, but they overpowered her and took her father for interrogation. Other members of the mob visited a pool hall operated by a sympathizer, Clay King, a site known to be a hangout for strikers. They piled the furniture in the middle of the floor and told the proprietor to "beat it" and never return. Like many others who fled Harrison that week, King landed in Branson, Missouri.[4]

The citizens committee kept up its work of questioning strikers and sympathizers. Evidently, the hanging of Gregor motivated some strikers to provide statements incriminating others. One striker, Dock Keeter, told the committee that Pete Venable and Charles DeGoche had ordered him to place emery dust in the axle boxes of train cars that were loading Walter Snapp's apple harvest at Bellefonte, just south of Harrison. Keeter said Venable threatened to take away his strike benefits if he did not follow through with the order. Keeter repeated this accusation before the Boone County grand jury. The citizens committee informed newspaper reporters that it had gathered evidence against about a dozen strikers who had committed depredations. In addition, the committee claimed to have collected materials, probably through the storming of Union Hall and the search of Venable's home, that implicated national union officials. Newspapers variously reported that the Boone County grand jury had indicted from ten to twenty-five strikers for bridge burning and other attacks on railroad property and that federal warrants were sought against the national union officials. However, a careful look through the Indictment Book and Criminal Record Book for Boone County shows no indictments for sabotage except those of Luther Wise, Verlin D. "Red" Orr, and Albert Stevens in the previous week. The grand jury did indict Dock Keeter on January 16, and again on January 20, for public drunkenness, based on witness statements provided by three members of the mob. This might give some explanation for Keeter's readiness to provide testimony against Venable and DeGoche.[5]

A steady stream of strikers, sympathizers, and their families exited Harrison on Tuesday. At daybreak, Fay Jines returned home to find that her house had been ransacked. She and her seven-year-old daughter left with some other wives and children of strikers early that morning for Bergman. They called for a taxi but were told that taxis were not allowed to make the trip. Knowing the roads were guarded, the women and children went on foot through the woods. About halfway to Bergman they came across a farmer who drove them the rest of the way. Pete Venable had called home Monday evening from St. Louis and learned about the events of the day in Harrison. Venable and Tillman Jines were due to arrive in Bergman at 12:58 p.m. on Tuesday, but instead they exited the train in Branson. Mrs. Jines joined her husband there, and they and other strikers made their way to Carthage, Missouri. Meanwhile, a squad of twenty-five men took Jennie Venable before the citizens committee. Snapp and McKinney were in and out of the room, she said, while she was questioned. The committee told her she must leave Harrison by nightfall. Under the guard of Carl Brown, a clerk for the M&NA, she returned home, where she replaced the front door, packed two trunks and a couple of grips, and drove away in her car. She took with her Ed E. Larimer, the brother of alderman William W. Larimer, who was also expelled from the town because of his sympathy for strikers. At Prosperity, fifteen miles north of Harrison, she picked up some other refugees, Dona Sebourn and her two children. Mrs. Sebourn said the mob had searched her home and run her out of town. Her husband was also returning from the union meeting in Chicago. Her feet were blistered from walking for miles in new shoes. Jennie Venable drove the group to Branson, where she met up with her husband, Pete.[6]

While the vigilantes directed most of their violence and deportations toward men, women and children also suffered. The railroad would not allow the strikers or their family members to exit Harrison by M&NA trains, thus necessitating difficult overland treks in January weather. Shelby Matthews, a striking brakeman, had fled at the beginning of the roundup. The committee ordered his wife, Nona, to get her husband back for questioning. She refused, for another wife of a striker had summoned her husband home under the promise of safety only to see him seized and flogged. Raymond S. Johnson departed Harrison on Sunday, January 14, when rumors abounded about a coming mob. He left behind a young wife, Thelma, who was nearing the delivery of their first child. When she went into labor on Tuesday night, she could not get a physician to come to her house to assist. Someone had cut their lights, and so four neighbor women helped Mrs. Johnson give birth to a baby boy by flashlight. Judge Shinn was Raymond Johnson's uncle. After some newspapers printed the story of Thelma Johnson's troubles, Shinn wrote to the *Boone County Headlight*, claiming that the story was manufactured out of whole cloth and that Raymond had left Harrison some months earlier for Oklahoma, where he was gainfully employed. Raymond, however, rebutted Shinn's story in the *Headlight*, declaring that he had fled Harrison in fear for his life and that the account of his wife's troubles was indeed true.[7]

By Tuesday evening, the crowds in the streets of Harrison had thinned, as many out-of-towners had left to clean up their own hometowns of strikers and sympathizers. Still, some three hundred armed men milled about the downtown area. A company drilled military style around the courthouse. Guards continued to man roadblocks to prevent strikers from leaving without going before the committee. The atmosphere remained threatening. One of Rev. John Kelly Farris's church members who wore the white ribbon, Andrew McAllen, spent the evening at Farris's house just in case the mob came calling there. Even Judge Shinn evidently feared the mob's wrath, for he went straight home after court and stayed inside all night. He admitted to the legislative committee that he "didn't want to be whipped."[8]

Shinn was back in the spacious second-floor courtroom by early Wednesday morning for the arraignment of Wise, Orr, and Stevens, charged with burning the Everton bridge the previous week. When he convened the grand jury the day before, Shinn was clearly appalled at the violence that had occurred in Harrison. "One man is killed," he said, "other men have been whipped publicly in broad daylight and others beaten with guns." He told the members of the grand jury that he had asked Governor McRae for help, but that if people's property "is taken possession of, and if people here are being mobbed and whipped we must do something to protect them." Shinn even admitted that he considered himself at risk of being beaten, whipped, or publicly humiliated because of his efforts to enforce the law. However, when the defendants stood before him on Wednesday, Shinn failed to acknowledge the threatening mob.[9]

Albert Stevens failed to show at 8:15 a.m. when the court convened, and his bond was declared forfeited. Luther Wise had appeared before Judge Shinn two and a half years earlier, in July 1920, when he was indicted for gambling. Wise and Red Orr now stood before Judge Shinn to plead, without knowing what evidence the prosecution possessed against them. It was flimsy and prejudicial at best: special deputy J. S. "Silby" Johnson's recollection that the tire tracks near the Everton bridge matched those of a Ford car owned by Wise, and a declaration by M&NA assistant superintendent Jack Halter that he had seen Stevens get in a vehicle that contained an oil can. Orr's wife, Josephine, had provided an alibi for her husband, swearing that he was home in bed when the bridge was reported burned. However, sometime before Wednesday, Mrs. Orr changed her story, saying she was asleep and had no idea when her husband had returned home. Mrs. Orr's brother, Almar H. Cooper, was staying in the home on the night in question. By Wednesday he had given a statement saying he had overheard Orr tell his wife that they had burned the Everton bridge. Moreover, the following day, while Orr was in the sheriff's office, his brother-in-law had told him through an open window—in January no less—that they had burned another bridge. However, once safely away from Harrison, Cooper repudiated this statement. He alleged that five carloads of men took him late on Monday night and drove him to a point south of the M&NA shops. There they tied a rope around his neck, threw the other end over a tree limb, and began to pull him up. Cooper said the men told him he would be killed if he refused to swear that Orr and Wise had burned the bridge. He was taken the next day to the courthouse, where he swore the false statement before the grand jury. One wonders whether Josephine Orr had been similarly threatened to change her testimony. By Wednesday, Mrs. Wise had escaped to safety in Crane, Missouri.[10]

A couple of days before their court appearance, Orr and Wise met with their lawyers for the first time: Elbridge G. Mitchell and Sam Williams, both of whom had represented Venable a few months earlier when the strike leader was charged with conspiracy to commit murder. Mitchell was a heavyweight lawyer, literally and figuratively, weighing in at 260 pounds and having under his belt two terms of experience as circuit judge and another two terms as representative from Boone County to the Arkansas General Assembly. Mitchell hated the Ku Klux Klan and willingly defended strikers. Mitchell told Wise and Orr that they could easily get a change of venue because of the bitter divisions within the community. But this would only delay the trial and cost more money. Most importantly, they would risk their lives if they stayed in jail in Harrison with a mob outside in the streets. Mitchell and Williams advised the prisoners to plead guilty, seek an expedited sentence, and be removed from Boone County before any harm could come to them. Mitchell expected that he would be able to get the sentence reversed on appeal because of the threatening mob outside the courthouse.

Orr and Wise followed their lawyers' advice. Before Judge Shinn and the packed courtroom of seated men, all wearing white ribbons of support for the railroad, Wise and Orr pleaded guilty. Wise added that he was innocent but would plead guilty to save his life. Shinn responded that he would not allow any man to plead guilty unless he were in fact guilty. He told the defendants he could place a hundred men to guard the jail if necessary. But Shinn must have known that Sheriff Shaddox's special deputies were members of the mob that had committed the illegal violence on Monday. The judge asked Mitchell to talk again with his clients, and they retired to the judge's chambers to confer. Mitchell later said: "I pointed out of the window at the hordes of men constituting the mob. These men had guns; their threats were audible; the defendants could see them and hear them." He said Orr acknowledged that he would be killed if he remained in Harrison any longer. Moreover, Orr knew that if they demanded a trial in Harrison they would lose, all their witnesses having been run out of town. Wise also reluctantly agreed to plead guilty to save his life. The two men and their lawyers returned to the courtroom and pleaded guilty unconditionally. Shinn immediately sentenced them to seven to ten years in the state penitentiary, rather than waiting the customary twenty-four hours for sentencing.[11]

Virtually admitting that Wise and Orr were in danger each moment they stayed in Harrison, Shinn ordered the sheriff to transport them immediately to Little Rock. Silby Johnson and fellow Klansman J. Walter Casey took the two prisoners by car to Bergman to catch the White River Line and then the Missouri Pacific on to Little Rock. Josie Gregor was at the station in Bergman with Bonnie Belle, Rev. Farris, and her husband's casket, waiting for the 10:00 a.m. train north to Missouri. She saw Johnson and his two prisoners as he was getting their tickets for Little Rock. Two days earlier, Johnson had promised Josie that her husband would be safe when he escorted Gregor from their house to Rotary Hall. She said she wanted to talk to Johnson, but he just tipped his hat and looked away.[12]

As Johnson and Casey brought Orr and Wise to Little Rock, Pete Venable was already in the capital city meeting with Governor McRae. After Venable met up with Mrs. Jines and other refugees from Harrison the day before in Branson, he had hurried to Little Rock. It is not clear how he managed to get an audience with the governor. Venable begged McRae to send troops to Harrison and other towns up and down the line to keep order. McRae said that the sheriff had things under control and there was no need for state intervention. According to Venable, McRae said the strikers "were getting just what we deserved." McRae made no public statement after his meeting with Venable.

Getting no satisfaction from the governor, Venable turned to the press. From his room at the Marion Hotel, he gave newspapermen exaggerated accounts of a drunken mob in Harrison, of Mrs. Jines's walk in her night slippers through a dark wood after inebriated men had wrecked her house, of Charles DeGoche's feet burned with a hot iron to get him to talk, and of DeGoche's wife beaten when she tried to intervene. Venable presented the mob violence in Harrison as premeditated, not spontaneous. Without using Festus J. Wade's name, Venable told reporters that a St. Louis banker knew all about the plans for mob action, to include some lynchings, days *before* the bridges burned and the vigilantes descended on Harrison. Venable hinted that he and union officials in Little Rock might organize a "relief expedition" to stop further persecution of strikers. Harrison newspapers expressed outrage over Venable's defamatory exaggerations and suggested that citizens would send a committee to "interview" him in Little Rock. After delivering Orr and Wise to the state penitentiary, Johnson and Casey spent Wednesday and Thursday looking for Venable, with the plan to arrest him and return him to Harrison. They failed to find him and went home on Friday empty handed.[13]

While the two deputies were searching for Venable on Wednesday, the Arkansas General Assembly passed a resolution calling for a legislative investigation into the Harrison troubles. The Senate had passed the resolution the day before, immediately after Governor McRae made his call for troops to be sent to Harrison. But on Wednesday the proposal met some resistance on the House floor. Boone County's representative, John H. Klepper, a farmer and Baptist preacher from Bellefonte, opposed it, saying that the people of the county would in no way benefit by legislative action. He offered some defense to strikers by suggesting that the bridge burnings were the work of a bolshevist minority element. Representative Neill Bohlinger, who had won his seat to represent Pulaski County on a Klan ticket, demanded immediate action, so Arkansas could avoid a repeat of the recent massacre in Herrin, Illinois, where striking miners killed nearly two dozen strikebreakers. Officials of the railroad brotherhoods in Little Rock sent a memorial to the General Assembly, calling for the legislature to investigate the violence against strikers. While it may not have been clear exactly whose violence was to be investigated, the House passed the resolution. The Senate president, Jacob R. "Jake" Wilson of El Dorado, and the Speaker of the House, Howard Reed from Heber Springs, would choose the members of the joint investigative committee. The committee began hearing testimony the following week in Little Rock.[14]

While the politicians in Little Rock discussed how to respond to the strike troubles, outsiders were already coming to Harrison to investigate and report on the events taking place there. Two sets of federal investigators came to assist the railroad in its battle against strikers, not to address the violence of the mob. Andrew J. Russell, a deputy US marshal in Fort Smith, arrived in Harrison on Tuesday, January 16, with directions from US attorney general Harry M. Daugherty to investigate conditions on the M&NA. Russell met first with Jack Murray. The railroad had asked for federal intervention, given that the alleged sabotage disrupted the delivery of mail and other essential government business. Russell's report to Daugherty recommended placing the railroad under federal guard. While Russell was in town, Murray left for Fort Smith to ask the federal judge of the US District Court for the Western District of Arkansas, Frank A. Youmans, for an injunction against interference with the railroad, reminiscent of the so-called Daugherty injunction, issued the previous September during the shopmen's strike. Later in the week, after Murray's visit, the federal court's district attorney sent C. E. Argabright and some assistants from the US Department of Justice to Harrison. When asked by the press whether they were there to investigate vigilante rule and violence, Argabright said his team planned to examine evidence uncovered by the citizens committee implicating high union officials in the sabotage against the railroad. On Friday they met with county officials and came before the committee to examine the evidence obtained by the illegal raids on Union Hall and Pete Venable's home. They left after three days of work.[15]

Harrison also experienced an onslaught by newspaper reporters throughout the week. Oden S. Williams of Little Rock's *Arkansas Democrat* was the first to arrive on Tuesday, in time to file a report for the afternoon paper. Upon arrival, he and all reporters had to appear before the citizens committee in Rotary Hall. If committee members found the person acceptable, they pinned the white ribbon. If the committee did not approve, the reporter received a deadline to leave town. Harry Robinson of the *Springfield Leader* said he asked the meaning of the white ribbon. Someone responded that it says, "Please don't kick me." Robinson understood the message. By the end of the week, reporters had arrived from papers in Fort Smith, Little Rock, Kansas City, St. Louis, Springfield, and Memphis. If the reporters did not show open hostility to the railroad and mob, the committee allowed them to send their reports freely.[16]

Three reporters made a difficult journey to Harrison on Wednesday: John Rogers of the *St. Louis Post-Dispatch*, Jack Carberry of the *Kansas City Post*, and Walter Casey of the *Kansas City Star* (no relation to the special deputy sheriff of the same name). Rogers had already staked out a reputation as a crusader against the Ku Klux Klan. Just two weeks before, he had been in Louisiana to cover the trials after the infamous Klan murders in Mer Rouge. He arrived in Arkansas with an axe to grind. The reporters met up in Eureka Springs on Tuesday evening, having arrived by train via Seligman, and set out by hired car Wednesday morning for Harrison. Carberry phoned Murray at 8:00 a.m. from Eureka Springs to let him know that the reporters were on their way. Their driver was Walter Suskey, a striker who had been running a jitney car service during the strike. Suskey had already been in the hands of the committee in Harrison and was in the bullpen with Ed Gregor when he was taken out to be hanged. It begs the imagination to know why he would agree to drive three reporters to Harrison.

They traveled uneventfully from Eureka Springs to Green Forest. There they appeared to enter a war zone. An armed crowd threatened to whip the reporters because they rode in Suskey's Ford car. After considerable argument, the mob allowed them to proceed with Suskey at the wheel. They arrived at Alpena, ten miles east of Green Forest, where fifteen armed men stopped the car about a hundred yards from the train station and ordered them out of the vehicle, with their hands up. The men searched each person, their luggage, and the

HOME EDITION

ARKANSAS DEMOCRAT

ASSOCIATED PRESS. INTERNATIONAL NEWS FULL LEASED WIRE REPORTS

FIFTY-SECOND YEAR

LITTLE ROCK, TUESDAY EVENING, JANUARY 16, 1923

MOB LYNCHES M. AND N. A. STRIKER

TROOP CALL TO LEGISLATURE

GOVERNOR M'RAE SENDS SPECIAL MESSAGE TELLING OF M. & N. A. SITUATION

Legislative action to send National Guard troops to Harrison and adjoining towns to take charge of the Missouri & North Arkansas railroad situation, loomed up as a probable local development here shortly before noon Tuesday.

MAN WHO RESISTED VIGILANCE COMMITTEE IS HANGED TO TRESTLE

Harrison, Jan. 16.—The body of E. C. Gregor, M. & N. A. striker, was found hanging from a railroad bridge near the railroad yards this morning. Gregor is the man that opened fire on officers and citizens who searched his home yesterday afternoon. It is stated he was called before the Vigilance Committee last night and that he defied them, vowing that a "day of reckoning" would come.

FRANCE SEEKING TO ANNEX TERRITORY, DECLARES CARAWAY

Arkansas Senator Says Occupation of Ruhr Imperialistic Move, and Reparations Collection Plea Only Subterfuge.

ROYAL PAIR WHOSE ENGAGEMENT WAS ANNOUNCED ON MONDAY

Duke of York — Lady Elizabeth Bowes-Lyon

PRINCE ALBERT PROPOSED THREE TIMES BEFORE GIRL CONSENTED

Mother, Praying for Sick Child, Causes Its Death

GERMANY DECLARED IN DEFAULT; FRENCH EXTEND OCCUPATION

BOARD OF COMMERCE HERE OFFERS HELP TO M. & N. A. HEAD

Letter to General Manager Murray Pledges Co-operation and Assistance of Trade Body Whenever Possible.

Today

No Peace, Sayeth the Lord. Lithuanians Fight Allies. English Mob Mosul. Turks Hang Christians.

PROMINENT MEN TO FACE CHARGES OF FRAUD IN OIL DEAL

12 PEOPLE INJURED IN LOUISIANA BLAST

SIX KILLED AS TRAIN STRIKES SCHOOL BUS

RESTAURANT OWNER SHOOTS TEXAS MAN

MEMBERS OF FLOGGING PARTY DECLARED KNOWN

M. & N. A. STRIKERS INDICTED AT SEARCY

BOOZE PROBE TO FEDERAL COURT

TENNESSEE HAS DEMOCRAT CHIEF

PRES. HARDING SLIGHTLY ILL

The Weather

MOTHER OF TEN KILLS HERSELF

12 INJURED IN DUBLIN RIOTING

CHAOS REIGNS IN CANTON CHINA

GERMANS PLAN TO "SIT TIGHT"

SENATOR AFTER BIG TAX DODGERS

F. S. & W. SALE HELD TUESDAY

FRENCH THREAT CAUSES PANIC

HERRIN TRIALS NEARING END

BOCHUM QUIET ORDER RESTORED

MARRY FIRST, GET APPROVAL LATER, POLICY

Are You Overlooking a Bet?

Phone 4-0321

Front-page newspaper coverage from the second day of the mob action in Harrison. *Arkansas Democrat, January 16, 1923.*

vehicle. Carberry asked whether he could call Murray in Harrison. He went into a store and phoned Murray, who instructed the armed men to allow the reporters to proceed. One man wrote out a pass and gave it to Rogers. Suskey would be taken again to the citizens committee in Harrison, a spokesman for the mob said, because he had violated the committee's edict that the competition of service cars with the railroad must cease. A member of the crowd volunteered to drive the three reporters the remaining thirteen miles to Harrison.[17]

Once they were in Harrison, their driver deposited them at a hotel, where they left their grips. The three reporters went directly to Murray's office. It was agreed that Carberry would be the spokesman for the three. Murray immediately launched into a lengthy description of the depredations that he alleged had been committed against the railroad. He brought out examples of bombs, emery dust, and other evidence of sabotage he kept in his desk. He estimated the damages to railroad property as amounting to a half million dollars. When asked who was in charge of Harrison, Murray said it was the citizens committee, but he said he did not even know who its members were exactly, as he had not been before them. He suggested that the reporters voluntarily present themselves to the committee, for they would be taken there anyway if they did not do it themselves. Murray leaned out of his office window and pointed across the street to show them where the committee was meeting.[18]

The three reporters crossed the street to Rotary Hall about noon. The committee had just come back after lunch and was questioning a woman and her teenage daughter. The journalists asked the woman some questions, but the guards told them they were not allowed to speak with witnesses. Again Carberry was to be the spokesman for the newsmen, and he tried to explain the problems they had experienced in traveling to Harrison. Rogers, however, could not contain himself and interrupted to declare that he had been physically assaulted and threatened with guns pointed in his belly and back. Rogers said that Sam Dennis spoke for the committee, telling him that "if he didn't like the town he could get out." Dennis tried to recite to the reporters a list of depredations against the railroad, as Murray had done. Rogers interrupted, saying they had come to investigate the hanging of Gregor, not destruction of railroad property. At this, a half dozen men in the room rushed at Rogers. They were called off by George McKinney, who recognized a button in Rogers's lapel showing that he was a veteran. McKinney came over, shook Rogers's hand, and placed a white ribbon on him. Asking about its meaning, Rogers was told that it meant he supported the committee. Rogers

WHAT HAPPENED IN ARKANSAS

Drawn for LABOR by Jack Anderson,
Vice President of the International Association of Machinists.

Labor's view of the mob action in the Arkansas Ozarks. *Labor, February 3, 1923.*

then refused to wear the ribbon. The committee denied the reporters' request to interview Mayor Clute. They asked to interview Judge Shinn and were told he was busy in court. McKinney ushered the three reporters out of the hall. Casey and Carberry were angry at their colleague. They feared that if they stayed around Rogers, all three would be killed.[19]

Rogers returned to the M&NA office, telling Jack Murray that he had received no satisfaction from the committee and would leave Harrison. Murray called in Walter S. Pettit, a bank cashier, and told him to instruct the committee to allow Rogers to interview whomever he wished. While they were waiting, Rogers said, a man came in the office asking Murray for permission to search a trunk removed from Pete Venable's house. Murray responded that it was a matter for the committee to decide. Rogers retorted: "Then why are men asking you, if you have nothing to do with the Committee?" Pettit returned with a response from the committee that Rogers was not allowed access to Clute; he might be able to interview Judge Shinn, but he would need to return to the committee to discuss the matter. This Rogers refused to do. Before departing, Rogers asked Murray whether he could take photographs as he was carrying a camera with him. The committee had denied Carberry's request earlier to take photographs. Murray opened the window. Rogers prepared to take a photograph of the crowd below, sitting around a log fire in the middle of the street. Murray asked whether the photo would show their faces. When Rogers responded probably so, Murray said he should best not take a photo. John Rogers clearly believed that Jack Murray was the guiding hand for the citizens committee, despite Murray's denial that he had any relationship with the body.

Rogers said he walked to the Western Union office to enquire about sending an article of four thousand words and was told the office was all "piled up" with other dispatches. He went to his hotel, collected his grip, and walked to the telephone office, where he phoned his managing editor and said he was leaving Harrison. He caught the M&NA's 4:20 p.m. train to Eureka Springs. Rogers said the train dropped burning coals from the engine and had to stop to fight fires all along the way to Eureka Springs. At one bridge before Berryville, Rogers said, a hunk of fire "as big as a table" dropped out of the engine and rolled on and under the bridge. The train got to Eureka Springs two hours late. Rogers returned to St. Louis the next day.[20]

Other reporters, such as Fletcher Chenault of the *Arkansas Gazette*, Oden Williams of the *Arkansas Democrat*, and Eugene Travis of the *Memphis Commercial Appeal*, took a much more conciliatory approach toward the actions of the citizens committee. Travis used his bylined article as an opportunity for the committee to deny Pete Venable's exaggerations about the mistreatment of women and other excesses. Travis wrote an investigative piece alleging that Venable was perpetuating the strike in order to make $300 a month as comptroller for the strikers' benefits, much more than his regular salary as conductor. Travis expected that the Boone County grand jury would indict Venable for embezzling funds from the unions. Fletcher Chenault, who had ridden on the M&NA's "booster train" from Helena to Eureka Springs the previous June, denied that the citizens committee interfered in any way with reporters as they filed their stories. He accepted the committee's denial that it used threats against strikers. He did not explain what measures, if not threats, could convince approximately two hundred strikers to abandon their homes and possessions in Harrison over a three-day period. Oden Williams was just a step more critical in the *Arkansas Democrat* by admitting that the actions of the committee were illegal. But they were necessary, he said.

By week's end, the three papers were running photographs of instruments of sabotage, such as boxes of emery dust, bags of blue vitriol, fuses, and bombs rolled in concrete and coal dust to look like lumps of coal. The photos were staged in front of the Boone County Courthouse, and the items were reported to have been taken from the homes of strikers. Yet a caption in the *Arkansas Gazette* said the fuse had been used in blowing up a water tank at Cotton Plant, an admission that the items came from the M&NA's collection. The two Harrison newspapers, the *Boone County Headlight* and the *Harrison Daily Times*, made even less effort toward objectivity and thoroughly supported the railroad and actions of the committee and mob. The editor of Berryville's *North Arkansas Star*, William J. Douglas, was even a participant, serving on the citizens committee. His editorials defended the actions of the mob, including the killing of Gregor.[21]

By the time the out-of-town journalists arrived in Harrison, the worst of the violence was over. Nonetheless, through the rest of the week, various members of the committee continued to huddle around the glowing base burner stove in Rotary Hall and do their work. By noon on Wednesday, January 17, they had questioned 150 strikers and sympathizers. Most strikers had left for Missouri. Some wives and children had departed, too, but others had been left behind to fend for themselves. The mob of armed men in the streets had dwindled but still numbered in the hundreds, drilling in formation and sitting around the log fire. Thirty-five men kept the roads in and out of town blocked and guarded. On Thursday, Mayor Clute was brought before the committee and said he and three city council members would present their resignations at the council's meeting on the following Monday. A group from Eureka Springs visited to get the committee's advice on how to perform a similar action on the twenty strikers who resided in that city. Later on Thursday, guards tracked down and apprehended some thirty strikers who had been hiding in the woods outside town since Monday. They were hauled into town for questioning.

The apprehension of a fresh group of strikers brought a new round of excitement. Rumors spread that union members were gathering in Springfield to the north and Cotter to the east, in preparation for a march on Harrison. Squads began a call-up for more vigilantes, and by nightfall some five hundred men were drilling military style in the streets, led by veterans of the Great War. The men stayed up all night, waiting for an assault that never came. The committee worked through the night questioning strikers and claimed to have gained valuable information about sabotage against the railroad. By the end of Friday, January 19, the tired men dispersed, having questioned 250 men and women in their week's work.[22]

After five days of mob rule, Harrison began to transition toward normalcy. Residents were returning to work and leaving their guns at home. The citizens committee presented a statement indicating that it would prepare evidence for the courts and the upcoming investigation by the legislative committee. It congratulated itself "on having wound up this situation with a minimum amount of tragedy and unpleasantness. What the civil and court authorities were not able to handle in the last two years," the committee declared, "the citizens have accomplished in two days' time. . . . The strike of railroad workers in Harrison is over." The committee, which had represented Boone, Searcy, Newton, and Carroll Counties, formally adjourned on Friday night and announced that it had been replaced by a new coordinating committee headed by Walter Snapp as chair and Troy Coffman as secretary. These two Harrison Klansmen then appointed local committees to continue the work in towns up and down the line. The *Harrison Daily Times* published the names of these new committee members for Leslie, Marshall, St. Joe, Western Grove, Jasper, Harrison, Alpena, Green Forest, Berryville, and Eureka Springs.[23]

The Boone County grand jury adjourned as the court schedule of Judge Shinn and prosecuting attorney Greenhaw moved to another county in the circuit. Before leaving Harrison, Shinn issued a statement that the citizens committee had no legal standing and had no connection to the grand jury. He said he had heard that it had turned cases over to the prosecuting attorney, but he had "no official information to that effect." This was clearly not true, as the grand jury had been working all week with "evidence" brought to it by the committee.

One striker, George W. Roberts, can serve as an example. Roberts had successfully hidden until Thursday, when Dr. Charles M. Routh took him to the committee for questioning. There he was accused of serving as Pete Venable's secretary, having been seen coming and going from Venable's house. Finding his denials unsatisfactory, the committee left him in the bullpen most of the day, with perhaps a dozen other men. In the evening, as the mob outside was tense with the expectation of an army of strikers that never came, the committee brought him back for further grilling. Roberts said that Walter Snapp, George McKinney, and others cursed him, hit him with guns, and threatened to turn him over to the mob if he did not confess. According to Roberts, Snapp and Sam Dennis took him before the grand jury the next morning and forced him to fabricate an accusation against Venable. With Dennis standing in one door of the courtroom and Snapp in the other, Roberts told the grand jury that Venable had asked him to grease tracks at Capps Hill, place vitriol in water tanks at Gilbert, break up some tracks near Marshall, and enact other assorted damage to the railroad. After making the statement, he was released, and as soon as he could, he left Harrison for good. With this sort of "evidence," the grand jury returned indictments against a number of strikers and sympathizers for offenses ranging from sabotage, disturbance of the peace, and concealed carry of a weapon to gambling and public drunkenness. Most of those detained posted bonds, were released, and, like Roberts, quickly left town. Sheriff Shaddox said that all the striker prisoners were out on bond by Tuesday, January 23. Newspapers reported that the grand jury also returned indictments against Pete Venable and other strike leaders in absentia.[24]

By the weekend, the neighborhoods where most of the strikers had lived, such as Eagle Heights just east of the downtown tracks and the Glines addition by the railway shops, were dark and deserted. Some two hundred strikers had left town, most for Branson, forty miles to the north. Probably another hundred women and children had also departed. The twenty-five or so strikers who remained all wore white ribbons. Every business now had its placard in the window proclaiming support for the open shop. A last step toward total victory was the takeover of the city government of Harrison. Two members of the city council (Fred Tyson and Walter Sims) were said to be part of the vigilante crowd, while the majority (George R. Cline, George Minicus, William Larimer, and William G. Daily) were supporters of the strike. Mayor Clute may not have supported the strike in principle, but he had become an adversary of the railroad and its supporters. In the eyes of the committee, these men had to go. On Monday, January 22, Mayor Clute resigned, as ordered, and the rump council appointed attorney John I. Worthington, an investor in the M&NA, to fill out his term. Troy Coffman and Luther "Clay" Holt, Harrison's two members of the citizens committee, were made council members, and Silby Johnson was appointed as the acting city marshal. Aldermen Larimer, Minicus, and Cline, and city marshal William Parr, had all fled Harrison. William Daily, who had been reported removed from the council, must have put on the white ribbon, for he survived and thereafter voted with the others.[25]

A last activity for the victors of the Harrison riot was to collect money to pay for it all. On Tuesday, January 16, more than $2,000 was raised in Harrison and towns along the line to provide an additional reward for those assisting with the arrest and prosecution of persons convicted of depredations against the railroad. The money was deposited in the Harrison branch of Citizens Bank, underneath the M&NA office. Another collection taken among the crowds in the courthouse square in Harrison collected $338.50 within fifteen minutes to defray the expenses of holding the vigilante court in Rotary Hall. Presumably the fund reimbursed members of the Mothers Club and other Harrison women who brought food all week to the citizens committee and prisoners in the bullpen. By early in the next week, citizens of Harrison began yet another fund drive, this time to raise money for the "relief" of families of strikers. Several wives and children of expelled strikers remained in town. The infrastructure for the strike benefits had vanished, and some families were in a desperate situation. With husbands afraid to return home to sell homes and household furnishings, and wives lacking resources to do so, the fund was proposed to assist them in moving out of Harrison. A finance committee, composed of merchants who were all members of the mob—Clay Holt, Paul Ellis, and Leslie Jackson—collected and held the funds. Rev. Farris, along with the Reverend William H. Albertson of the Baptist church and the physician and Klansman David E. Evans, was in charge of disbursing the funds.[26]

Farris said he came up with the idea of a relief fund after visiting the wife and children of a striker who had been run out of town and finding their kitchen empty of food, save for a handful of flour. He went to a shop and had some meat sent to their house. Besides the need for food, fuel for heat was a necessity. While the week of the mob action had been abnormally warm for January in the Ozarks, the following week turned bitterly cold. Farris went to the office of the chief attorney for the railroad, J. Sam Rowland, who was a member of his church, and explained the need for a relief fund for the remaining families of strikers. Rowland agreed, and the two of them drove to the needy family's house, where the two men each gave the woman money to buy more food. The next day, Rowland and Farris organized the committee that planned the collection and disbursement of funds. They eventually raised $550.

While the fund had begun with altruistic motivations, the execution of the project served less noble goals. Farris said that while he, Albertson, and Evans were visiting a striker neighborhood, a woman who was a member of Albertson's church told him that some strikers were still hiding out in the woods by day and returning to their cottages at night. Albertson said to Evans, "Doctor, this makes a situation that must be looked into." The doctor agreed. Two days later, Farris stopped by these strikers' homes to see how those families were faring, and he found the houses to be vacant. With sarcastic understatement, he said, "Evidently the situation had been very carefully looked into." Farris said he disbursed only ten dollars, to help two women pay for transporting their household possessions by truck to Bergman and then train to Branson. Dr. Evans said the committee sent a few family members out on the M&NA and took a small number of others to Bergman to buy tickets on the White River Line.

J. Sam Rowland, the M&NA's lawyer. *Courtesy of Boone County Library Archival Photo Collection, no. 11.*

Strikers' families got little of the money said to be raised for them. The relief committee turned down several women Farris recommended for assistance, including one striker's wife who needed help paying for the cost of giving birth. Farris said the relief committee told those who needed help with moving to sell their houses and use those funds to get out of Harrison. Approximately three-quarters of the strikers in Harrison owned their homes outright or were paying on mortgages. Some simply abandoned their homes, and others sold at a considerable loss. Jennie Venable said she returned to Harrison and sold her home for a third of its value. She found it had been repeatedly entered and ransacked after her January 16 departure. Farris said he saw the five-room cottage of a striking dispatcher sell for $35. The town was glutted with secondhand furniture and other household goods, even canned foodstuffs, chickens, and cattle. Farris said one relief committee member told him that almost all of the $550 was used for coffee and sandwiches to feed the guards that continued to patrol the town for months. Farris soon quietly dropped off the committee. His days in Harrison would be numbered.[27]

By the time the "week of the mob," as Farris called it, had ended, several patterns had become apparent. Harry Robinson, who wrote for the *Springfield Leader*, boasted about mingling with the men in charge while he reported from Harrison. He suggested that the mob action had been a premeditated and well-planned event: "Their plan of action was not formed in a hurry, but carefully conceived and executed by the very best professional and business men of that community. City, county and state officers were fully advised and then things started to move." He would have received this impression from those in charge of the mob, for reporters were not allowed to question strikers or sympathizers. Jesse Lewis Russell, editor of the *Boone County Headlight*, later recalled that both sides were arming themselves in the later months of 1922, anticipating a final showdown. Pete Venable alleged that the St. Louis owners of the railroad at least knew about the plans for a mob, even if they did not originate the plan. He believed that attorneys Rowland and Worthington were the masterminds and that others simply played their part. Venable had gone away from his interview with the governor, he said, with the impression that McRae, county officials, and railroad executives had all been in communication before the mob even assembled. Special agents for the railroad Walter Snapp, George McKinney, and J. C. "Bud" Baker had gone to towns up and down the line to organize men to come to Harrison. Jack Murray arranged for the special train. Venable believed that the plan was to kill a couple of strike leaders, most likely him and Tillman Jines, and throw a couple more in prison for burning bridges, thereby frightening the others into submission. Gregor was hanged because the others were not available.[28]

One factor that facilitated the organization of the mob was infrastructure provided by the Ku Klux Klan. Harrison's Kerr-Harrell Klan no. 101 was probably large and well organized by January 1923. In the summer of 1924, the Klan in Arkansas and nationally began to abandon much of the secrecy and anonymity to which it had once subscribed. Previously, only high-ranking Klan officials, lecturers, and political candidates seeking Klan votes had revealed their membership. In contrast, on August 7, 1924, Klansmen paraded through the streets robed but not masked, and the *Harrison Times* named the men who led the procession. Also that month, the paper identified Harrison Klansmen who attended Klan meetings in neighboring Hopewell, Alpena, and Valley Springs. These articles allow the identification of forty-four members of the Harrison Klan out of a total membership the newspaper estimated at one thousand. But these forty-four included sheriffs Silby Johnson and Bob Shaddox; railroad officials such as J. Sam Rowland; Harrison's two members of the citizens committee, Clay Holt and Troy Coffman, who then took seats on the city council along with Klansman Walter Sims; leaders of the mob such as Walter Snapp and Doyle Woodruff; the bank cashier who had acted as Murray's messenger, Walter Pettit; and the deputy who had guarded Orr and Wise in the county jail, J. Leo Godwin.

Clearly some men in the mob were not members of the Ku Klux Klan, but it is reasonable to think that most of the vigilantes were members of the Klan chapters in Harrison, Eureka Springs, Berryville, Marshall, Leslie, and Heber Springs. The $338 that Harrison citizens donated in fifteen minutes around the courthouse square had been billed as a drive "to feed the visiting 100 percent Americans," a euphemism for the Klan. The citizens committee asked strikers and sympathizers whether they were "100 percent Americans" when trying to get them to don the white ribbon, clearly a code for supporting both the Klan and the railroad. As we will see in the next chapter, Klansmen had a significant role in expelling strikers in Leslie and Heber Springs. A year after the dust had settled from the strike, Pete Venable noted ironically that the leader of the St. Louis investors, Festus J. Wade, a Roman Catholic, had been shrewd enough to use the Klan, an anti-Catholic organization, to fight his battles.[29]

CHAPTER 7

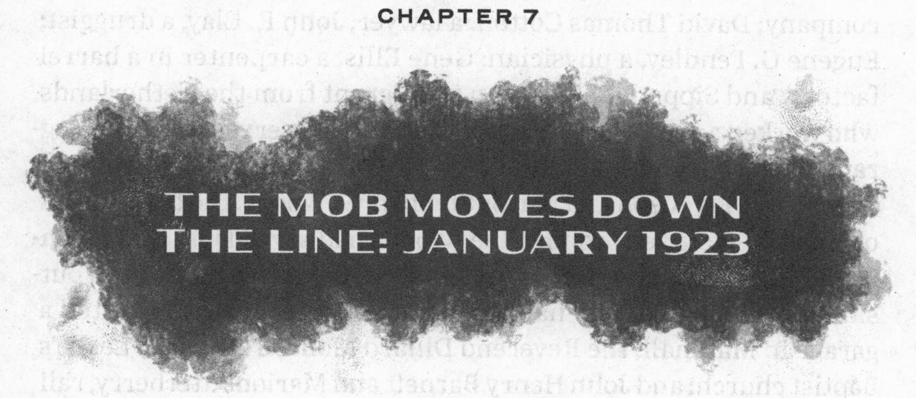

THE MOB MOVES DOWN THE LINE: JANUARY 1923

WHILE THE MOB WAS consolidating control over Harrison, some members returned to their hometowns to continue the purge of strikers there. The largest number of strikers outside of Harrison lived in Leslie, with the high volume of shipments of wood products, and Heber Springs, where crew changes took place for the 360-mile route. Railroad supporters in these two towns reprised the kangaroo courts that had been so successful earlier in the week in Harrison. Before the week was over, strikers would be expelled along the entire line of the M&NA through the Arkansas Ozarks, from Eureka Springs to Kensett.

Evidently, men from Searcy County who were in the Harrison mob on Monday, January 15, planned to convene in Leslie on Tuesday evening to clear out the twenty-five strikers who lived there. Some of the men arrived on the afternoon train, while others came by automobile. Ed Treece, a Leslie garage owner, said the vigilantes arrived brandishing shotguns, rifles, and pistols. By the late afternoon, the men were traveling around Leslie, giving notice to strikers and sympathizers to appear at city hall. James Taylor, a striking brakeman, said the five men who came to get him told him that he was summoned to a public meeting. When he arrived at city hall, he found a crowd of more than two hundred, with some men going in and out of the building and others milling about in the streets and around a bonfire. A citizens committee had already been formed, including the following men from Leslie: Noah Webster Redwine and Augustus Garland Killebrew, two merchants; William W. "Bud" Fendley, a former postmaster; J. Marshall Lack, the manager of a wholesale grocery company; David Thomas Cotton, a lawyer; John R. Clay, a druggist; Eugene G. Fendley, a physician; Gene Ellis, a carpenter in a barrel factory; and Sippe J. Pekema, an immigrant from the Netherlands who worked as auditor for a barrel factory and served as the stenographer for the group. Additional members on the Leslie committee were Zeb V. Ferguson and Mayor Stephen W. Woods, the two officers of Marshall's citizens committee. Woods had served just that morning as part of the committee in Harrison. In charge of the mob outside the doorway of city hall were Dorsey Treece, who operated a garage in Marshall; the Reverend Dillard Monroe Carter of Leslie's Baptist church; and John Henry Barnett and Marion Atterberry, railroad employees in Leslie.[1] Carter, one might recall, had applied the lash to George O'Neal's behind in Harrison earlier in the day. Pete Venable had named Atterberry as one of the three men who took Ed C. Gregor to his death in the wee hours of the morning.

Leslie's citizens committee operated in much the same fashion as the committee in Harrison. Members of the mob evidently searched homes of some strikers, for Mayor Woods noted that two switch keys were found in the possession of Leslie strike leader Charles Clark, who had escaped to the woods the day before. As strikers came forward, the group asked about depredations against the railroad. They were given the choice of tearing up their union cards or leaving the area. When James Taylor refused to surrender his strike benefits, he said, they threatened to turn him over to the guards. Ferguson told him, "Don't you realize you're in danger. You may leave here and never come back." Taylor said he was given thirty minutes to leave town. When he protested that his wife was sick and he needed more time, they gave him four days. He left for Little Rock after two days.[2]

Several sympathizers were also forced to appear before the Leslie committee. On Tuesday evening, January 16, the members asked Ed Treece to sign a statement declaring that he was for the M&NA. He signed it and was given a white ribbon. But this did not satisfy the committee. Rev. Carter and some other men, Treece said, punched and shook him as they escorted him out of the room. Carter marched Treece west down Main Street and then south to the depot, where a crowd surrounded him and pulled out a leather strap, about two feet long and an inch and a half wide. Carter ordered Treece to pull down his pants. When he did not do so, Carter jerked his trousers down so hard that the buttons popped off. Carter held his head while Atterberry applied the strap. Treece said the men flogged him until he fell to his knees, then pulled him back up and continued whipping. Rev. Carter choked him and hit him on the head with his pistol. The men were asking him questions about the whereabouts of strikers Charles Clark and Dick Kimbrell, as well as others who apparently had managed to escape. Treece was so traumatized that he could not speak. Finally, about 11:30 p.m. they let him go, telling him that they would see him in church on Sunday. His right hip was so damaged he could hardly walk.

Two weeks later, as Ed Treece testified in Little Rock before the legislative committee investigating the violence surrounding the strike, he still had strap marks from the beating and a large scab. He was hospitalized at some point for damage to a kidney sustained during the beating. He eventually moved sixty miles south to Conway, from where he filed suit in January 1926 for $70,000 in damages from the beating in Leslie. The case was dismissed under a statute of limitations.[3]

Ed's cousin Abe Treece, the proprietor of the People's Mercantile in Leslie, was forced to close his store and come to city hall. After keeping him waiting an hour, the committee questioned him for about twenty minutes. When asked whether he supported the M&NA, he responded that he would go out of business without the railroad. The committee questioned why he would allow strikers to congregate at his store. Abe answered that they had been his friends since birth and were his customers. He put on the white ribbon. As he was leaving, the mob outside announced that they were going to "learn him to be a better citizen." Rev. Carter ordered him to pull down his pants and bend over a box, and gave him eight to ten licks with the strap. At around 2:00 a.m. on Wednesday, Carter and the mob finally let Abe Treece go.[4]

Several men who served on the Leslie committee and some who were part of the mob outside city hall gave testimony before the legislative committee. John Clay insisted that all the witnesses were treated with courtesy, while Augustus Killebrew insisted that the committee neither made threats nor used violence. At the end of Killebrew's testimony, names were read into the record of four other members of the committee, and three members of the mob, who were present and corroborated Clay's and Killebrew's accounts: Zeb

Ferguson, Noah Redwine, Bud Fendey, Dr. Eugene Fendley, Thad Rainbolt, Auda A. Hudspeth, and John Henry Barnett. A few members of the mob who testified were more forthcoming. A. L. Barnett, who owned a cooperage business, admitted that "some of them got a licking." Delania E. "Pegleg" Decker said he saw Abe Treece get "a pretty good tanning" and even identified Carter and Atterberry as applying the lash. Decker minimized the beating by suggesting that Abe put on his clothes afterward, stayed for a while, and then went home. Abe was still in Leslie running his store two months later, Decker said. He admitted, however, that Ed Treece had packed up and left Leslie after his beating. Even Rev. Carter testified before the legislative committee. While he first said he knew of no acts of violence or lawlessness that took place in Leslie during the week in question, under more pointed questioning he admitted to having seen Abe Treece whipped. When asked who whipped Abe, Carter's answer was, "I would not like to say."

At least seven men—Abe and Ed Treece, Dow Shipman, a striker named Jackson, John Steelman, Floyd Harrison, and Hiram Gibson—were flogged in Leslie over Tuesday and Wednesday, January 16 and 17. Carter and other leading citizens suggested that the men who received whippings were men of low character and thus in essence that they deserved the treatment. Ed Treece was a bootlegger, Killebrew alleged. Dow Shipman had taunted the mob and called them cowards before he was whipped. Jackson had been prosecuted in Judge Jacob Trieber's court the year before. While members of the committee denied making any threats, Killebrew admitted when asked how many strikers remained in Leslie, "I don't suppose there are any."[5]

As the men of Searcy County wrapped up their business in Leslie on Wednesday afternoon, many of them caught the late afternoon train to Heber Springs. Mayor Woods said they received a telegram asking them to come help in the neighboring town. A mob action in Heber Springs was not a spontaneous event, however, for plans had begun the previous Saturday. In response to a telegram from M&NA general manager Jack Murray, most of the town's businessmen gathered on Saturday morning, January 13, to prepare an action against the strikers. In charge of the meeting were the president of Arkansas National Bank, William C. Johnson; former county judge James L. Bittle; the mayor of Heber Springs, Marcus E. Vinson; and a local real estate man,

Tom Underwood, who had the telegram from Murray in his possession. They called James W. "Jim" Beer, the local leader of the strikers, to appear before the group. Beer assured the assembly that the strikers of Heber Springs had nothing to do with the recent burning of bridges, including the one at Latona, just across the White County line. The group assembled again that evening at around 8:00 p.m. at Johnson's bank, but finding the crowd too large to accommodate, they moved to the courthouse. Streets and sidewalks were filled with people in an atmosphere of excitement. The leaders announced that it was a meeting of the chamber of commerce to keep any strikers from wandering in. The men raised $200 to buy out the license of Happy Gunn's lunch wagon, considered a hangout spot for strikers. The next day, Gunn was summoned, presented with a check, and told to get his wagon off the streets. The tension only rose as the summons for citizens to come to Harrison was communicated in towns up and down the railroad. Mayor Vinson said he learned on Sunday from hardware merchant (and city marshal) Howard Bridewell that strikers were buying all the ammunition they could find.[6]

While the mob convened on Harrison the next day, a squad put Heber Springs under armed guard. One downtown merchant, Chester Casey, said his wife got up at 3:00 a.m. on Monday and was surprised to see the streetlights on in the town. Normally they were turned off at midnight. Casey said he learned later that day that men had guarded the town all night. On Wednesday, January 17, Captain Sam C. Herrin of the Arkansas National Guard arrived on orders from Governor Thomas C. McRae. After meeting with Mayor Vinson and Cleburne County sheriff Emmett Baldridge, Herrin mailed a report to Little Rock recommending that his 121st Machine Gun Battalion be mobilized in Heber Springs to prevent the sort of events (presumably lynching) that had occurred in Harrison. The sheriff and mayor did not think it was necessary. By Wednesday afternoon, Sheriff Baldridge and county judge Brose Massingill had received notice that men from Searcy County were on their way to Heber Springs after the cleanup in Leslie. Baldridge and Oscar B. Robbins, the owner of the local Ford dealership, met the men as they arrived on the evening train. More than two dozen Searcy County men stepped off the train, saying they had come to arrest the strikers. Robbins took the men to a restaurant to feed them supper, charging the bill to the chamber of commerce.

Meanwhile, men in Pangburn, the next town down the line in White County, received telephone calls requesting assistance. More than a dozen men from Pangburn drove into Heber Springs to augment the mob. Arthur N. "Poe" Hilger, a former agent for the M&NA, said he was sick in bed with the flu on Wednesday night when he received the call, but got dressed anyway and drove to Heber Springs.[7]

By 8:00 p.m., after the visitors from up the line had been fed, they made their way to the courthouse, where some 150 armed men had already gathered in the street. Some of them crowded inside the courtroom on the second floor, where Robbins was elected chair of the proceedings. Some speechmaking followed by Robbins and by Mayor Woods of Marshall about the need to end depredations by strikers against the railroad once and for all. The local men would recognize some irony here, given that no bridges had been burned or other damages inflicted in Cleburne County, except for a few hoses that had been cut. Clearly the reason for an action in Heber Springs came from the fact that some fifty strikers resided there, the largest number outside of Harrison. Robbins and Sheriff Baldridge appointed fifteen men to serve as the citizens committee to interrogate strikers, following the model of Harrison and Leslie. The committee included Cloyd E. Olmstead, a stave mill operator; Guy E. Basye, the manager of a handle factory; Poe Hilger, who lived in Pangburn but also owned land in Cleburne County; Judge Massingill; Mayor Vinson; Thomas M. Andrews, the manager of a cotton gin; Joe Taylor and Arthur A. Hodges, both grocers; William E. Huie and William R. Griffin, both druggists; Ollie Baker, who owned a lumber company; Roy Raywinkle, an abstracter and insurance man; Nicholas A. "Nick" Speed, who operated a slaughterhouse and meat market; Howard Bridewell, the city marshal who also ran a hardware store; and Mayor Woods of Marshall. Woods had the distinction of being the only man to serve on all three citizens committees—in Harrison, Leslie, and Heber Springs.[8]

The committee then organized the squads that would guard the town and bring in strikers and sympathizers for interrogation. Robbins again seems to have been in charge; he appointed seven captains, who each chose a squad of five to eight men: A. G. "Guy" Morris, the assistant prosecuting attorney for Cleburne County; Richard H. Dickenhorst, a bank vice president; Frank Haywood, a merchant; Neill Reed, a young lawyer (and the brother of Cleburne County's representative to the General Assembly, Howard Reed, who had just been chosen Speaker of the House); Frank C. Loving, a real estate agent; and William L. "Billie" Thompson, a farmer.[9] In giving testimony before the legislative committee a week later, these men claimed that they operated under the direction of Sheriff Baldridge. They said Baldridge had declared the squad members "deputized," although clearly no oath was taken and nothing was put in writing. One legislator asked squad member Frank Stewart of Pangburn whether it was normal for a citizen of White County to be deputized in Cleburne County. The Cleburne County court records show that Baldridge actually deputized only five men during the mob action: Emery L. Sherlock, William A. Cobb, and Hilger, Huie, and Olmstead of the citizens committee. Yet Robbins suggested that as many as four hundred men operated under Sheriff Baldridge's authority that week.[10]

Before disbanding at 11:00 p.m., the group inside the courtroom made plans to arm the men who had not come with their own weapons. Sheriff Baldridge instructed those who needed weapons to get guns from the armory. Frank Stewart said a Captain Smith went with the men to disburse weapons, and others said Captain Herrin oversaw the distribution of weapons on the sheriff's orders. This Smith may have been Captain Harry Smith, who, the evening before, had been prepared to lead National Guard troops to Harrison, until, at the last minute, Governor McRae decided not to send them. Smith apparently accompanied Herrin to Heber Springs on Wednesday. Frank Stewart and Odie Logan both said they received Colt 45 pistols and that all the boys in their squad were issued army pistols from the armory. Logan said that after the whole affair ended, he returned his weapon to the bank president, William Johnson.[11] The organization and arming of this mob in Heber Springs on Wednesday, January 17, was thus accomplished through the collusion of town, county, and state militia officials, along with the chamber of commerce and other prominent citizens.

Before those in charge headed home to sleep, the citizens committee instructed squad members to stand watch through the night, letting no automobiles leave town. Mortimer Frauenthal said his squad patrolled Main Street, while Frank Stewart was sent to guard Vinegar Hill, north of downtown. Some Pangburn men guarded the courthouse. Searches and arrests of strikers were to wait until morning. One exception was the arrest of T. J. "Jeff" Garner, whom Frauenthal's squad arrested in the early morning hours when he came to draw water at the spring in the city park. The guards instructed Garner to go home but to report to the courthouse in the morning for interrogation. As he returned home, he saw armed guards standing on each street corner and milling about the streets. After breakfast with his wife, Garner came out of his house, and waiting guards escorted him to the courthouse. Garner would be among the first of a large group of strikers and sympathizers who were interrogated as the committee began its work at around 7:00 a.m. on Thursday, January 18, at the courthouse, the symbol of authority in Cleburne County.[12]

One subject of much discussion in the testimony before the legislative committee concerned arrest and search warrants. In response to legislators' questions about warrants, most committee members, squad members, and county officials said they thought warrants existed. Judge Massingill and Mayor Vinson said that a justice of the peace, Miles M. Irwin, had issued warrants on Wednesday at the request of the assistant prosecuting attorney. Robbins said that Sheriff Baldridge claimed to have a pocket full of warrants. No one, however, admitted to having ever seen a warrant on that day.[13] Strikers uniformly testified that warrants were neither presented nor read when they were arrested or their homes searched.[14] As with the alleged deputizations, members of the mob simply presumed that they were working under the authority of the justice system, even if they were not following written protocols.

As morning broke on Thursday, the squads began their rounds to bring strikers to the courthouse. Committee members had handed out names of nearly fifty men they wanted to see, and squads went to get them. Just before daylight, Ura Russell, a striking fireman, was walking to a store to buy a loaf of bread when a group of twenty men accompanying Guy Morris's squad approached him and told him to return to his home, for they were going to search his house. Russell said the men went through his trunks and drawers. Then, while Morris and his squad went on to other houses, some men he did not know took him off to the courthouse. Just after daylight, the squad pounded on the door of Charles L. Woolard, a striking brakeman. When he opened the door, someone stuck a gun in his face and told him to put up his hands. Others were coming in the back door at the same time and began searching his house. Finding nothing, they told him to get dressed and marched him to the courthouse.

The squad then went on to the homes of two sympathizers known to be friendly with strikers and took both men away to be interrogated. At 8:00 a.m., Odie Logan's squad went to the house of Jim Beer, the local head of the strikers, and pulled him out of bed. They allowed him to put on his clothes and then took him away to the courthouse. John Byes, a striking fireman, had seen the congregation of men on the streets Wednesday. With men patrolling and streetlights burning all through the night, he said, he got little sleep. After breakfast, he went to the courthouse on his own accord. By midmorning some of the squads were driving outside of town to get strikers who lived in rural areas. Charles E. Black, another former fireman, was clearing brush on his farm at Tumbling Shoals, seven miles northeast of Heber Springs, when a car pulled up with Neill Reed and three prominent businessmen. They told him he must come before the committee at the courthouse. Black asked whether they had an arrest warrant, a subpoena, or a summons. They answered no. They allowed Black to shave and change clothes, then drove him to town and marched him down Main Street to the courthouse.

Charlie L. Goff, a striking conductor who lived three miles south of Heber Springs, had heard rumors about the arrival of a mob and had given his shotgun to his father-in-law so that it would not be taken. Goff was sitting by his fire at 10:00 a.m. when several cars drove up. A man named Jack Satterfield and several other men from Marshall came to his porch and demanded to search his house. The men went through six trunks looking for written material from the unions, before taking Goff away for interrogation. Goff's four orphaned nieces and nephews played on a wagon outside while the Searcy County men were searching through his house. This process continued for dozens of strikers and sympathizers all day on Thursday.[15]

The searches and arrests were generally peaceful. Strikers, aware of what had occurred earlier in the week in Harrison, offered no resistance. There was one exception. As Chester Casey arrived at his father's dry goods store on Thursday morning, he saw the crowd of men carrying rifles and pistols in the streets. He recognized some of the local men, but others had come from towns up the line. Squad leader Billie Thompson instructed Chester to report to the courthouse, apparently to participate in the mob action. The men had already taken his younger brother Paul to the courthouse. Instead, Chester went inside the store. At that point some of the Searcy County men, led by Dorsey Treece, demanded that Chester and his father, James Casey, close the store. Treece called James "every name that could be called," grabbed him by the throat, and began shaking him, while another man jerked off his glasses and threw them to the ground. As Chester came forward from behind the potbellied stove, Treece told him to put his hands up and then smacked him with the barrel of his Winchester rifle, causing a head wound that bled profusely. Treece forced Chester, James, and an employee, William Steed, to line up against the wall and then marched them into the street. He kept them standing until Robbins arrived from the courthouse and vouched for the Caseys as "one hundred percent American."

Local squad leader Richard Dickenhorst took Chester Casey to a physician's office to get patched up, then Robbins escorted the father and son to the courthouse. A week later, Chester gave testimony before the legislative committee in Little Rock, a bandage still covering the wound on his head. The legislators managed to get Robbins to admit that neither Sheriff Baldridge nor any of his "deputies" made any effort to arrest Treece, or anyone else, who had assaulted the Caseys. When questioned two months later in Harrison, Treece said his squad leader had ordered him to Casey's store and that Chester was going for a gun when "he was stopped." When asked pointedly whether he had hit Chester with a rifle, Treece answered: "I believe I have a right to refuse to answer."[16]

It is not entirely clear what motivated the mob to attack James and Chester Casey. Chester had attended the meeting of businessmen the previous Saturday in response to Jack Murray's telegram and contributed money, but he was not part of the Wednesday meeting that organized the committee and the squads.[17] By Robbins's comment that the Caseys were "one hundred percent American," it could be inferred they were members of the Heber Springs Klan. Both James and Chester Casey made efforts to blame the violence on the outsiders from Searcy County, rather than on their neighbors in Heber Springs.

The precipitating factor may have been the Caseys' display of support for a farmers union. Judge Massingill testified that in the search of the home of local strike leader Jim Beer, written documents were found and given to the committee indicating that Beer was also secretary of the local chapter of the United Farmers of America. Chester

Casey, too, was a member of this union. Chester explained that organizers for the farmers union had come around asking merchants to purchase trade cards and display them in their windows. The elder Casey said that he, like other merchants, had been asked to display cards declaring whether he was for or against the strike. He had resolutely refused, he said, for he traded with men from both sides. He said that Dickenhorst had been asking him to remove the United Farmers card, but he declined to do so, for he had paid $47.50 for that card. When Dorsey Treece assaulted James and Chester Casey, he demanded that they take down the United Farmers card. Treece then went to the window and found that Dickenhorst had already taken the card.[18]

An additional nine business establishments in Heber Springs held trade membership in the United Farmers organization. The mob forced others to remove cards from windows, including the confectionary/millinery shop owned by John and Roxana Hicks, the Irvin Shoe Store, and the Miller Barber Shop. A farmers union man at the barber shop was punched with guns and carted off to the courthouse. David I. DeBusk managed the United Farmers store in Heber Springs. A squad marched him at gunpoint to the courthouse for questioning at about 9:00 a.m. on Thursday. When he returned to the store in the afternoon, the squad returned and forced him to paint over the store's sign. Thirty minutes later, Sam Rector, a bank cashier, came with an M&NA open-shop card to replace the card for the United Farmers. DeBusk testified that the armed mob had announced that they had come to clean up organized labor in general, first the railroad strikers and then the farmers.[19]

The local office for the United Farmers was located on the second floor above the Caseys' store. Supporters of the railroad, led by real estate agents Frank Loving and William J. Short, had been circulating petitions denouncing the strike and raising money to pay for guards to protect railroad property. About forty local farmers had been meeting in the office for several weeks to organize resistance to these efforts. Fearing retaliation from railroad supporters, the farmers asked Sheriff Baldridge for protection, which he refused to give. James Casey had hired one of the organizers, Henry Newman, to guard his store on rumors that it was going to go up in smoke. Newman was standing ten feet away when Dorsey Treece and the mob assaulted the Caseys. Heber Springs was clearly already bitterly divided before the mob action of January 18, 1923. Robert Moor Stewart, a disabled veteran of the Great War, testified that he had been commander of the Saxon Willis Post 64 of the American Legion in Heber Springs until one-third of the members got mad and ran the others off at gunpoint.[20]

The citizens committee and squads expelled most of the strikers from Heber Springs and further alienated the members of United Farmers who remained in the area. The committee interrogated strikers and sympathizers all day on Thursday and into the night. Mayor Vinson said he arrived at the courthouse at 7:00 a.m. and stayed there for the next twenty-two hours, except for a quick bite in the afternoon. He said the committee examined 116 strikers and sympathizers before the long day ended. When Charles Black was brought into the courtroom before noon, he found from fifty to seventy-five men being held by four guards equipped with high-powered rifles. The committee conducted its interrogations in the jury room in the southwest corner of the building, a sixteen-by-sixteen-foot space with a big wooden table in the middle. William Johnson served as the inner guard. Oscar Robbins appears to have operated in the role of Walter Snapp in Harrison, going between the committee and the squads/mob assembled outside in the courtyard and streets. Robbins said he was acting as the right hand of Sheriff Baldridge, who was present in the courtroom and made no efforts to disarm any of the men carrying weapons. If, after questioning, any men were then detained, they were kept under the guard of three men in the bullpen, a small room in the northeast corner, adjacent to the courtroom.[21]

Many men were kept waiting for the better part of the day. Squads had brought in Ura Russell so early that he missed breakfast. When he asked for food, Pegleg Decker allowed him to go to a restaurant with a guard, John Barnett, who sat with gun in his lap while Russell ate. The guards allowed John Byes to go home for lunch with the promise that he would return. He got his turn before the committee at 3:00 p.m. Charlie Goff, who was taken from his home at 10:00 a.m., did not go before the committee until nearly dark.[22] Besides people, the squads brought to the courthouse a variety of so-called contraband. Most of this was in the form of guns and ammunition, which the guards had no legal right to confiscate. In their searches of homes, the squads also took emery dust, blue vitriol, and some switch keys, items that could potentially be used to sabotage the railroad. Dickenhorst said he searched the home of Harry Maloy, the assistant secretary for the strikers, and brought written records to the citizens committee.[23]

As strikers came before the committee, the process followed much the same formula as the citizens committees in Leslie and Harrison. Striker Charles Black said that Mayor Woods of Marshall seemed to be in charge of the committee's proceedings in Heber Springs. Committee members interrogated strikers about their knowledge of sabotage against the railroad. Uniformly strikers denied any involvement and reminded the committee that hardly any such acts had taken place in Cleburne County over the two years of the strike. Ultimately, strikers had to make a choice at the hearings: renounce the union and support the railroad under Jack Murray's administration, or leave Cleburne County as well as any of the other fifteen counties through which the M&NA ran. In Heber Springs, the committee had some additional time to prepare for the interrogations. It presented strikers with two preprinted forms. One directed them to renounce the strike and surrender their union cards, and thereby preserve the possibility of staying in their homes. A signature on the other form indicated a refusal to do so, with the understanding that they must exit Cleburne County by the following Monday, January 22.

The majority of strikers signed the second form. Mayor Vinson said about a dozen signed the form to renounce the strike and stay. But some of these left anyway. Charlie Goff left behind his wife and four orphaned nieces and nephews on their fully owned eighty-acre farm. His wife told him he was doing the right thing by leaving, saying, "I would rather live on cornbread and water as to yield to them people." Jessie B. Davis, a striking brakeman who had lived in Heber Springs since he was a boy, said he signed to stay because his wife was sick and he needed to care for her. But he later left anyway for Little Rock and planned to go to Oklahoma. Several men who signed the form to leave did not wait until the deadline of Monday. Jeff Garner went home directly from the courthouse, packed his grip, and left town on the evening train. Others were afraid to travel on the M&NA and headed out on foot. Striker Woodrow Wilson left his wife and nine children behind on Sunday and walked to Conway, catching a few wagon rides along the way. After his encounter with the committee,

Emmett Crosby went home, put on his overalls and overcoat, and walked sixteen miles to Quitman, where he caught a ride on a mail truck to Conway. From there he traveled by train to Pine Bluff, where he found work as a bricklayer.[24]

Mayor Vinson testified before legislators that members of the citizens committee had made no threats against the men they interrogated and that "not one discourteous word was said." He denied that the committee had forced anyone to leave their homes and insisted that the strikers had done so voluntarily. The committee had made it clear, Vinson said, that strikers' safety could not be guaranteed if they refused to renounce the strike. He even bragged about the compassion displayed by the committee toward one striker, a Mr. Duncan, who was allowed to remain an extra week because he had a sick child. Jeff Garner, however, testified that two automatic rifles leaned against the wall in the committee's interrogation room, an implied threat. Charles Woolard said committee members were armed with rifles and pistols and noted that at one point during his time with the committee, a pistol fell out of Joe Taylor's pocket, in full view of Sheriff Baldridge, who was in the room. According to Woodrow Wilson, one member of the committee pulled out a leather strap and gave him one minute to decide which form to sign. He signed to renounce the strike, but after going home he changed his mind and came back and signed to leave. Emmett Crosby said when he went before the committee at around 3:30 a.m. on Friday, Mayor Vinson pointed to a leather strap, four inches wide and several feet long, that lay across a large man's lap. The unnamed man pulled it between his hands. Crosby said Poe Hilger made the motion to give him fifty lashes. All members of the committee raised their hands in support. In his testimony before legislators, however, Hilger denied that the committee was armed or ever used a strap. All he knew about whippings, Hilger said, was what he had read in the newspapers. When the legislators questioned Vinson about the threats with a strap, he did not answer and changed the subject.[25]

Despite this contradictory testimony, it is clear that Emmett Crosby and another man received whippings. Crosby said the man with the strap took him from the courthouse down the street to the ballpark, where he was strapped to a post and told to take off his jumper and pull down his trousers. He did not know the man's name, but he heard someone call him "Treece." Treece whipped him until he was exhausted, Crosby said, at which point others took over, including Odie Logan. As Crosby was standing and assembling his clothes, the men hit him over the head with a pistol and told him to get out of town by sundown. Dewey Webb, an eighteen-year-old who had never worked for the railroad, was interrogated by the committee shortly before Crosby, then sent to the bullpen. After sending away Crosby, the committee brought Webb back. He watched, he said, as the whole committee, except Stephen Woods—"the old man from Leslie or Harrison"—voted to whip him.

At the front of the courthouse, a group of around ten men, led by Jack Carter, Frank Stewart, and Odie Logan, took charge of Webb. They took him to the ballpark where Crosby had just been whipped a few minutes before. Logan snatched Webb's hat and, when he saw a union label on the sweatband, tore it in half and threw it on the ground. Stewart strapped Webb to a post, wrapping barbed wire around his knees and head. Each man took about two licks with the strap. Dewey said he counted nineteen licks total. At around 5:30 a.m. they turned him loose, telling him to leave town. He asked to go home first and was told no. Dewey Webb began walking to get out of Heber Springs. About four miles outside of town, he came across his older brother Clyde Webb, a striking fireman who earlier had signed to leave. Clyde and Dewey stayed in the woods for two days. Dewey could hardly walk, and his brother had to carry him part of the way to get to Kensett, where they caught the train to Little Rock.[26]

A week after his assault, Dewey Webb sat before the legislative committee at its hearing in Little Rock, with visible wounds on his forehead where he had been wrapped with barbed wire to the post. In their testimony, members of the mob defended the treatment of Webb and Crosby on the grounds of their poor character. Mayor Vinson testified that he had sworn warrants against Webb months earlier for public drunkenness and the use of offensive language. Vinson said Webb and another young man had stood by in the city park as an outdoor religious service was taking place. Each time the preacher would pray, the two young men would yell out "Amen God Dam," disturbing the worshippers. Vinson fined each twenty-five dollars but then sent them to jail because they had no money to pay the fine. Mortimer Frauenthal agreed that Webb was "one of the toughest young son of guns that ever lived." If one would give him fifty cents or a drink of whiskey, Frauenthal said, Webb would cut a hose or do anything else. Vinson said Crosby was no better. Oscar Robbins, when asked pointedly whether he had participated in the whipping of Dewey Webb, declined to answer by pleading the Fifth Amendment. Sheriff Baldridge testified that he had investigated Webb's whipping but did not learn who did it.[27]

After meeting continuously for twenty-two hours and interrogating more than a hundred strikers and sympathizers, the Heber Springs citizens committee adjourned on Friday. Those men like Mayor Woods and Pegleg Decker who had been part of the mobs in Harrison, Leslie, and Heber Springs must have been exhausted after missing many hours of sleep since Sunday. The out-of-towners returned to their homes in Leslie, Marshall, St. Joe, Gilbert, Pangburn, and areas of Van Buren and Stone Counties on Friday. Locals stayed on guard to make sure the strikers left town by the Monday deadline. Almost all business establishments were closed, and all but one displayed a placard saying, "We are 100 percent for the M&NA and against all strikers and their sympathizers."

Some prominent citizens of Heber Springs continued to meet and morphed into a permanent organization, the Cleburne County Railway Labor Board. Robbins served as its chair, and Mayor Vinson was a member. Vinson announced that his group had secured a quantity of evidence that could lead to indictments for sabotage. Circuit court records for Cleburne County, however, show no prosecutions when the grand jury convened in the following month. Vinson admitted that most of those who could be indicted had left the county. Vinson also tried to make peace with members of the United Farmers, who interpreted the mob action as directed against them as well as strikers. At least one member of the farmers union was brought in for interrogation like the strikers. Arch Cathey said he had come into town to buy plow points and get a haircut. Around the time that the mob went after the card in the window of Casey's Dry Goods, a group burst into the barber shop and jerked Cathey out of the chair, just as the barber's clippers were over his head. Cathey said he was a United Farmer, not a striker, but his assailants responded: "they are the kind of damn sons of bitches we are hunting." The men took Cathey to the courthouse, where he waited from 9:00 a.m. until 4:00 p.m., before he finally went before the committee and was sent home wearing a white ribbon. By the weekend, Vinson's Railway Labor Board put an announcement in local papers that it had no issue with the farmers organization or businesses' right to display the trade cards.[28]

Rumors circulated that the Heber Springs committee planned to move down the line and clean out strikers in the towns of Searcy and Kensett, in White County. Robbins said that some eight or nine striking section workers who lived in Pangburn had come to Heber Springs and surrendered their union cards to the committee. One committee member, Ollie Baker, had telephoned White County sheriff Ben Allen, who told Baker that he had the situation under control and did not want their assistance. Harrison's strike leader Pete Venable gave the sheriff of White County his highest compliment, saying, "Ben Allen had the nerve to Buck the Game and defied the Mob and they failed to go to Searcy." On the other hand, the mob may not have been needed, for newspapers were reporting that by the weekend strikers had fled from their homes in Searcy and Kensett, even though they had not been molested.[29]

Strikers elsewhere could read the handwriting on the wall. Mayor Woods said a committee was not needed in Marshall; strikers there left of their own accord. They knew, he said, that the town "isn't a good healthy place for strikers that don't behave themselves." Likewise, most of the twenty-five strikers in Eureka Springs had left voluntarily by the weekend of the riots. On the following Monday evening, January 22, some two hundred citizens of Eureka Springs gathered in the courthouse, commended the actions that had taken place elsewhere, and created a standing citizens committee to protect the railroad. Armed men stood guard at the stairway to the courtroom and allowed no one to pass unless the person pledged support for an open-shop railroad. Festus O. Butt, a lawyer and bank president, drafted a resolution for the committee, published the following week in the *Eureka Springs Daily Times Echo*. It declared that no resident who still participated in the strike was welcome in Eureka Springs. The committee told three remaining strikers that their safety could not be guaranteed if they refused to leave town. When the dust settled, only the strikers who gave up their union membership remained.[30]

The mob violence in these other towns along the railroad, as in Harrison, involved the Ku Klux Klan. One wonders to what extent the Klan facilitated the organization and work of the vigilantes. It is hard to be certain, given that membership in the Klan was to remain a secret—at least until the summer of 1924, when Klansmen and women began to appear in public without their masks. However, the charter for Pat Cleburne Klan no. 126 of Heber Springs, dated December 18, 1922, has survived. The handsome nineteen-by-twenty-one-inch document, suitable for framing, had the names of the thirteen officers inscribed in elegant calligraphy. Five officers—Mayor Vinson, Judge Massingill, William Griffin, Roy Raywinkle, and the exalted cyclops of Klan no. 126, Arthur Hodges—served on the citizens committee that interrogated strikers and sympathizers. Two other Klan officers, Neill Reed and Richard Dickenhorst, led squads, while a third, the banker William Johnson, served as the guard at the door for the committee. One additional Klan officer, a dry goods merchant named Ruben R. Morton, was noted by a striker as being part of the mob when he was detained. Klan officer Tom Underwood had been one of the organizers on the previous Saturday, holding in his hands the telegram from Jack Murray calling for citizens along the line to rise up against the strike. In addition, one old-timer in Heber Springs, speaking before his death in 1982, remembered seeing from a distance the cross burnings of evening Klonkaves on the farm of Nick Speed, another member of the citizens committee.[31]

One can speculate that Jack Murray and those who planned the riot used the Klan network to communicate. Otherwise, why would Underwood, a real estate agent, have Murray's telegram? Also suggestive is that members of the citizens committee and squads, when asked at the legislative hearings to identify the members of the committee, failed to include the name of Arthur Hodges, the exalted cyclops of the Heber Springs Klan. Strikers and sympathizers, when asked this question, noted Hodges's membership on the committee and described specific comments he had made. Newspaper accounts of the Heber Springs riot spoke of a committee of fifteen, yet the perpetrators consistently only identified fourteen. This apparent deception mirrors what happened in Harrison, where Walter Snapp operated as part of the citizens committee, but perpetrators obscured this fact when questioned by legislators.[32]

The historical remembrance for years afterward associated the Ku Klux Klan with the vigilante violence that ended the strike. Elderly residents of Heber Springs interviewed in the early 1980s for a county history blamed the Klan for the mob violence. Similarly, Hallie Ormond of Elba, a stop on the railroad in Van Buren County between Heber Springs and Leslie, remembered the violence of 1923 as an action of the Klan. Hallie was seventeen when the strike ended, and he and his older brother, Arthur, had guarded bridges and worked at the Elba station. Years later, Hallie wrote that "the citizens up and down the railroad organized themselves under the Ku Klux Klan and took it upon themselves to literally run the union and their sympathizers out of the country." In neighboring Searcy County, the oral tradition within the Treece family cast responsibility on the Klan for the whippings of Abe and Ed Treece in Leslie. Mollie Thomas, who lived in Leslie in 1923, said years later that the Klan had whipped Ed Treece, but she did not wish to name perpetrators, for they were all local men. Another local resident, Dale Lee, later recounted the story of his uncle Charles Kuykendall, who was summoned to appear before the Leslie committee. When his uncle got to town, Lee said, he saw men in Klan robes and masks flogging strikers on the street with horsewhips. They had started to whip him when a storeowner vouched for him, and after much discussion he was dismissed. Kuykendall was so traumatized by the event, Lee said, that he left for California and did not return to Searcy County for nearly thirty years, finally visiting in 1951.[33]

Even participants in the mob action revealed an awareness of the connection between the Klan and vigilantism. Ed Treece said that while he was still reeling from the pain of his flogging with a leather strap, Rev. Carter explained to him that it was the citizens, not the Klan, that did the whipping. Carter appears to have been a member of the Klan, for after moving later in the year to Berryville, he was giving public lectures on "Americanism," a code for the Klan agenda. He and Mrs. Carter took a group of their church members to Eureka Springs to see *The Birth of a Nation*, a Klan favorite film, in the Commodore Theater. But even Klan members understood the relationship between the Invisible Empire and the actions of the mob. According to Orville J. McInturff, an amateur historian of Searcy County, Abe Treece's brother Hugh, a bank cashier in Marshall and former county judge, was the exalted cyclops of the Marshall Klan. During the week when the violence was coming down in Harrison, Leslie, and Heber Springs, Marshall's Bear Creek Klan no. 88 passed three resolutions: (1) blaming strikers for destroying property with the intent to shut down the railroad, (2) affirming support for the railroad under general manager Murray, and (3) pledging assistance to county and state officials in bringing to justice those who committed depredations. This last resolution virtually declared the Klan's participation in the actions that were taking place against strikers. Yet, according to McInturff, when Hugh G. Treece learned of the whipping of his brother, he resigned his membership in the Ku Klux Klan. Treece's resignation serves as admission that the whippings in Leslie took place on behalf of the Klan.[34]

By the end of January most of the strikers and many of their sympathizers along the railroad's line in the Arkansas Ozarks, from Eureka Springs to Kensett, had fled, leaving their families and homes behind. It does not appear that strikers were expelled in the Missouri portion of the line, or where the railroad ran through the Arkansas Delta, from Kensett to Helena. Some members of the mob, especially men from Searcy County such as Mayor Woods of Marshall and Pegleg Decker of Leslie, had spent the entire week cleaning out strikers in Harrison, Leslie, and Heber Springs. Clearly there was coordination between the vigilantes up and down the line, most likely through the Klan chapters in each of these towns. They were successful, for the mob actions effectively brought an end to the strike, even though the national officers of the railroad brotherhoods would not declare the strike officially over until eleven months later.

CHAPTER 8

INVESTIGATIONS: 1923

As the violence was unfolding in Harrison, Leslie, and Heber Springs, both federal and state governments sent representatives to examine the situation. Assistant district attorney C. E. Argabright came to Harrison on behalf of federal judge Frank A. Youmans and the US Department of Justice, while US attorney general Harry M. Daugherty dispatched deputy US marshal Andrew J. Russell. But they worked *with* the M&NA and the citizens committees to examine the actions of strikers and higher union officials. Governor Thomas C. McRae sent officers of the Arkansas National Guard to Heber Springs to survey the situation there, but they passed out weapons from the armory to the vigilantes who were rounding up strikers and sympathizers. These representatives of state and federal governments facilitated the actions of the mobs that supported the railroad. As the dust settled from the riots in the last week of January, the vivid reporting in newspapers throughout the country prompted probes by national organizations such as the American Federation of Labor (AFL) and the American Civil Liberties Union (ACLU). At the same time, the Arkansas General Assembly's special committee began preparations for what would be the most thorough investigation of the strike and riot. The investigations that began after the riots held out the prospect of bringing members of the mobs to justice. In all cases, they failed to do so.

The special legislative committee was getting organized in Little Rock as the vigilantes were still at work in the Arkansas Ozarks. The Ku Klux Klan exercised enormous influence over the new General Assembly and the elected county, judicial district, and state officials who took office that same week. Harrison's Klan no. 101 was organized by the time of the August 1922 primaries, and it received its charter before the state general election in October. Because charter numbers were consecutive, at least a hundred Klan chapters existed in the Klan Realm of Arkansas at the time of the elections within the state's seventy-five counties. In many of these counties, the Klan endorsed slates of candidates that went before voters. In Boone County, the Klan ticket included both Republicans, such as Robert "Bob" Shaddox for sheriff, and Democrats, such as incumbents James M. Shinn and Karl Greenhaw for circuit judge and prosecuting attorney, respectively.

The Republican Party was hardly viable in most Arkansas counties outside the Ozarks. In counties that lacked a competitive two-party system, the Klan held its own preferential primary before the August Democratic primary, to choose which Klan candidates would get the vote of Klan members. This preferential primary system worked most notoriously in Pulaski County, where the Little Rock Klan no. 1 was not only the oldest Klan in the state, receiving its charter in October 1921, but the largest, with approximately ten thousand members. The Little Rock Klan had voted as a block in the municipal elections of April 4, 1922, to sweep all city positions, including the mayor. Through the preferential primaries for sheriff, senator, and representatives in July, the Little Rock chapter prepared a Klan ticket for all county and legislative positions to present to voters in the August 8 Democratic primary. All the Klan-endorsed candidates, except for two representatives to the lower house of the state legislature, won over other Democratic opponents in the primary. They handily defeated Republicans in the October election and took their offices in January 1923. These officials then selected a new list of grand jurors to serve for the calendar year.

Evidence suggests Klan politicking in many other Arkansas counties, though none as dramatic as in Pulaski. The grand dragon of the Realm of Arkansas, James A. Comer, also endorsed a slate of candidates for every state constitutional office, from governor on down. All the Klan-endorsed candidates won, including incumbent governor McRae and Heartsill Ragon, a Klansman sent to Washington as congressman to represent the Fifth District of central Arkansas.[1]

The changing of the guard in January 1923, after the Klan's success in the state and local elections, may have directed the timetable for the mob actions that ended the strike. Pete Venable certainly believed so. He asserted that Governor McRae was a Klansman and that he knew in advance of the plans for January 15. While the Klan publicly endorsed McRae in the 1922 election, it is unclear whether McRae was a member of the Invisible Empire. Some Klansmen suggested that McRae was "Klan friendly" and that they could control him through his personal secretary, Clarence P. Newton, who was a member of Little Rock Klan no. 1. Newton would later win the Klan preferential primary in 1924 and serve two terms as Pulaski County judge.[2]

As one additional example of what a difference a month could make in the Arkansas court system, consider the case of John G. Spurgeon, a striking machinist for the Missouri Pacific Railroad. Spurgeon was arrested in North Little Rock in October 1922, during the shopmen's strike, for dynamiting the home of a strikebreaker. When his case went before the Pulaski County circuit court in December, the jury could not come to a verdict and so the presiding judge declared a mistrial. After the jury had been out for more than sixty hours, the vote still stood nine to acquit versus three to convict. However, the prosecuting attorney, a Klansman reelected in October, brought the case for a second trial in January, after the newly elected officials were sworn in. Spurgeon's lawyers accused the new county sheriff, Klansman Homer Adkins, who would later become governor of Arkansas, of handpicking a Klansman-only jury. The new jury convicted Spurgeon on Sunday, January 14, the day before the mob descended on Harrison. Spurgeon was sentenced to a year in the state penitentiary. The Klan was well known generally for its attempt to pack juries and solicit the cooperation of justice officials.[3] Such a posture toward railroad strikers lends some support for Venable's claim that the January date for a mob action against the strike was planned well in advance.

The Ku Klux Klan also exercised considerable influence over the state legislature that convened on January 8 and a week later created the special committee to investigate the M&NA strike violence. While it is unknown specifically which or how many legislators in the 1923 Arkansas General Assembly were members of the Klan, one can reasonably assume that most were Klansmen. The kligrapp (secretary) of the Realm of Arkansas, Clio Harper, served as the calendar clerk for the session, and his company received the contract to print the journals of both houses. Either the *Arkansas Gazette* or

Arkansas Democrat had formerly always published these official documents. Klansmen pushed through several bills reflecting the Klan agenda. Paul Grabiel, a Klansman senator elected from Pulaski County, sponsored an "Americanization" act that required all public and private schools to fly the American flag and teach American history in every primary grade, in addition to a full year in high school. The law also mandated that no student could graduate from an institution of higher learning in Arkansas without a course in American history or government. The representative from Johnson County, Paul McKennon, who also served on the committee for the M&NA investigation, introduced a bill that required the registration of all handguns at the county courthouse. While it might appear on the surface as a progressive gun control measure, the law required individuals to go before county officials, who were likely to be Klansmen, to demonstrate their "good moral character" to possess a pistol. African Americans viewed the law as a clear attempt to disarm them. A group of Black citizens left St. Francis County for Chicago in the spring of 1923 on account of the law and their fear of the Klan.[4]

One of the most lasting acts of the forty-fourth session of the Arkansas General Assembly was its modification of the state flag, a banner designed and approved just a decade before. The flag had a blue band of stars in a diamond shape on a red background. Inside the diamond were three stars representing the three countries to which Arkansas had belonged before statehood: France, Spain, and the United States. Neill Bohlinger, a Little Rock Klansman, introduced a bill to add a fourth star to represent the Confederate States of America. The bill became law, but still Bohlinger was not satisfied. In a special session of the same legislature the following year, he sponsored another bill that moved the star representing the Confederacy to reside above the other three stars, including the star representing the United States. This same Bohlinger, like Paul McKennon, served on the special M&NA committee. As its secretary, he would write the report presented to the governor. The Americanization law of 1923 still guides education in Arkansas, and the revised Arkansas flag flies above all schools and government buildings in the state today.[5]

On Wednesday, January 17, the General Assembly passed the act creating a special joint committee to investigate conditions along the M&NA line, relative to "certain acts of lawlessness alleged to have been committed." One might note that the language of the act did not specify which acts of lawlessness would be examined, leaving the door open to review actions of strikers as well as the mob. By the next day, the special committee had been constituted, with Howard Reed, the Speaker of the House, choosing four members from the lower house, and Senate president Jacob R. "Jake" Wilson appointing three senators. Representatives included Ernest Chaney, a teacher from rural Woodruff County; Paul McKennon, a lawyer from Clarksville; Neill Bohlinger, a Little Rock lawyer; and Fred Harrelson, a lawyer from Forrest City. From the Senate were the committee's chair, M. B. "Brooks" Norfleet, another Forrest City lawyer; G. Otis Bogle, a lawyer from Brinkley; and William H. Abington, a physician living in Beebe. Senator Wilson, from El Dorado, and Speaker Reed, of Heber Springs, were to serve as ex officio members of the committee. Reed asked to be excused, presumably because his brother Neill had been a squad member in the vigilante mob in Heber Springs, while his brother-in-law Brose Massingill, the Cleburne County judge, had served on the citizens committee. Given that both Neill Reed and Brose Massingill were officers of the Heber Springs Klan no. 126, it is likely that Howard Reed was also a member. Pete Venable alleged that all eight members of the legislative committee were Klansmen. Of the entire committee, only Wilson was disposed to favor the strikers; he had worked as a railroad conductor for some years before and still held membership in the Order of Railway Conductors. But even Wilson had been initiated into Little Rock Klan no. 1, despite his home being in El Dorado. Unlike Reed, Wilson did not recuse himself, and he took an active role in the committee's inquiry.[6]

The investigative work of the committee began on Monday morning, January 22, when it took testimony in the Senate chambers of the State Capitol exactly a week after the mob assembled in Harrison. As its first witnesses, the committee questioned Luther Wise and Verlin D. "Red" Orr, brought over from the state penitentiary on Roosevelt Road. After adjourning at noon, the committee reconvened in the evening in the second-floor ballroom, room 212, of the Marion Hotel, where many legislators stayed while the General Assembly was in session. For the rest of the week, the committee's hearings took place there in the evening hours after the legislature's regular sessions had ended for the day. The room was large and usually crowded

Members of the joint committee of the Arkansas General Assembly to investigate the M&NA Railroad strike and riots. *From top to bottom, left:* Sen. G. Otis Bogle, Sen. William H. Abington, Rep. Fred Harrelson; *center:* Sen. Brooks Norfleet, chair; *right:* Rep. Neill Bohlinger, Rep. Ernest Chaney, Rep. Paul McKennon. *Pine Bluff Daily Graphic, February 9, 1923.*

with strikers waiting to testify, M&NA officials, newspaper reporters, and curious spectators. Most of the men who gave testimony in these first meetings were strikers and sympathizers from Heber Springs and Leslie, and a few from Harrison, who had congregated in Little Rock after being expelled from their homes. So many strikers were present wishing to testify that on Wednesday evening, Chairman Norfleet asked for the record to note that the committee had chosen not to take testimony from some twenty strikers present whose testimony the committee deemed repetitive of the other witnesses. On Thursday evening, the committee heard testimony from Albert Raash, Chester Casey, and Dewey Webb, whose wounds from beatings the week before were still visible on their bodies.[7]

After a weekend break, the investigation reconvened on Tuesday evening, January 30, with meetings each evening thereafter in that second week. The special committee cast its net wider, interviewing additional strikers and sympathizers; victims of beatings, such as Abe and Ed Treece of Leslie, and George W. O'Neal of Harrison; a number of vigilantes from Heber Springs; John Devaney, who testified to the alleged conspiracy of the railroad to burn its own bridges as a pretext for an uprising against the strike; and John Rogers, the reporter from the *St. Louis Post-Dispatch*, who recounted his experiences in Harrison. By the end of the second week, a division within the committee had become apparent. Senator Wilson was only an ex officio member, but he took the leading role in questioning strikers and demonstrated his sympathy for labor. His questions gave strikers the opportunity to display their patriotism, good citizenship, and opposition to the damaging of railroad property. Questioning by Senator Abington and Representatives Bohlinger, McKennon, and Chaney gave a velvet glove to the vigilantes and showed antagonism to strikers.

Senator Bogle was downright hostile and argumentative when questioning strikers and their sympathizers. For example, he insinuated that Albert Raash was a member of the Industrial Workers of the World (IWW). He went beyond asking questions and directly accused Raash of moving from Wisconsin to Harrison with the deliberate plan of raising Cain with the M&NA, even though Raash had never worked for the railroad. He also accused Raash of loitering in the lobby of the Marion Hotel to eavesdrop on a conversation between himself and Senator Abington. Senator Norfleet even called out Bogle for badgering the witness. During the questioning of John Rogers, Bogle was sitting with the attorneys for the M&NA and kept interrupting and objecting, until Wilson finally intervened to allow Rogers to finish his statement. Bogle and Wilson clashed also when Wilson refused to allow J. Sam Rowland, attorney for the railroad, to challenge Rogers's testimony. Abington, presiding in the absence of Norfleet, twice threatened to clear the room because of loud outbursts among the crowd of approximately a hundred people.[8]

Several of the legislative committee's actions suggest an overall bias toward the railroad and its supporters. In the few moments when witnesses were poised to name individuals guilty of the worst crimes, the committee went into executive session, thus keeping the most incriminating material to itself. John Hughey was present with Ed C. Gregor when the three masked men stormed into Rotary Hall to take Gregor away to his death. Hughey testified that Walter Suskey, another prisoner in the room, recognized one of the men. But Suskey was never questioned by the committee. In its first few days, the legislative committee did issue subpoenas to members of the Harrison citizens committee, a few railroad officials, and some Boone County elected officials. Jack Murray and three members of the citizens committee, in fact, traveled from Harrison to Little Rock, and were expected to sit for interviews on the following Monday, January 29. However, Murray asked the legislative committee to take his testimony and that of others from Boone County in Harrison instead. The committee on Monday heard no witnesses and announced it would travel later to Harrison to question residents of the town. Strikers indicated that it was not safe for them to go to Harrison to rebut testimony or to witness the proceedings.[9]

After two weeks of nearly daily hearings, the committee paused. The 1,400-page record of the hearings contains testimonies and affidavits of witnesses, but none of the committee's internal discussion. It is therefore not known how the committee made its plans. While the legislators announced their intention to travel to Harrison, they left the date for their visit uncertain. Newspapers reported that citizens, even mayors, along the line from Eureka Springs to Leslie showered Senator Norfleet with phone calls, telegrams, and letters inviting the committee to visit their towns to take testimony. Norfleet announced that the committee would give citizens every chance to tell their side of the story, probably after the General Assembly concluded its session on March 8. Senator Norfleet asked Judge Shinn for the use of his courtroom in Harrison for the hearings. On February 28, part of the special committee convened in Senate chambers under Representative McKennon as acting chair to hear testimony of three Heber Springs men who complained about harassment directed toward them as alleged sympathizers, intimidation that had continued in the weeks following the January riot.[10]

One of the last actions of the General Assembly was to pass an act authorizing a $5,000 reward for the arrest and conviction of the lynchers of Ed Gregor. Sometime after the legislature adjourned, the special committee set its plans for the hearings in Harrison. Senator Wilson would later allege that the other legislators chose to go to Harrison at a time they knew he could not attend because his wife had fallen ill in Little Rock. The committee, minus Wilson, left Little Rock early on Monday, March 19, to travel by train to Harrison. Newspaper reporters and J. W. Bishop, representing the sixteen railway brotherhoods, tagged along. In Heber Springs, a group of vigilante leaders, including Mayor Marcus E. Vinson and Judge Brose Massingill, boarded the train and rode along to give their testimony in Harrison, even though the town was nearly twice as far away as Little Rock. The train arrived at Harrison at 5:00 p.m. on Monday, over an hour late. A short meeting of the group determined that Bohlinger and McKennon, both of them lawyers, would do all the questioning to make most efficient use of time. Because Harrison's hotels were expected to be filled, the M&NA's lead attorney, J. Sam Rowland, arranged for residents who had extra beds to take in the out-of-town guests.[11]

The legislative committee convened its session in Judge Shinn's courtroom on Tuesday morning, with the room crowded with spectators and witnesses. Chairman Norfleet made some introductory remarks and reminded those present, many who had been part of the mob, that the committee's purpose was to ascertain the facts and report to the governor, not to make a "judicial determination." In other words, the committee was simply recording information, not prosecuting anyone for illegal activities. It was the committee's pleasure, Norfleet said, to come before the community and its public officials, and the legislators appreciated their kindness and hospitality.

Norfleet was, besides Wilson, the only committee member in Little Rock who had not shown hostility to the strikers and sympathizers, but his tone in Harrison sounded downright obsequious. He concluded his speech: "We are more than willing to do anything we can to aid and assist the citizens and the general public."[12]

After Norfleet's comments, the hearing began by calling the railroad's general manager, Jack Murray. Instead of questioning him, the committee allowed Murray to read a prepared statement in which he gave a history of the railroad, a rationale for the wage reductions, and a narrative of the strike in which he cataloged depredations committed against the railroad over the two-year period. With great drama Murray pulled out relics of sabotage and dramatically placed them on a table in the courtroom: two bombs he said had been placed in coal chutes, cans of emery dust, a pack of blue vitriol, and a horseshoe and bolts said to have been placed on tracks to derail trains. Some of these items, Murray said, had been found at the home of strike leader Pete Venable. When Murray placed a box of two hundred blasting caps on the edge of the table, Representative McKennon objected that they might explode in the courtroom. Further excitement ensued when a spectator dropped a long blue-barrel pistol on the floor of the courtroom. A deputy sheriff promptly warned all to strap their holsters tight so this would not happen again, a telling statement, given that carrying a concealed pistol was illegal in the state of Arkansas and Boone County had prosecuted numerous strikers for this offense. Another highlight was when Mayor Stephen W. Woods of Marshall, who had been part of the vigilante committees in Harrison, Leslie, and Heber Springs, compared their work to the Boston Tea Party, a comment that brought a round of applause from the crowd.[13]

Over four days, the committee took testimony from more than sixty individuals, most of whom had been directly involved in the actions against strikers and sympathizers. Consistently, the committee, as with Jack Murray, let witnesses control the narratives. They allowed prosecuting attorney Greenhaw to read into the record thirty pages of gossipy grand jury "evidence" against strikers, while they failed to push him to reveal any information about who might have lynched Gregor or beaten men in Harrison, Leslie, or Heber Springs. They hardly questioned Sheriff Shaddox about his failure to act against mob violence, and they let pass his cooperation with the vigilantes by guarding illegally detained men in Rotary Hall.[14]

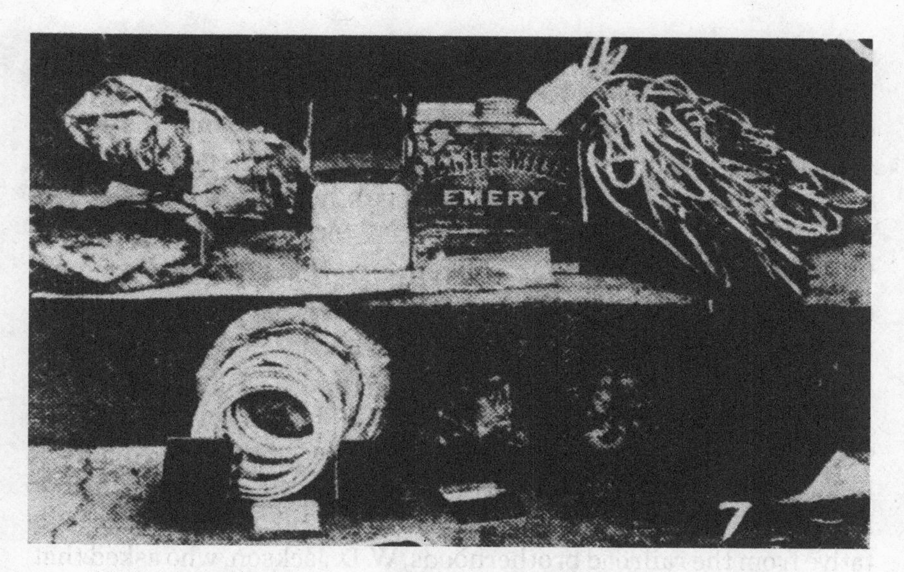

M&NA general manager Jack Murray's collection of alleged articles of sabotage. *Memphis Commercial Appeal, January 21, 1923.*

The Harrison hearings ended with a virtual lovefest between the committee and community. On Thursday, the committee, stenographers, and newspapermen were feted by Harrison's Rotary Club at a luncheon prepared by the Mothers Club, the same women who had fed the vigilantes for a week back in January. The local newspaper reported that after some piano numbers and two vocal solos, the legislators' speeches made Harrison citizens feel that they were being investigated "by our friends" and that the committee's opinions were "altogether pleasing to our citizens." J. Sam Rowland, a past president of Harrison's Rotary Club, said citizens looked forward to a good report from the committee "because we folks here believe we have earned it." As far as they were concerned, "the strike is off forever." The next day, Friday, March 23, Chairman Norfleet, with a fit of purple prose, gave a concluding address before leaving the courtroom. He declared that the committee had heard from "each and every citizen" who desired to testify, ignoring the fact that the committee in Little Rock had dismissed twenty strikers who wished to make a statement on the grounds that their testimony was repetitive. While the committee made no concluding statement in Little Rock, in Harrison Norfleet praised the "the splendid American citizenship as developed by the people of this section of our great state, a citizenship in which the independent spirit of Jackson and Cromwell has been shown." The issue of capital and labor, he said, will be settled by American citizens "as it was settled by the people of Boone County and North Arkansas." The audience responded with thunderous applause. Miss Anna Fitzpatrick, Judge Shinn's stenographer, read a closing statement praising the "brilliant committee" for its fair and impartial hearing. With the committee finishing work on Friday afternoon, after the daily southbound train had already departed, the M&NA provided as a final gesture of goodwill a special train to take the legislators and newspapermen back to Little Rock.[15]

Three additional meetings in March and April would conclude the work of the special legislative committee. After arriving back in Little Rock, on Monday afternoon, March 26, Bohlinger, Chaney, McKennon, and Harrelson met in Senate chambers with a representative from the railroad brotherhoods, W. D. Jackson, who asked that the unions receive time to look over the stenographer's record and summon any witnesses to rebut testimony given in Harrison. Jackson and five other union representatives met with the legislative committee in Little Rock on Friday, April 13, at which time they must have received a transcript of the testimony. Ten days later, the committee met again with representatives of the brotherhoods in the Marion Hotel. With Senator Wilson present to guide the testimony, the union men brought additional witnesses, including several more men who had been summoned before the citizens committees in Leslie and Heber Springs. Martin C. Carey, the vice president of the Order of Railway Conductors, who had been run out of Harrison in 1921 and subsequently met with President Warren G. Harding, made a statement. And the sheriff and county judge of White County testified that they had managed to prosecute strikers for criminal offenses without the need for a mob.

The union representatives submitted climatological data and reports by inspectors from the Interstate Commerce Commission (ICC), asserting that the shoddy safety standards of the M&NA had caused the fires along the line, rather than striker sabotage. The union men also provided a copy of the January 12 editorial in the *Marshall Mountain Wave* calling for telephone poles to be "decorated" with strikers as evidence that lynchings had been planned in advance of the riot. Finally, the union men presented a host of notarized affidavits taken in Oklahoma, Missouri, and other states from strikers, such as Pete Venable and Charles DeGoche, who feared for their lives if they returned to Arkansas to testify in person before the committee.[16]

All the extra information may not have mattered, for five days after this meeting, on April 28, word leaked that Representative Bohlinger had already prepared the report and that it placed no blame on anyone and made no recommendation for action to Governor McRae. On May 6, the committee filed the report with the governor's office and the press, signed by all members except for Wilson. After taking three months and assembling nearly 1,400 pages of evidence, the committee had put out a report that was remarkably brief, less than 6,000 words. The report provided a short history of the railroad, the two-year-long strike, and the events that ended it in January. The committee report considered the damages to railroad property, on the one side, as comparable to the illegal searches of property, the detention and expulsion of strikers, the floggings, and a lynching, on the other. After walking a balance holding neither side accountable, the report ended with a backhanded Klanish compliment to the citizens of the Arkansas Ozarks, considering it a tribute to their "Anglo-Saxon blood" that only one man, Ed Gregor, lost his life.[17]

The legislative committee's report would have put the strike and mob action largely to rest, were it not for one last spat between Sen. Jake Wilson and Rep. Neill Bohlinger, who spoke for the rest of the committee. Wilson had reportedly said that as an ex officio member of the committee, he was not required to sign its report. But two days after the report was filed, Wilson gave an address in Little Rock before the Arkansas Federation of Labor. He complained that the other legislators had chosen a time to take testimony in Harrison when members knew he would not be able to attend. Wilson called the work of the vigilantes in northern Arkansas "high treason," and he said they should be dealt with by the courts. Instead of a real investigation, the committee's work, he said, was a whitewash. In a press release the next day, Bohlinger, who wrote the report, shot back that Wilson had never made his complaints known to the committee. The report was anything but a whitewash, Bohlinger said. Governor McRae remained silent, apparently ready for the public discussion of the matter to come to an end. The Boone County authorities landed a parting shot at Wilson a year later, when he was running for the

Senator Jake Wilson. *Arkansas Gazette, December 17, 1922.*

Democratic nomination for governor. In his stump speeches he had apparently claimed that if he were elected governor, the truth would come out about the Harrison troubles. Wilson received a subpoena to appear before the Boone County grand jury to address his comments, and he had to interrupt his campaigning to appear behind closed doors in Harrison on July 23, three weeks before the primary. Wilson would lose the election, coming in fifth out of six candidates.[18]

As the special legislative committee was investigating the violence associated with the railroad strike, representatives of organized labor put pressure on Governor McRae. On Thursday, January 18, Warren S. Stone, the chair of the coordinating committee for the sixteen railroad brotherhoods, sent McRae a telegram from Chicago saying that Harrison still was under mob rule and had treated strikers shamefully, but yet the state did nothing. McRae wired Stone back, saying that conditions along the railroad were back to "normal" and authorities were in control of the situation. A news report circulated nationally on Monday, January 22, announcing that the AFL was investigating the violence in Arkansas and launching an effort to impeach Governor McRae for his inactivity. The Federated Shop Crafts Union, affiliated with the AFL, issued a call for all union workers to give 1 percent of their earnings for the next thirty days to create a fund for the investigation and prosecution of those responsible for the violence in Harrison.

On the following day, Tuesday, January 23, AFL president Samuel Gompers issued a public demand for Governor McRae to stop the mob violence and bring those who were guilty to justice. The editor of the *North Arkansas Star*, who was a member of the citizens committee in Harrison, mocked the "Canadian Jew" who thought he had put "a great fright on the people of North Arkansas," missing that Gompers was actually born in London, England, and had immigrated to the United States when he was ten years old. Lewis W. Lowry, a Little Rock labor leader, was sending reports to the AFL in Washington, DC, summarizing the testimony before the legislative committee. Gompers on Friday issued another statement declaring that city and county officials in Heber Springs had been part of the mob that illegally expelled strikers from their homes. Further, two days before that, Gompers wrote letters to the *Washington Post*, *New York Times*, and *Philadelphia Public Ledger*, as well as to several other influential newspapers in the Northeast, asking for them to provide more coverage to the outrageous actions committed by the mobs in Harrison and other towns along the M&NA. The editor of the *Baltimore Sun* responded that the news services had stopped providing information for fuller reports. Gompers then wrote to the Associated Press, United Press, and International News Service on January 31 and February 2, asking them to review their coverage of the Arkansas case. Perhaps Gompers might have kept the pressure going, but later in February he fell gravely ill with influenza and pneumonia and was unable to work for several weeks. Officials of the railroad brotherhoods, however, continued to follow the legislative committee's investigation to the very end. After the disappointing report in May, Warren Stone, speaking again for the railroad brotherhoods, complained about the failure of state and local officials in bringing perpetrators to justice. He announced an additional $5,000 reward to add to the $5,000 already appropriated by the state legislature.[19]

The mob actions in the Arkansas Ozarks that ended the M&NA strike clarified the stance of organized labor in the United States toward the Ku Klux Klan. Formerly, the Klan and labor had each held ambivalent attitudes toward the other. In some locations the Klan had supported white workers who perceived competition from Black, Catholic, and foreign-born laborers. In many communities, skilled workers joined the Klan in great numbers. With the outrages in Harrison, Leslie, and Heber Springs, the labor press, including the *Garment Worker*, the *Federated Press Bulletin*, and *Labor*, identified the mob actions as planned and led by Klansmen. In November 1923, Arkansas's District 21 of the United Mine Workers added to its constitution a ban on Klan membership. Even Gompers and his executive council of the AFL declared after the actions in Harrison that union members could not participate in the activities of the Ku Klux Klan.[20]

Simultaneous with the attacks on Governor McRae by organized labor, officials in the ACLU began what would be a prolonged campaign alleging the complicity of state and county officials in the mob violence. Established just a few years earlier, in 1920, with its office on Fifth Avenue in New York City, the ACLU was led by its founding executive director, Roger Nash Baldwin. A greater contrast could not be found between the Boston-born, Harvard-educated Baldwin and the Arkansas politicians he engaged. Baldwin had spent nine months in jail for refusing to register for the selective service during the Great War. He joined the IWW and consorted with the likes of Emma Goldman and Norman Thomas, some of the country's most notorious communists. Baldwin's ACLU quickly established a reputation for radical Left politics, raising money for the defense of anarchists Nicola Sacco and Bartolomeo Vanzetti in the 1921 show trial. Baldwin came under continued scrutiny of Attorney General Daugherty and the director of the Bureau of Investigation, William J. Burns, who called Baldwin a "paid agent" of the Third Communist International and Moscow.[21]

Roger Baldwin had several items on his plate in 1923, but he began a crusade for accountability for the vigilante violence in northern Arkansas and the acquiescence of elected officials on the state and local levels. On Wednesday, January 17, while the mobs still controlled Harrison and Leslie, Baldwin wired Governor McRae, asking for an explanation of measures taken to bring to justice those who had committed the floggings and Gregor's lynching. He even offered McRae the services of the ACLU's investigators and attorneys. McRae responded with a telegram that same day, explaining that he had condemned the lynching and other acts of violence at Harrison and had asked the circuit judge and sheriff to direct a thorough investigation through the grand jury. Sheriff Shaddox admitted later that he had made no investigation. If Boone County's grand jury did so, its findings never became publicly known. As the legislative committee began taking testimony in Little Rock, union representative Lewis Lowry began sending Baldwin information about the committee's work, just as he was reporting also to AFL headquarters in Washington, DC. Baldwin and the ACLU even agreed to pay Lowry's expenses, up to seventy-five dollars, as he covered the legislative committee's meetings. While on the run, Pete Venable was also writing to Baldwin, sharing his narrative about what had transpired in Harrison. Venable had left Little Rock after his audience with Governor McRae on January 17, fearing that he would be arrested and hauled back to Boone County for prosecution. By mid-February, he had landed in McAlester, Oklahoma, where his wife, Jennie, had family.[22]

Both Venable and Lowry coached Baldwin about the sluggish work of the legislative committee and behind-the-scenes manipulation by the Ku Klux Klan. After the committee had concluded its hearings in Little Rock, with no announced plan to conclude the probe, Baldwin wrote to McRae a stinging public letter, chastising state officials for their inaction. Was it not true, he asked, that they had failed to provide exiled strikers with protection to return to their homes to collect families and possessions? Have M&NA officials not influenced the legislative investigation, Baldwin asked, as evidenced by Murray convincing the committee to take his testimony and that of others subpoenaed from Boone County in Harrison rather than in Little Rock? And finally, Baldwin asked, was it not true that the Ku Klux Klan had played a role in organizing the violence and in curbing the legislative investigation thereafter? After a few days, McRae gave Baldwin's lengthy letter a two-sentence response. "Your letter received. Waiving the discourteous tone of it, I answer all of your questions in the negative, so far as I have information." Baldwin wrote back with implied irony that he was glad to know that none of his charges were founded on fact. But he said the ACLU would continue its own investigation with its man on the ground.[23]

Baldwin continued to monitor the work of the legislative committee through press accounts and missives from Lowry and Venable. Soon after the committee returned from Harrison, Baldwin once more wrote to Governor McRae, expressing his dismay with the state's "investigation." Again, he did not mince words. Apparently referencing Senator Norfleet's closing speech in Harrison, Baldwin said that the committee had glorified the terrorism inflicted by the citizens of north Arkansas as acts of patriotism. And he noted that floggings and deportations had continued in Heber Springs, Harrison, and Eureka Springs during the very weeks when the state was examining the violence. Baldwin charged that McRae, by his failure to protect citizens' basic civil rights, had acquiesced to the carefully organized and lawless violence of the mob. It appears that Governor McRae did not bother to reply to Baldwin's letter.[24]

On the same day that Baldwin wrote to McRae, April 6, he told Pete Venable that the ACLU was anxiously waiting for the report of the legislative committee before hiring its own investigator. Ten days later, Baldwin asked John Rogers, the reporter for the *St. Louis Post-Dispatch* who had given riveting testimony in Little Rock in January, to write up an account of his trip to Harrison, implying that the ACLU would publish it as a pamphlet. Rogers apparently did not respond. After the legislative committee's unsatisfactory report came out in May, the executive committee of the ACLU voted to hire Charles Finger, a writer in Fayetteville, Arkansas, to help it conduct its own investigation of the mob violence in the state.[25]

Finger was a peculiar and ultimately unsuccessful choice for the ACLU. Born in England in 1867, Finger came of age in the 1880s as part of a homosexual literati set in London. He left the country in 1890, before the prosecution of Oscar Wilde and other gay intellectuals later in the decade. He bounced around South America and the American Southwest for fifteen years, earning a living as a part-time musician, newspaper reporter, and fiction writer. In 1905 he married and moved to Ohio, where he found steady employment as an office worker for several railroad companies. In 1920 he bought a 115-acre farm three miles west of Fayetteville, with the intention of establishing an artists' colony he named Gayeta. He began a literary journal, *All's Well*, which published mostly his own work. A few of Finger's articles were picked up by national literary journals, such as *Century*

Magazine and the *Nation*. Oswald Garrison Villard, a longtime friend of Baldwin's and member of the ACLU's executive committee, was the editor of the *Nation* and probably suggested Finger's hiring. Finger might have appeared to be a good choice, given that he had worked in the railroad industry for fifteen years and lived just seventy-five miles from Harrison. Baldwin sent him information Pete Venable had collected, and Finger promptly went to work. The report was in the hands of the ACLU by the last week of September, and on October 1, the executive committee voted to release it.[26]

Finger's eighteen-page typed report turned the investigation of the strike violence into a literary exercise. Finger narrated the M&NA's history and the two-year strike, much like the legislative committee's report had done. He did not hold strikers accountable for any damages to the railroad. Instead, he emphasized that the shoddy construction of the M&NA bridges had made them a tinderbox with the exceptionally dry weather in 1922. He noted fires on the Frisco and other lines in the Ozarks during the same time. Finger described the actions of mobs in Harrison, Leslie, and Heber Springs but concluded that the identity of Ed Gregor's killers, and their motivation, remained unclear. Finger did not even lay particular blame on the Ku Klux Klan. It was fashionable, he said, to do so, and many members of the mob doubtless belonged to the Invisible Empire. But the events of the week were larger than the plan of any one organization. Finger's rambling report, filled with flowery and pretentious language, added nothing new. It ended abruptly, making no real conclusions or recommendations. McRae acknowledged receipt of the report, and the matter dropped. The newspapers in Arkansas appeared to have lost interest by October 1923. In a short article, the *Arkansas Gazette* acknowledged the Finger report and McRae's response but managed also to discredit the ACLU by noting its activities to defend "Bolshevists, I.W.W., Left Wing Socialists, and other Reds."[27]

The strikers and their supporters were losing the war of public opinion as the distance grew from the events of January 1923. With no apparent impact from the report, the ACLU shifted its strategy toward preparation for legal action. Pete Venable, from his home in McAlester, did much of the groundwork for a civil lawsuit. In January 1924, he sent Baldwin a list of 207 members of the Harrison mob whom he judged the "cream of the lot." Venable's list included Jack

Murray, J. Sam Rowland, and J. Loyd Shouse of the M&NA; Judge Shinn, prosecuting attorney Greenhaw, and Sheriff Shaddox and his deputies; and even eight women of the Mothers Club who had provided meals for the mob. Through the winter months and into the spring of 1924, Venable worked with a Tulsa lawyer, Robert J. Boone. Boone even traveled to New York to meet with the ACLU attorney Walter Welles to discuss the case. Boone estimated the cost of a lawsuit to exceed $27,000, which Welles thought unaffordable. Baldwin advised Venable to find another lawyer with less grandiose ideas about the case. Venable then entered discussions with a lawyer in McAlester, Emilio C. Marianelli, who proposed that they whittle down the list of defendants to the top seventy-five with the greatest ability to pay. The arrangement with Marianelli also went nowhere. Both Marianelli and Baldwin suspected that Venable preferred a lawyer who would split the fees sent by the ACLU.[28]

Finally, Venable and the ACLU settled on Charles West, a Tulsa lawyer who had formerly served as the first attorney general of Oklahoma. West spent the better part of a week reading the 1,400-page transcript of the legislative hearings. The ACLU wired $1,000 to a joint account of Venable and West for up-front expenses. The two strategized. The plan was to bring a case in federal court in Fort Smith against the St. Louis owners of the railroad for conspiracy to execute the illegal mob action. A separate case would be filed in Missouri for damages brought by the lynching of Ed Gregor and whipping of George O'Neal. Mrs. Josie Gregor was then living in Cabool, Missouri, while O'Neal had fled with his family to Springfield. O'Neal agreed to go back to Harrison to get affidavits from some women who worked at the Harrison telephone exchange, who he believed had overheard conversations between St. Louis owners and M&NA officials. Nothing apparently came of this investigation.

The main evidence for a federal case rested on Venable's account that Edward J. Manion, the president of the Order of Railway Telegraphers in St. Louis, had told Venable of plans for an uprising against strikers at the Chicago meeting on January 14, a day before the event took place. Manion had said that Festus J. Wade, the chief investor of the M&NA, had called him to his office earlier in the week to warn him that a mob would be coming to Harrison to end the strike and that strikers would be lynched. However, a year and a half later, when Venable and the ACLU tried to put the legal case together, Manion got cold feet and changed his story. By this time, Manion had become president of a bank in St. Louis, which, according to Venable, had dealings with Wade's Mercantile Trust and Savings Bank. With Manion unwilling to give evidence, West decided to wash his hands of the matter. The evidence against the railroad was too weak, he said, and the distance made it too difficult to bring a case in Missouri. Running up against a two-year statute of limitations, the ACLU and Venable finally let the cases go. The ACLU would find bigger fish to fry, for later that year Baldwin hired Clarence Darrow to travel to Tennessee to defend John Thomas Scopes in what would become perhaps the century's most famous trial.[29]

Over a two-year period, considerable human and financial resources had gone toward investigating the violence that had ended the M&NA railroad strike. The continued taking of testimony and affidavits, the digging for new evidence, and the prolific correspondence the event engendered might have kept hopes alive for justice among strikers and sympathizers whose lives had been disrupted. The investigations created a rich record for historians, but they led to no actions by public officials at the local, state, or federal level. The supporters of the railroad, with a clean sweep removing anyone who might hold contrary opinions, simply consolidated their hold over their communities in the Arkansas Ozarks.

CHAPTER 9

AFTERMATH: 1923–1924

THE WEEK FOLLOWING JANUARY 15, 1923, effectively brought an end to the strike on the M&NA Railroad. But the strike would not officially end until the executive committee of the railroad brotherhoods voted to terminate the strike eleven months later. While the legislators conducted their investigations, the citizens committees kept control over their communities by armed force, terrorizing strikers who dared to return and sympathizers who had remained. Government officials on the local, state, and federal level maintained their support for the railroad and antipathy toward strikers. Just as the Civil War divisions in the Ozarks had taken a generation to heal, the resentment following the strike lingered for years.

Three weeks after the January riots expelled strikers and some sympathizers from their homes, thirty-nine refugees penned a letter to Governor Thomas C. McRae asking him to guarantee their safety in returning home. Some wanted merely to reclaim their possessions, withdraw funds from local banks, and sell their property. They told the governor that they feared to return, for the committees still controlled the towns along the railroad. Armed guards had checkpoints on roads in and out of Harrison. Two union representatives in Little Rock, Owen Kendrick and James M. Brickhouse, reported that one woman, Enola Stewart—whose husband, James, was a striking brakeman—had returned to Harrison with a letter from McRae guaranteeing her safe passage, but had nonetheless been forced to sell her rooming house and leave town. McRae responded, saying that he was sending a letter to sheriffs in counties along the line with the instruction to put an end to the alleged injustices and give all citizens the protection of the law. He asked the sheriffs to report on conditions in their counties. Yet with the detailed newspaper reporting of the testimony of strikers before the legislative committee, McRae would have known that the sheriffs of Boone and Cleburne Counties were in league with the vigilante mob. The governor's response did not satisfy, Kendrick and Brickhouse said.[1]

The sheriffs apparently ignored McRae's request. The following week, the citizens committees in Eureka Springs, Leslie, and Heber Springs, in a coordinated effort, passed resolutions of support for the M&NA under Jack Murray's management, declaring that any persons who refused to sign the pledge of support were considered "undesirable citizens" not welcome to remain in their communities. On the evening of February 15, several men and women testified before the legislative committee, saying that the deportations had continued of individuals deemed sympathetic to the strike. Mrs. Henry Porch explained how she and her husband, a druggist, had been forced to leave Eureka Springs because he and several other men had given affidavits on behalf of striking brakeman Omar N. Pritchett. Mrs. Stewart recounted her financial losses when forced to sell out in Harrison. A striking fireman, Edward W. Griffith, testified that Walter L. Snapp had informed him that he—along with his mother and father, who had moved to Harrison four years before from Ohio—must leave town. Five days after the Leslie committee threatened expulsion of strike sympathizers, Cecil P. Ruff, who had lived in Leslie since birth, feared "for bodily harm" and left for Tulsa, Oklahoma. He would reside there the rest of his life. As they announced their threats to deport "undesirable citizens," the committees in Leslie and Heber Springs set up "investigating committees," similar to Klan chapter Klokanns, which aimed to continue the policing of their communities.[2]

As the legislative committee prepared to visit Harrison in March to take testimony of community leaders and railroad supporters, the town still functioned like a war zone. Kansas City newsman Jack Carberry, who had covered the riot in January, was called to Harrison to rebut John Rogers's Little Rock testimony alleging censorship during the reporters' sojourn in the town. Carberry said before the legislative committee that the journalists had been treated with courtesy in Harrison and that no censorship had occurred. But while he was in Harrison to testify, Carberry wrote an article describing the current situation in the town—and the International News Service immediately sent it off to newspapers nationwide. Carberry said that while the legislators were taking testimony in the courthouse, two months after the riot, Harrison was still like an armed camp under a revolutionary guard. A citizen army of 350 men, divided into seven companies, guarded the town twenty-four hours a day in eight-hour shifts. Machine guns were posted on every road leading in or out of town and along the draw of Crooked Creek. Carberry said rumors were circulating that a thousand union men threatened to descend on the town, driving in motorcars from Branson, Missouri, to hurl bombs and dynamite. Every man in the street, Carberry said, had a rifle slung over his shoulder or a pistol buckled to his hip. Some thirty families, relatives or friends of strikers, he said, had left the town in the previous week.[3]

Of all the communities along the railroad, Heber Springs probably saw the most conflict in the months that followed the January riot. Hundreds of farmers in Cleburne County were riled up about the mob's hostile gestures toward the United Farmers of America. On Monday, January 22, just three days after the riots ended in Heber Springs, some two hundred farmers of Cleburne and White Counties assembled and drafted a letter of protest to Governor McRae. The farmers complained about the assault against their union by the businessmen and officials of Cleburne County, aided by an armed mob from other counties. The farmers asked for the protection of the law and the prosecution of persons guilty of the outrages. A few days later, members of the Heber Springs citizens committee declared to the press that they had not intended any accusations against the farmers union. They alleged that out-of-towners, not local men, had removed the farmers union trade cards from the windows of businesses. These words did not appease the farmers. Just a few days later, at the legislative hearings on January 25 in Little Rock, J. G. Brown, the organizer for the United Farmers, testified how the committee had held him in custody for five hours on Thursday, January 18. Brown gave evidence that Heber Springs men had taken down some of the cards in windows and were directing the actions of the men who had come from Searcy County. Brown submitted a resolution passed by the executive committee of the farmers union; it denounced the armed mob, assisted by county officers and prominent men of Heber Springs, for attacking the union's members, entering their places of business, and taking their trade cards.[4]

The strife in Heber Springs continued into the next month. On February 20, city marshal Dick Wallace arrested Brown for a minor traffic violation when his wife parked their car on the wrong side of the highway. When he went before Mayor Marcus E. Vinson, Brown said, he received a discourteous lecture about the railroad. That same week, a strike sympathizer, G. F. Wilmer, was terrorized after he returned from Little Rock after testifying before the legislative committee. Wilmer said a posse tried to batter down his bedroom door. He fired a gun toward them, and the men returned fire, about twenty shots in all. On February 26, Ura Russell and Fred Bell, two deported strikers who had been staying in Little Rock, returned to Heber Springs to pay their taxes and visit family. As they paid taxes they had a friendly chat with Sheriff Emmett Baldridge, then walked to William C. Johnson's bank to get some money from their accounts. They visited the barber shop and went to Russell's home. There they found that some person or persons had torn the locks from his doors. A group of men, including Mayor Vinson and several of the citizens committee members and squad leaders from January 18, immediately arrived, asking for Russell and Bell. Just as it appeared that the mob was poised to take them away, five carloads of farmers arrived. The railroad supporters then departed. The next day a larger armed group appeared at the home of Bell's brother, who said that the two strikers had left for Little Rock just thirty minutes before. The mob headed up the mountain south of town but failed to catch Russell and Bell. In his testimony to the legislative committee, Mayor Vinson justified the actions against the returned strikers. He said that farmers, meeting in the United Farmers Hall in Heber Springs, had organized a "Defense Club" that was rumored to have received a case of firearms. He and others believed trouble would follow if the strikers returned.[5]

Another exiled striker who had the poor judgment to return to Heber Springs was Clyde Webb, the brother of Dewey Webb, who was severely beaten on January 19. Clyde Webb had come home to visit his mother, who was gravely ill with pneumonia, and his seventeen-year-old wife, Golda, who was seven months pregnant. While in town, Webb said, he never left his mother's home or yard, which was located two blocks from the depot. On the night of Thursday, March 15, some thirty men in seven automobiles came to get him, marched him away, and then forced him to bend over a log. Oscar B. Robbins appeared to be in charge as he had been in the January 18 riot, and he pulled out a strap and gave Webb two licks. According to Webb, each of the other men, except city marshal Dick Wallace, took a turn—Richard H. Dickenhorst, Arthur N. "Poe" Hilger, Brose Massingill, Odie Logan, William R. Griffin, and others—the same men who had led the vigilante actions two months before. When they got around to Boone Sparkman, he declined to take his turn. Robbins insisted that he must participate or get on the log himself. Webb said Sparkman applied the lash but jerked just as it hit his backside, to do no harm. Afterward, the men marched Webb to the depot to catch the train, but, finding that the M&NA was running four hours late, they allowed him to go home, eat supper, and visit his mother. A member of the mob accompanied him the whole time and then took Webb and his wife to the depot to catch the train. Webb said Robbins told him that when he got back to Little Rock, he could tell "that dam Legislative Committee" all about it.[6]

On April 23, 1923, not long before the legislative committee's work was done, J. G. Brown appeared again before the legislators. He presented a resolution directed to Governor McRae and signed by more than six hundred farmers of Cleburne County, denouncing the continued lawlessness that prevailed there. The statement also rebutted claims in the press that farmers had formed a large part of the mob (purportedly out of a desire for cheap transportation to ship farm products). Governor McRae responded that he could not help the farmers and that they should just "grin and endure it and stop making faces at one another." Brown asked that the document be incorporated as evidence in the transcript of the investigation. The legislative committee, in one of its last acts, declined to add the statement, on the grounds that it was addressed to the governor, rather than to the committee.[7]

While the legislative committee was at work in February and March, the courts were hearing the cases of strikers accused of having burned bridges near Letona and Eureka Springs in the week before the riots. The trials of George Welcher and Omar Pritchett in February and March kept the opposing sides riled up. And the appeal cases for Luther Wise and Verlin D. "Red" Orr, accused of burning the Everton bridge, came up in the Arkansas Supreme Court and then federal court in July. Orr and Wise claimed they had pleaded guilty before Judge Shinn to get away from the angry mob that encircled the courthouse. These court cases for these four men kept the M&NA strike in the news for the better part of the year.

Welcher's case came to trial on February 8 in circuit court in Searcy. Welcher may have been fortunate that Letona was in White County, in the First Circuit, not in Judge Shinn and prosecuting attorney Karl Greenhaw's Fourteenth Circuit, which spanned all the way from Harrison to Heber Springs. The evidence against him was primarily the claim by Verne Dodge that he had accompanied Welcher, C. H. "Straight Air" Smith, and H. T. Jones when they burned the bridge. The prosecution added circumstantial evidence of emery dust, acid-eaten overalls, and correspondence with Pete Venable found in Welcher's car and his room in Searcy. Other witnesses testified that they had seen Welcher with a five-gallon oil can near the bridge. Jack Murray testified that he had observed Welcher manning a picket line in 1921, as if that was relevant. Notably, while Dodge was in jail awaiting his own trial, he told other prisoners that a mob had placed a rope around his neck and threatened to hang him if he would not accuse Welcher and Smith. When in court in Searcy, Dodge first stuck to his original story. Under cross-examination on the witness stand, however, Dodge admitted that he had told Sheriff Ben Allen that William K. Gaines, a Kensett dry goods merchant, had paid him $200 to tell the fabricated story implicating Welcher. Pete Venable alleged that Gaines, like Walter Snapp and George McKinney, was a special agent of the M&NA. Even the prosecution admitted that Dodge was a weak witness.

Welcher's defense was primarily an alibi that he had been in Stuttgart, nearly eighty miles away, on the evening the bridge was burned. Three separate witnesses testified that Welcher ate in a restaurant, went to a movie, and spent the night in a rooming house in Stuttgart with another man from Heber Springs, E. E. Ganns. Welcher's lawyers presented his signature on the register of the rooming house as evidence. H. T. Jones also presented an airtight alibi. In rebuttal, the prosecution claimed that Welcher could have slipped out, burned the bridge, and returned to Stuttgart in time to check out in the morning. Other witnesses claimed to have seen Ganns in Heber Springs and Welcher in Kensett at the time they claimed to be in Stuttgart. The jury deliberated only an hour and a half before acquitting Welcher. The cases against Dodge, Smith, and Jones were apparently dropped, deemed as having little chance of success following Welcher's acquittal.[8]

George Welcher. *Arkansas Gazette, February 10, 1923.*

But Welcher's difficulties were not over. Five months later, in July, several citizens of Heber Springs prevailed on Sheriff Allen to arrest Welcher once again, insisting that they had seen Ganns in their town at the time he was said to be with Welcher in Stuttgart. The grand jury of White County indicted Welcher for perjury, a second count of arson, and two counts of night-riding. While they were at it, the grand jury indicted for perjury the people who had provided Welcher's alibi: two restaurant operators who said he ate dinner in Stuttgart, the boardinghouse manager who provided the register, a garage operator who said he took car of Welcher's car on his way, and Welcher's girlfriend, Stella George, who said she had gone with Welcher to a movie. The trial was scheduled to come before the court in Searcy in February 1924, but apparently the prosecution dropped the case.[9]

Just as Welcher's case lingered on, Omar Pritchett's similarly divided the community in Carroll County. Pritchett had been arrested on mostly circumstantial evidence for the burning of the 240-foot bridge near the Eureka Springs tunnel. The presiding judge of the Fourth Circuit, William A. Dickson, agreed to a change of venue for the case to be heard in Huntsville, in neighboring Madison County. Dickson said that he believed that Pritchett could receive a fair trial in Eureka Springs, but, because many of the jurors had that very week in February signed the resolution of support for the M&NA, he concluded that the case would likely be appealed to the Arkansas Supreme Court and there be overturned. Pritchett's trial began in the Madison County Courthouse in Huntsville on Wednesday, March 7. The M&NA's lead attorney, J. Sam Rowland, assisted prosecuting attorney John N. Nance for the state. The prosecution's case depended on claims that Pritchett had been seen with an oil can on the day the bridge was burned. Carroll County sheriff Ed McShane testified that footprints near the bridge were of the same size and make of shoe as those worn by Pritchett. A local farmer, Ertie Weston, testified that Pritchett stopped at his house on the night of the fire, attempting to buy whiskey, and said he was on his way to do some damage to the railroad. General manager Murray gave a lengthy account of sabotage against M&NA property and testified that the bridge was clearly burned intentionally, using a combustible substance placed in multiple locations on the bridge and ignited at once.[10]

The atmosphere of Pritchett's trial was reminiscent of the Orr and Wise case in Harrison six weeks before. A large number of men from along the line, including Walter Snapp, Luther "Clay" Holt, and Dr. Charles M. Routh, had come to Huntsville for the trial. Rumors circulated that Pritchett's supporters planned to forcibly take him away if he was convicted. Pritchett and his friends, on the other hand, believed that the hostile crowd intended to mob him. During the trial, two deputies, Bill Vaughan and Jones Brown, sat in a window of the courtroom with guns in hand to protect against a mob. The jury returned a verdict of guilty late on Saturday night. Pritchett was taken under guard to the Madison Hotel to await sentencing Monday morning. One of Pritchett's defense witnesses received a call to come to the porch of the hotel, where two men tried to seize him. A scuffle followed. One attacker dropped a pistol, and the crowd of forty men dispersed. Fearing for his life, Pritchett ran to the back of the hotel. The next morning, some of the railroad supporters asked Judge Dickson that Pritchett be taken to jail in Berryville. Dickson rejected this suggestion, anticipating that Pritchett might be lynched there. On Monday, Dickson sentenced Pritchett to two years in the state penitentiary.[11]

The trial was done, but the case was not over. Pritchett's lawyers announced their intent to appeal. By the end of March, newspapers reported, sheriffs McShane and Shaddox had claimed the reward offered by the state for the arrest and conviction of those committing depredations against the M&NA. They shared the reward with two men who they said gave information leading to Pritchett's arrest. Just days later, it was reported that a party of armed men, thought to be supporters of Pritchett, were spotted in the neighborhood of Ertie Weston, the farmer who had testified against Pritchett. Weston said he had received threats from Pritchett's friends. On Monday evening, April 2, a band of fifty masked men in Eureka Springs stripped and severely lashed Fred Smith, said to be Pritchett's star witness in Huntsville. Smith fled to Missouri for safety. A group of men there gave an affidavit to the legislative committee that they had examined Smith without his clothing and found his body from his hips down to be "one solid blood shot mess, black and blue." In addition, Smith's nude body was exhibited before Governor McRae in his private chambers at the Capitol Building, showing the mass of discolored and swollen bruises. All roads into Eureka Springs were guarded as rumors circulated that Pritchett's supporters in Missouri had purchased dynamite in Seligman and were planning an invasion of Eureka Springs and neighboring towns, in retaliation for the attack on Smith.[12]

The Arkansas Supreme Court finally heard Pritchett's appeal in October. The court ruled that the state had erred in allowing Jack Murray to catalog the depredations committed against the M&NA because no evidence connected Pritchett to any of those acts. Murray's testimony probably had some influence on the jury, the court concluded. Also, the prosecution had introduced as evidence the testimony of individuals who were not present to be cross-examined. Some of the key evidence was also discredited. Ertie Weston, it turns out, was in jail for selling whiskey and was released without charges after he agreed to testify against Pritchett. Also, in the matter of the shoeprints found at the scene, questioning established that the prints were found two days after the bridge was burned, after twenty to thirty men had walked around the crime scene. These mistakes caused the high court to nullify the verdict and call for a new trial. This trial would never take place.[13]

While the Welcher and Pritchett trials kept the kettle boiling, the Wise and Orr case received the most attention in Arkansas and nationwide. After their guilty plea before Judge Shinn on January 17, the two men had languished in the state penitentiary, except for their brief appearance the next week as the first two witnesses before the legislative committee. The union lawyers in Little Rock advised Orr and Wise to wait for the conclusion of the legislative committee's investigation before taking any further legal action. But when the report in May brought no results, Orr and Wise filed an appeal to the Arkansas Supreme Court. Their case came before the state's high court on July 9. The union lawyers secured the services of two Little Rock attorneys, M. Edwin Dunaway and Edgar L. McHaney, to argue the case before the Supreme Court. An extensive portfolio of exhibits on behalf of the two prisoners was presented, including statements by George W. O'Neal, Jennie Venable, and former mayor Jasper L. Clute about the lawless conditions in Harrison on the morning that Wise and Orr appeared in Boone County circuit court. The most important evidence was a lengthy statement by their lawyer Elbridge G. Mitchell, describing in detail his advice to his clients to plead guilty to save themselves from the angry mob assembled on the grounds of the courthouse. Mitchell explained that he and his clients could, from the window, see the men carrying guns and hear their threats. He said he had told the court of his belief that Wise and Orr would be mobbed if they remained overnight in Harrison. Another key statement was by Almar H. Cooper, Orr's brother-in-law, who had given testimony incriminating Wise and Orr before the grand jury. In his statement to the Supreme Court, Cooper explained that in the early morning hours of January 16, eight men had placed a rope around his neck, swung the other end over a tree limb, and threatened to hang him unless he told the grand jury that Wise and Orr had burned the Everton bridge. The Supreme Court ruled that it had no jurisdiction over the case and dismissed the petition the same day. Two days later, Orr and Wise filed a writ of habeas corpus for a hearing in the US District Court for the Eastern District of Arkansas.[14]

Judge Jacob Trieber agreed to hear the case and set the hearing for July 17, less than a week away. With Trieber hearing the case of Orr and Wise, his role with the M&NA and strike had come full circle. Trieber was born near Breslau, in Prussia (now Wrocław, Poland), and immigrated to the United States at age thirteen. His family came first to St. Louis in 1866 but then, two years later, moved to Helena, Arkansas. He studied law under the tutelage of a retired Arkansas Supreme Court judge in Helena, Marshall Stephenson. Trieber was the first Jew to serve as a federal judge in the United States, having been appointed by President William McKinley in 1900. He had a reputation for progressive causes, championing women's suffrage and civil rights for African Americans, especially in employment. Believing railroads to be essential for economic development, Trieber consistently favored railway companies in his rulings. He could hardly claim to be without some bias in any matter relating to the M&NA Railroad. He had a supervisory role over the line for the ten years it was in receivership, between 1912 and 1922, and had much association with the St. Louis owners, the management in Harrison, and, especially, the railroad's lawyer, J. Sam Rowland. Trieber had approved the wage reduction that precipitated the strike on February 1, 1921.[15]

Trieber's docket allowed six days to schedule the witnesses and prepare them for oral testimony. Besides witnesses hustling to get to Little Rock from various locations in Missouri, Oklahoma, and Arkansas to testify on behalf of Wise and Orr, many railroad supporters and spectators on the other side traveled from Harrison for the two-day trial. Pete Venable and his wife, Jennie, traveled from Oklahoma to support the defendants. Venable came at some risk, given that Boone County had outstanding warrants for his arrest. Testifying for Orr and Wise were Mitchell and O'Neal, as well as St. Louis newspaper reporter John Rogers, who described the environment in Harrison on the day of the trial. Two longtime Harrison lawyers who had both moved to Oklahoma after the January troubles, George J. Crump Sr. and Oscar W. Hudgins, gave their opinion that the accused would have met violence had they stayed in Harrison. Both Wise and Orr took the stand on their own behalf. For the state, Judge Shinn, prosecuting attorney Greenhaw, circuit clerk Walter Cotton, and special deputy J. S. "Silby" Johnson all testified that while Harrison did experience troubles, the men in the courtroom were

Lose Again in Second Effort of Week to Regain Their Freedom

LUTHER WISE.

VURLEN ORR.

Luther Wise and Verlin D. "Red" Orr. *Arkansas Gazette, July 19, 1923.*

at all times safe. Shinn said he saw only one man carrying a gun in Harrison that entire day, a schoolteacher who was going hunting. Evidently the judge never looked out the window of the courthouse.[16]

Just as Trieber's rush to schedule the hearing is puzzling, the ending is also indicative. After more testimony on the trial's second day, Trieber presented his ruling at noon. He must have drafted the document before the trial had begun, for it was eighteen pages long. He denied the petition of Orr and Wise and discharged the case. In his ruling, he stated very simply that he believed the testimony of Shinn and Greenhaw and did not believe the accounts of the same events given by Orr, Wise, Mitchell, and the other witnesses for the defense. He even praised Judge Shinn as a man who could not be intimidated by a mob. Orr and Wise were returned to the state penitentiary to serve their seven-year sentences.[17]

Right after Shinn and Greenhaw returned from Little Rock, they convened the summer session of Boone County circuit court. One case before them concerned a strike sympathizer, Charles D. Allison, whose crime was carrying an army pistol on the streets of Harrison back in January. Allison testified that he and some other men had been deputized by the city marshal, William Parr, on the Thursday night before the riot, when rumors began circulating that Albert Stevens and Red Orr were about to be lynched. Luther Wise and Perry Ingram were also indicted, but both were unavailable, Wise being in prison and Ingram having been run out of the state. Much irony surrounded Allison's charge of carrying a pistol, when hundreds of men in the mob carried weapons just a few days later. Nonetheless, Allison was found guilty and fined seventy-five dollars. Later that week, Allison wrote to the American Civil Liberties Union (ACLU), saying, "You people on the outside cannot realize that we have no Constitutional or civil rights and are absolutely at the mercy of the 'Citizens.'" He asked the ACLU to send any correspondence in a plain envelope sealed with wax, as two post office employees were "Citizens" and did not hesitate to open mail. Such was the state of justice in Boone County.[18]

The decisions of the Arkansas Supreme Court and Judge Trieber, coming after the inaction by the legislature and governor, only further convinced the railroad's supporters of their impunity. The former Harrison city attorney Oscar Hudgins, after he testified in Little Rock for Wise and Orr, traveled to Harrison to check on his invalid father, Benjamin Brice Hudgins. The citizens committee, still functioning in July, informed him that he would be flogged if he did not leave town at once. The committee, composed of Walter Snapp, Troy Coffman, Clay Holt, and ten other men, grilled him for two hours after he lunched with his father. The committee members told him to communicate with his friends in the railroad unions about the horrors they would face if they returned to Harrison. Joe Lineberry, who had lost his job in a hardware store the summer before because his brother was a striker, had been deported on January 15. Like Hudgins, he returned to Harrison in late July. The committee summoned him to appear and then ordered him to leave town and never return. In Eureka Springs, the last striker, a former conductor named Charles Ross, had steadfastly remained after repeated warnings to leave the town. The sixty-seven-year-old Ross had worked for the line since it had begun as the Eureka Springs Railway in 1882, and he was determined not to leave his home of forty years. The citizens committee there told him that if he did not leave by August 19, he would be "properly taken care of" by men on an excursion train from Harrison.[19]

The ACLU sent out a press release detailing abuses, but newspapers in Arkansas had apparently tired of reporting the continued lawlessness by supporters of the railroad. No Arkansas newspapers seem to have picked up the story, although a German-language newspaper in New York City carried the headline, "Mobherrschaft besteht immer noch in Arkansas" (Mob Rule Still Continues in Arkansas). The ACLU press release suggested that the Klan controlled Harrison's citizens committee. It also blamed the Harrison Klan for lynching a sixteen-year-old boy, Henry Lean, whose decomposed body was found in the woods near his home in the last week of July. The Boone County coroner, Dr. David E. Evans, a Klansman, ruled that Lean's death was caused by an accidental gunshot. But Lean's family and neighbors suggested that his death followed the alleged Klan whipping of four other boys for stealing chickens and other petty crimes. One of these boys, Ewing Sansing, was said to have become insane because of the beating. Hearsay evidence placed undertaker Doyle B. Woodruff and M&NA attorney J. Sam Rowland among the eleven men who did the whipping.[20]

While it is unclear whether the Klan had a role in the killing of young Henry Lean, that summer Harrison's power establishment and the M&NA made public their support for the Klan. Walter Snapp, exalted cyclops of the Harrison Klan and mob boss in the January riot, appears to have functioned as an occasional deputy to Sheriff Shaddox, a fellow Klansman. In the week following the riot in January, Troy Coffman and Clay Holt, two Klansmen who were on the citizens committee, took the seats of strike sympathizers on the city council. At its meeting on June 5, Harrison's city council, in a unanimous vote, reversed the ordinance passed a year earlier prohibiting masked men from appearing on the streets of Harrison. The week before, a prominent Klan lecturer, the Reverend Harry Knowles of Little Rock, had delivered a speech to a packed crowd at the courthouse. After the council's action, Harrison could host parades and public events with Klansmen in full regalia.[21]

On August 2 in Heber Springs, 116 miles down the line from Harrison, the Pat Cleburne Klan no. 126 marched solemnly in the annual reunion parade, right behind the Boy Scouts and the local members of the Arkansas National Guard. The hoods and robes covered many members of the Heber Springs citizens committee, which apparently still functioned. The week after this reunion parade, Harrison's Klansmen were preparing to attend a Klan extravaganza in Joplin, Missouri, even creating a float for the parade. The M&NA provided a special train that left Harrison at 12:05 p.m. on Saturday, August 11, with 150 Klansmen. The train picked up Klansmen along the way at Alpena, Green Forest, Berryville, Eureka Springs, and points in Missouri. The railroad offered a special Klan rate, at three dollars round trip from Harrison, half the normal fare. The train arrived in Joplin at 6:10 p.m., with 336 Klansmen aboard. The first car carried members of Harrison's Klan band and cold soft drinks. As the train pulled into Joplin's station, the band played its rendition of "The Gang's All Here." Thirteen hundred robed Klansmen from Missouri, Arkansas, Oklahoma, and Kansas marched in an evening parade through downtown Joplin as thousands lined the streets to watch. An airplane encircled the city displaying an electric fiery cross. Fireworks in red, white, and blue and fiery crosses erected on the tops of buildings added to the festive atmosphere. The day concluded with a Klansman-only gathering in a ballpark, featuring an address by Hiram Evans, the imperial wizard, who had come from headquarters in Atlanta. The M&NA's return train left Joplin at 1:30 a.m. on Sunday, getting the Klansmen back to Harrison at 8:30 a.m., just in time for church.[22]

The Reverend John Kelly Farris of Harrison's Methodist church struggled through the summer and fall because of the stand he had taken on the strike. On Sunday evening, August 19, while a guest preacher, Rev. Albritton of Kensett, was assisting Farris with a revival service, forty-two robed knights of the Ku Klux Klan entered the church in dramatic fashion. They had erected an electric fiery cross in the door, and it blazed as they processed in. They pointedly gave a letter of commendation and a cash gift of twenty-five dollars to Albritton, not Farris. They knelt as one Klansman led a prayer, and then they filed out in silence to their automobiles. In November, Farris lost his job and was forcibly retired, "superannuated," from the ministry. Pete Venable explained to the ACLU that Farris was fired because

The Heber Springs reunion parade, August 1923.
Courtesy of Cleburne County Historical Society.

he would not preach sermons endorsing the actions of the Klan and Harrison's citizens committee. Farris returned to his former home in Wynne, Arkansas, where he did some occasional preaching but never again had his own congregation. He began work on his book, *The Harrison Riot*, which appeared in January 1924. He sent a copy to the *Harrison Daily Times*, but as one might expect, the editor, Tom Newman, panned Farris's book as insufficiently informed. The *Times* said that Farris thought strikers did no wrong and held the citizens as wholly responsible for the troubles.[23]

With few strike sympathizers left in the Arkansas Ozarks to pick on, the violence slowed. Frank Thornton, a blacksmith who had been forced to leave on January 17 because he sympathized with the strike, returned in October to Berryville, where he owned a home. But on October 18, a week after his arrival, he received an anonymous letter telling him that he could not stay, on account of his sympathy for labor unions. He left the following day. The violence could go the other way as well. In early November, citizens committee member Clay Holt and Harrison businessman Roy W. Milum had left a car for repair in Branson, when they came across two exiled strikers, John D. Jones and John Dobbins. Jones reminded the two men that Holt had personally told him he had to leave Harrison ten months earlier. Dobbins struck Holt in the face, knocked him down, and continued beating him. Holt managed to escape and ran into the woods to hide. A farmer later found him and helped him return to Harrison, albeit badly bruised, with a broken nose and several loose teeth. Jones must have later attempted to return to Harrison, for Pete Venable reported to the ACLU that J. D. Jones was expelled on December 28. Another striker, Major Robertson, had also been whipped and deported from Harrison the week before, Venable said.[24]

By the end of the year, efforts coalesced for a compromise conclusion to the straggling issues left from the strike. With the publication of Charles Finger's report in October, the ACLU announced a campaign to free Luther Wise and Red Orr from prison. Sheriff Shaddox and M&NA officials had already taken steps to put the Wise and Orr case, and the strike, behind them. In September, Shaddox made application to Governor McRae for himself; deputies Bryan Holt, Walter Snapp, and Silby Johnson; M&NA officials Jack Murray and Jack Halter; and George McKinney to receive the state's reward for the capture and conviction of the two men for burning the Everton bridge. When news about the reward got out, Murray withdrew his name.[25] The previous month, Wise and Orr's Little Rock lawyers, McHaney and Dunaway, had made an application of their own, seeking to get the men's sentences reduced from seven to two years. Meeting with McHaney and Dunaway in Harrison, Judge Shinn and officials of the M&NA insisted that in exchange for a sentence reduction the unions must officially terminate the strike. The lawyers said they could not achieve this, and the attempt failed.[26]

However, in December negotiations began once more. Frank Mulholland, a lawyer from Toledo, Ohio, who represented the railway brotherhoods, visited Harrison with another offer. He met with Greenhaw, Shinn, Murray, and Rowland, and the two sides came to a compromise just before Christmas. The railway brotherhoods agreed to terminate the strike in exchange for the release of Wise and Orr from prison and the dismissal of all criminal and civil cases involving strikers and sympathizers pending in the Boone County circuit court. The latter part constituted a sticking point, for the county would forfeit some $19,000 in bonds, including the $10,000 posted by George O'Neal for Albert Stevens. Greenhaw and Shinn negotiated a $500 payment by the unions to cover costs for the cases to be dismissed. Mulholland wrote a check for that amount, and the deal was done. Thirty-five court cases were dropped, including four against Pete Venable, four against Norman Stevens, and two for Albert Stevens. These cases were moot, for the defendants had fled the state and were not available to prosecute. It appears that the compromise included the dropping of trials outside Judge Shinn's circuit for George Welcher and Omar Pritchett, as well.[27]

Shinn and Greenhaw had no authority to undo the sentences of Wise and Orr, so they asked Governor McRae to pardon the two men. That same week, McRae received a letter from several prominent board members of the ACLU, also appealing for a pardon of the two strikers. The group included Jane Addams, founder of Hull-House in Chicago; Jeannette Rankin, a suffragette and the first woman elected to Congress, taking office in 1917; Father John A. Ryan, a well-known liberal priest in Washington, DC; Norman Hapgood, writer and former editor of *Harper's Weekly*; the Reverend John Haynes Holmes and progressive lawyer Frank P. Walsh, two longtime protégés of Roger Nash Baldwin; and Harry F. Ward, a professor at Union Theological Seminary in New York. The letter asserted that the conditions in Harrison had made a fair trial impossible for Orr and Wise and that their guilty plea was made under duress. McRae responded that the legislative hearings had contradicted this opinion, but he furloughed Wise and Orr anyway on December 21. Orr and Wise walked away from prison as free men. A full pardon followed on January 31, 1924.[28]

The strike technically ended on December 21, 1923, with the last benefits paid to strikers on January 1, 1924. Murray announced that all claims on the railroad had been satisfied. The railroad brotherhoods' newspaper, *Labor*, however, inquired at the US Department of the Treasury and the Interstate Commerce Commission (ICC), which both said that the $3.5 million borrowed in 1922 was unpaid and that the railroad was in default on $95,000 of unpaid interest. Mulholland asked Murray to hire back former strikers. Murray responded that the railroad would consider employing those who were on strike, providing they were willing to accept the terms of wages and work. Elsewhere, Murray said the M&NA would continue with its present employees. The official end of the strike did not come through negotiations with the railroad, which gave up nothing. The M&NA would continue to operate on an open-shop basis, with employees receiving wages 25 percent below the rate before the strike. The railroad unions made their deal with the Boone County circuit court and the state of Arkansas. The dismissal of indictments and pardon of men in prison implied that the strikers were hostages rather than criminals.[29]

With the strike officially over nearly three years after it had begun, the railroad rolling again, and the strikers gone, continuing conflict in the area revolved around the Ku Klux Klan. The public perception was that Klansmen had dominated the actions that brought the de facto end of the strike in January and that they controlled local governments thereafter. Anti-Klan movements coalesced in Boone and Searcy Counties in 1923 and 1924.

In the summer of 1923 in Marshall, William Franklin "Frank" Reeves, a Republican lawyer who had lost to Judge Shinn in the circuit judge race the previous October, began organizing what he called the "Anti-Poke-Noses." In July, Reeves wrote to the ACLU that his group outnumbered the Klan, especially in rural precincts of Searcy County. This was a bold claim, for a joint Klonkave of the Marshall and Leslie Klans had met earlier in the month in a field between the two towns. With three hundred robed Klansmen present, the two chapters inducted a large class of new members, after which an address was delivered and refreshments served. Reeves said his organization was working hard to keep these Klansmen from dominating juries and school boards in the county. He suggested that if the ACLU brought a legal case to Boone County, it might be possible to secure a change of venue and have the case transferred to a more friendly jury in Searcy County. Any Klansman, Reeves said, who served as a juror on a case against the railroad would support the M&NA. Reeves explained that his group was launching a newspaper called "Common Horse Sense" to provide an alternative to Marshall's two other newspapers, which both supported the Klan, the Democratic-leaning *Marshall Mountain Wave* and the *Marshall Republican*. The two papers were losing subscriptions because of their support for the Klan, and a boycott had begun of businesses in sympathy with the Klan. Jackson F. Henley, one of the lawyers who had served on the citizens committee in Harrison, had apparently had a change of heart, for he had dropped his subscription to the *Marshall Mountain Wave*, owing to its persistent propaganda in favor of the Klan.[30]

In October 1923, Reeves purchased equipment of a defunct newspaper, had it shipped to Marshall, and began publishing the *Eagle*, apparently deemed a better name than "Common Horse Sense." On its masthead, the paper made its perspective clear with the heading: "The Idea of an Invisible Empire in a Free Republic Is Nothing Less Than Visible Nonsense." Unlike the other two Marshall newspapers, the *Eagle* claimed to be affiliated with neither the Republican nor the Democratic Party. Reeves's associate editor was a young lawyer, Andrew Jackson Parks, who would become the chairman of the county's Democratic Party organization. Also serving on the board of directors was Jackson Henley.[31]

In late October 1923, a squabble between Klan supporters and detractors in Searcy County erupted into a fight that cost one man his life. The Klan lecturer Dr. L. M. Copeland had come from Little Rock and spent the week lecturing around the county at Marshall, Leslie, Snowball, and Horton Bend. By Friday, October 26, he arrived in St. Joe to give his regular talk in the opera house. A crowd that was equally divided between Klansmen and opponents of the Klan had assembled from various parts of the county. About three minutes into his lecture, a scuffle began in which one of the anti-Klan folks, Albert Love, pulled out a pistol. As Klansmen tried to subdue him, the revolver discharged, striking him in the abdomen. The shooting broke up the meeting. Love died the next morning.[32]

The anti-Klan forces in Searcy County stepped up their opposition to the Klan and the railroad in 1924. In the October 1922 election for sheriff, Dan J. Patterson, a Democrat living in Zack, had defeated deputy sheriff John Henry Barnett, the Republican candidate. Barnett, a Marshall Klansman, would be a leader of the mob in Leslie three months later. Sheriff Patterson, however, played no role in the riots, unlike his counterparts in Boone and Cleburne Counties, Shaddox and Baldridge. The next year, in January 1924, Patterson arrested five Klansmen who had battered down the door of the home of Frederick Houghton (an unsuccessful candidate for tax assessor), dragged him out of bed outside in the dead of winter in his underwear, and whipped him severely. In early March, Patterson announced in the *Eagle* his campaign for reelection on the agenda of fighting the Klan. In the same issue, Patterson named a number of local men who, he claimed, were part of Klan whipping parties. In addition, the previous year he had gathered evidence for grand jury indictments of four men on the charges of whipping strikers and sympathizers in Leslie. These four men—the Reverend Dillard Monroe Carter, Jerome Cotton, Dick

Highland, and Henry Nation—were the only persons held accountable in any way for the illegal actions committed by the mobs. In August 1924, Carter, Highland, and Cotton pleaded guilty in Searcy County circuit court; Nation did not show up for his trial. Highland and Cotton were fined ten dollars and Carter fifty dollars for their crimes. Their case immediately followed the guilty pleas and fines for the men who had whipped Fred Houghton. But while these cases were being heard in Marshall, someone burned Houghton's house to the ground.[33]

Sheriff Patterson would not live to see the trial of these men, for seven weeks before, on the morning of June 6, 1924, he was found dead in the courthouse in Marshall. He had gone into the courtroom on the second floor, reportedly alone; he took off his coat and hat, sat in a chair, and died from a single gunshot fired behind his right ear. The thirty-six-year-old father of seven was said to have been ill for several months. Others said his books as county tax collector did not balance. A coroner's jury ruled the death a suicide from his own gun. Family members believed that the Klan had murdered him. Two weeks after his death, Governor McRae appointed Harvey Helm as sheriff of Searcy County. The *Eagle* charged that McRae had never heard of Helm until he was suggested by the local Klan. Patterson's estate became a shareholder in the *Eagle*.[34]

The animosity toward the Klan expressed itself in politics, as 1924 was an election year. The Marshall municipal elections in April hinged on the issue of Klan versus anti-Klan, and the antis won in nearly every instance. The former exalted cyclops Hugh G. Treece, who had turned against the Klan after his brother Abe was whipped in Leslie, defeated William Wenrick, editor of the *Marshall Mountain Wave*, in the race for mayor, with Andrew Parks, associate editor of the *Eagle*, elected as recorder. In the August primary election in Searcy County, the anti-Klan ticket endorsed by the *Eagle* carried the Democratic side, including for sheriff, with Dan Patterson's deputy, William M. McCall, soundly defeating Harvey Helm, McRae's Klan appointee. Most of these Democrats, however, except for McCall, were defeated by Republican opponents in the October 7 election. The county committees for the two political parties were also reshuffled. Frank Reeves, editor of the *Eagle*, was chosen as chair of the Republican Central Committee. Sam G. Daniel, a stockholder in the *Eagle*, became chair of the Democratic Central Committee, with Andrew Parks chosen as secretary, replacing former mayor Stephen W. Woods and William Wenrick, respectively. The anti-Klan element was making a clean sweep in Searcy County.[35]

In neighboring Boone County in both the August primaries and the October general election, candidates positioned themselves as for or against the Klan. When votes were counted in the Democratic primary, Klan candidates won over anti-Klan candidates in all races except that of treasurer. The Klan-backed candidates won again in October, with Bob Shaddox taking the county judge position and Silby Johnson once again becoming sheriff. Two Harrison men, Elbridge G. Mitchell and Virgil Willis, made their opposition to the Klan the center of their primary races for wider offices. Mitchell, the defense lawyer for Pete Venable and later Orr and Wise, was an elder statesman of the county bar who had previously served as circuit judge and representative for Boone County and was now running for US representative of Arkansas's Third District. He ran against the incumbent congressman, John Tillman of Fayetteville, who had served in that office since 1915, and Claude Fuller, the former mayor of Eureka Springs. Willis, a brash newcomer, was a twenty-five-year-old Harrison lawyer, with more conviction than experience. He aspired to Greenhaw's position as prosecuting attorney in a race against J. C. "Charlie" Smith, a lawyer in Jasper. In a speech at the Boone County Courthouse, Mitchell launched his campaign with a blistering attack on the Klan. He held the Klan accountable for the murder of Ed C. Gregor, referring to the black masks worn by Gregor's assailants as "the K. K. insignia of death." He claimed that both Fuller and Tillman were Klansmen. Tillman declared his Klan membership with pride. Fuller admitted that while he had joined the Ku Klux Klan, his campaign was neither pro- nor anti-Klan. Tillman, Mitchell said, had spoken to robed Klansmen under a fiery cross in Bob Shaddox's field outside Harrison. Willis bluntly declared the Klan to be a criminal organization. Both Mitchell and Willis charged that the Klan had engaged illegal night-riding in Boone County during the railroad strike.[36]

In a letter to the newspaper, the Harrison Klan no. 101 called the allegations of Willis, Mitchell, and other candidates "premeditated libel and slander." Evidently, most voters agreed, for Rep. Tillman, with nearly 9,000 votes, defeated Fuller, who polled 7,500, and Mitchell, who trailed a distant third with 3,592 votes. Willis fared better, losing to Smith by fewer than 300 votes. Willis and Mitchell lost in Boone

County, but both men carried Searcy County. Another measure of the strength of the Klan versus anti-Klan issue in the August primary was the vote tally in the governor's race. In a statewide Klan "primary" in May, several Klansmen had competed for the Klan vote. Lee Cazort of Clarksville was the winner, and the other candidates were to stand down and back him in the August Democratic primary. Three Klansmen, however, refused to step aside, including Jim G. Ferguson, who had grown up in Searcy County and was the brother of Zeb V. Ferguson, who had served on Leslie's citizens committee in January 1923. Only one candidate in the August primary, Little Rock chancery judge John Martineau, took an explicitly anti-Klan position, running against the four Klansmen and another candidate who took no position on the Invisible Empire. Of the counties along the M&NA, Martineau won only in Searcy County, defeating, in the process, native son Jim Ferguson. In Boone County, the Klan's anointed candidate, Cazort, came in first, followed by Martineau a distant second. Martineau came in fifth of six candidates in Cleburne and Carroll Counties.[37]

On the weekend before the August 12 primary, Harrison's Klan had already begun to celebrate. Cooks prepared three thousand pounds of meat, scores of cakes and pies, and gallons of lemonade for a barbecue at the city park that served five thousand people. A concert followed by Harrison's Klan band, assisted by one Klanswoman. The band then led a parade through the streets of Harrison, followed by Doyle Woodruff, Troy Coffman, Walter Snapp, the Reverend Walter F. Bradley, and the Reverend William Green Winans, pastor of Harrison's Baptist church, all of them riding on white-robed horses. Snapp had borrowed his horse and saddle from young Henry Vance Kirby. More than a thousand Klansmen from Harrison and surrounding communities followed in autos and on foot. It was a sea of white, although by August 1924 the Klansmen had stopped hiding their identities under masks. After the parade, Klansmen "and their women folk" adjourned to Bob Shaddox's farm, where a large class of new members were initiated after a picnic supper of leftover barbecue and boiled ham, accompanied by music from the Klan band.[38]

Just as Elbridge Mitchell linked the Klan to the murder of Ed Gregor, other anti-Klan activists considered the M&NA and Klan to be standing together as one. Writing about the August 1924 primary election in Harrison, the *Daily Times Echo* of Eureka Springs charged that M&NA employees had received tickets already made out, with instructions to vote for the Klan candidates from state representative on down to constable. If they did not, they would lose their jobs. The newspaper asserted that the present railroad management was controlled by Harrison's exalted cyclops, Walter Snapp. Marshall's anti-Klan *Eagle* added that the M&NA management encouraged its present employees to join the Klan as a protection of the railroad. While most employees were members of the Klan, the paper wrote, a good number refused to join. The *Eagle* concluded that the railroad "should not worship at the feet of an Imperial Wizard or bow to the dictations of Walter Snapp, Cyclops or any other cyclops, kleagle or kligrapp." The editors, Reeves and Parks, denied the allegation that they and other opponents of the Klan wanted the railroad to fail. They said they wanted the M&NA to run and prosper. But they did not wish to be dominated by a railroad or to suffer the sort of Klan outrages as experienced in the Arkansas Ozarks.

Even the former exalted cyclops of the Harrison Klan, Rev. Bradley, publicly drew a connection between the Klan and railroad. In June 1924, he gave a talk to a capacity crowd on the topic "Why I Joined the Ku Klux Klan." He declared that the Klan issue in the local elections was a smoke screen, for the real issue was the M&NA strike. Those who claimed to be anti-Klan, he said, were actually sympathizers of the strike. Pete Venable, he said, was in league with all the anti-Klan candidates. Bradley thus virtually admitted that "Klan" and "pro-railroad" were two faces of the same coin.[39]

Thus, while the M&NA strike effectively ended in January 1923, the local conflict continued through the rest of the year and beyond. Henry Vance Kirby recalled years later that the committee continued to control Harrison, with the streets guarded by armed men, for eighteen months after the riot. Railroad supporters consolidated control over their communities and celebrated their success. With the strikers and many sympathizers expelled, only a few courageous citizens, like Elbridge Mitchell and Dan Patterson, continued to take a stand against the illegal actions of the supporters of the railroad. Only in Searcy County did these citizens form a sizable-enough group to win elections, right wrongs, and bring some perpetrators to justice.

CONCLUSION

IN 1938 THE M&NA purchased two gleaming gasoline-powered "streamliners," rail motor coaches painted blue and white, from the American Car and Foundry Company. The newest thing in railroading, the streamliners carried passengers in air-conditioned comfort daily between Neosho and Kensett. The coaches would connect the railroad's past to its future. The company named one the Thomas C. McRae in honor of the former governor who had stood by the railroad during the strike. The second was christened the John E. Martineau, for the federal judge who had directed the receivership of the M&NA after Judge Jacob Trieber's death in 1927. Eight years after the coaches' purchase, on a Friday morning, August 23, 1946, the Thomas C. McRae left Neosho as usual. As it approached Harrison, coming downhill at about thirty-five miles an hour, it crashed into a milk truck at a crossing. The streamliner derailed and the truck was demolished, killing both drivers. The Thomas C. McRae was junked and dismantled for parts, and never ran again. The crash was perhaps an omen. Less than a month later, the M&NA shut down for good.[1]

While the railroad strike ended in 1923, the hard feelings would last for years. Even without the presence of strikers, resentment toward the Ku Klux Klan kept communities divided. The issue of Klan versus anti-Klan continued to dominate politics in Searcy and Boone Counties into 1926. Antis held the upper hand in Searcy County, sweeping Marshall's municipal elections in 1925 and most positions in the county elections in 1926. In Boone County, the dominant Democratic Party was divided into a Klan faction, headed by M&NA attorney J. Sam Rowland, and an anti-Klan group, led by Lewis Dowell, the unsuccessful candidate for sheriff against Klansmen Robert "Bob" Shaddox in 1922 and J. S. "Silby" Johnson in 1924.[2]

But by 1925 the Ku Klux Klan in Arkansas and nationally was declining about as fast as it had risen. A public relations nightmare would lead to a free fall in the last half of the year. In Arkansas, Grand Dragon James A. Comer had married his former secretary Robbie Gill, whom he had elevated to the position of imperial commander of the Women of the Ku Klux Klan. Comer was behind the creation of a women's Klan and secured the national headquarters of the organization in Little Rock. The women's Klan became a cash cow, with the initiation fees and annual dues of a million Klanswomen pouring into Little Rock. In August, several women's Klan leaders filed suit, claiming that Gill had taken the reins of power illegally and that the couple had enriched themselves by bilking the coffers of the women's Klan. Once the case was in court, Klan secrets become lurid newspaper reading. Most members of the Little Rock Klan no. 1, the state's first and largest Klan chapter, were so disgusted with the Comers that they voted to secede and set up a rival organization: the Mystic Knights of Arkansas. The secession started another round of lawsuits and newspaper articles as the two groups, like a married couple going through a divorce, squabbled over the property.

As the meltdown took place in Arkansas, the national Klan had its own scandals come to light. In March 1925 one of the most powerful Klan figures, David C. Stephenson, was arrested for kidnapping, raping, and torturing a young woman onboard a private train between Indianapolis and Chicago. The woman died a few weeks later, from a staph infection from bites Stephenson had inflicted on her body and some poison she consumed in an attempt to take her own life. The trial of Stephenson, a serial rapist and drunkard, played out in November as the courts in Arkansas dealt with their own Klan cases. Membership in the Klan plummeted nationwide after the scandals of 1925. The last Klan gathering in Harrison covered by the newspapers was a May 1925 lecture on "Americanism," delivered to a large crowd at the courthouse by national Klan speaker John H. Moore. The last Klan event in Marshall seems to have been a rally at the opera house in August 1925 for both Marshall's Klan no. 88 and a chapter of the women's Klan.[3]

As the Ku Klux Klan declined after the strike, the M&NA continued to struggle. The company's trains ran normally in the last eleven months of 1923 without the presence of strikers, yet the railroad still ran a deficit for the year of $87,307. In 1924 the net loss grew to $139,236, and the following year it reached $239,329. The Bureau of Locomotive Inspection of the Interstate Commerce Commission (ICC) inspected fifty of the M&NA's locomotives in 1924 and found forty of them defective. After the locomotives failed repeated follow-up examinations, inspectors ordered eight of the engines out of service. On the first day of 1926, Charles Gilbert, the leader of the St. Louis owners, announced the replacement of Jack Murray as general manager with W. Stephenson (no relation to David C. Stephenson). W. Stephenson was the former manager of the Jonesboro, Lake City, and Eastern Railroad, an eastern Arkansas railroad that the Frisco Line had recently acquired. The termination of Murray was an unpopular move, especially in Harrison, where he had many supporters. Stephenson's eccentric manners kept both employees and the community at a distance. He went by the initial *W.* and refused to tell anyone that the letter stood for his given name, Wellington. An unmarried man, he arrived in Harrison with a Black servant. The two men lived in a thirty-four-foot rail car pulled onto a spur track and connected to electricity. When Stephenson wanted to travel the line, the electric lines were disconnected, and his home became a private motor coach. Stephenson's living arrangements must have raised some eyebrows in a town that had forcibly expelled all but one of its Black residents in two waves of ethnic cleansing, in 1905 and 1909.[4]

Stephenson promised to make money for the railroad by an ambitious rehabilitation program of the line's facilities, roadway, and rolling stock. Under his leadership, however, the railway continued to bleed money. The great flood of 1927 did considerable damage to the company's infrastructure in eastern Arkansas, and the M&NA went back into receivership. New federal loans kept the M&NA going. Stephenson put some of his own money into the railroad, and a new investor, Frank Kell of Wichita Falls, Texas, began to buy out shares of the St. Louis owners. By 1929 Kell held a majority of the company's stock. The Great Depression intensified the hard times. By June 1933, employees had not been paid in four months. With no unions to represent them, a delegation of three employees made an appointment with Stephenson, and in a heated discussion demanded his resignation and that of the traffic manager and general superintendent he had brought with him from Jonesboro. The delegation accomplished what sixteen brotherhoods had failed to do in 1921. Stephenson agreed to a suspension of a 10 percent pay cut, and then he and the other two officials resigned. Stephenson and his servant rolled out of Harrison in his private car, bound for Kansas City.[5]

Stephenson's replacement in 1933 as general manager was Lewie Watkins, the first Boone County man to lead the railroad. He had begun work in the M&NA as a transportation clerk and errand boy in

1917. During the strike, in 1922, he became general auditor. The company was reorganized in 1935 as the Missouri and Arkansas (M&A) Railroad. Frank Kell, the largest stockholder, convinced federal judge John Martineau to foreclose and sell the railroad. Kell then bought the newly reorganized railway for a mere $350,000, wiping out some $5 million of the federal loan debt. Lacking this debt burden and operating under Watkins's able leadership, the railroad began making a modest profit, and it would continue to do so for the next decade. Judge Martineau's role in this sweetheart deal explains why the company's second streamliner would bear his name.[6]

As World War II ended, with greater competition with the trucking industry on the nation's highways, the M&A began again to lose money. At some point the railroad brotherhoods returned and represented workers in collective bargaining. When employees represented by the Brotherhood of Railroad Trainmen in July 1946 demanded a wage increase of eighteen and a half cents an hour, the president of the railroad, Malcolm Putty, the late Frank Kell's son-in-law, said no. Two weeks after the Thomas C. McRae streamliner crashed, the trainmen went on strike. They were soon joined by union enginemen, firemen, and other employees. Ironically, some of these men had been the strikebreakers who joined the M&NA twenty-five years before. By the middle of September 1946, Putty abandoned the railroad, terminating the M&A's five hundred employees, half of them in Harrison. A few pieces of the line, from Seligman to Harrison and from Helena to Cotton Plant, returned to freight service under new ownership, but the company was no more. While it had endured the long strike of the early 1920s, the railroad was killed off by the short strike of 1946. With access to a network of paved roads that had been constructed in the years since 1923, the "citizens" accepted the shutdown of the railroad in 1946 with no apparent wrath against the strikers. Former employees of the railroad readily found work on other lines. It was said that any man who could work under conditions like those on the M&A could railroad almost anywhere.[7]

So much for the railroad. But what of its supporters and detractors? After the owners sacked Jack Murray as general manager in 1926, he moved to Little Rock, where he became the traffic manager for the city's chamber of commerce. He and his wife returned to Harrison frequently, often staying with their friends Walter L. Snapp and his wife, Stella, who had been next-door neighbors when they lived in

Harrison. Murray would be central Arkansas's leading authority on freight rates and all things transportation until his death in 1956. Snapp moved to Fort Smith, where he sold insurance. J. Sam Rowland stayed with the M&NA as its lawyer until his death in August 1933. Both Snapp and Murray returned to Harrison for Rowland's funeral. Silby Johnson and Bob Shaddox won additional terms as sheriff and county judge and remained active in Harrison until their deaths in 1952 and 1965, respectively. James M. Shinn, after stepping back from the position of circuit judge, returned to his law practice in Harrison. Karl Greenhaw ran for US Congress in 1926, losing to incumbent John Tillman. Two years later, he moved to Fayetteville and opened a successful law practice. In 1941 he was appointed by Governor Homer Adkins, a former Klansman, to the Arkansas Supreme Court, and he served nearly two years. He died in 1967.[8]

While the supporters of the railroad for the most part stayed close to home and continued to play leading roles in their communities, strikers and sympathizers scattered in all directions. Their homes and possessions were abandoned or sold for pennies on the dollar. Strike leaders James E. Queen, Charles DeGoche, and Albert and Norman Stevens found work with other railroads in Missouri, Kansas, Oklahoma, and Texas. Tillman Jines had left railroad work and moved from Missouri to California by 1930. The fate of Pete Venable is one of the saddest stories. For two years he lived in his wife's hometown of McAlester, Oklahoma, and pushed forward the American Civil Liberties Union (ACLU) lawsuit against the M&NA and the perpetrators of the Harrison riot. When this opportunity for compensation had failed by early 1925, he was blacklisted from employment with other railroads in the region. He found work as a yard switchman for a railroad in Orlando, Florida. On March 26, 1926, while riding the pilot, he was thrown under an engine as it split a switch. His left leg was severed at his hip, and his right leg was fractured. He died within minutes from loss of blood. His body was brought back to McAlester for a funeral and burial. His wife, Jennie, never remarried. She lived with her mother and brother there until her death in 1978. Josie Gregor also never remarried and in 1940 was laid to rest next to her husband, Ed, in a cemetery in Fremont, Missouri.[9]

The sympathizers who were whipped in Harrison, Leslie, and Heber Springs fared little better. Ed Treece, mercilessly flogged in Leslie, moved sixty miles south to Conway, where he worked as

Jack Murray in his later years. *Courtesy of Arkansas State Archives, Shrader Negatives, SH42-2531-001.*

a truck driver. Three years after the attack, he filed suit in Judge George W. Carr's court in Conway against eighteen individuals of Searcy County, whom he held responsible for his beating, including members of the citizens committee and the mob outside who inflicted the blows. He asked for $70,000 in damages. The judge dismissed his case, however, citing the state's statute of limitations and the amount of time that had passed since the offense. Ed's cousin Abe Treece lived in Leslie a few years, but by 1928 he had moved to Little Rock, where he worked as an agent for the Missouri Pacific Railroad. Other men who were beaten in Leslie and Heber Springs mostly stayed in Arkansas, but they did not return to their home counties. Albert Raash, Ed C. Gregor's friend in Harrison, moved to Milwaukee, Wisconsin, a city more friendly to German immigrants. George W. O'Neal relocated to Springfield, Missouri, where he lived for many years. Of the men forcibly expelled from the town, it seems only William Parr, the town marshal, returned. He and his wife were back in Harrison by 1926, and he died there ten years later.[10]

These participants in the strike on both sides are all long gone. One wonders what they would think years later. Was it worth it? Supporters of the M&NA would likely say yes. In their view, they had saved the railroad and, in so doing, the well-being of their towns. Jesse Lewis Russell, the editor of the *Boone County Headlight* in the early 1920s and a staunch supporter of the railroad, reminisced at length about the strike twenty-four years later. He still placed blame on the strikers and had no remorse about the actions taken by citizens. Even the radical measures of illegal violence used to end the strike brought no negative consequences for perpetrators, except for the small fines levied on the four men who carried out floggings in Leslie. While no one publicly defended the slaying of Ed Gregor, the Reverend Walter F. Bradley ultimately put the blame on Gregor himself, saying, "his defiance and abuse of the citizens in carrying out the proceedings of the investigations were undoubtedly the cause of his death." The Reverend John Kelly Farris, in his book *The Harrison Riot*, noted how the legislative committee gave the citizens of Harrison a clean bill of health, closing its hearing in Harrison with a banquet given by the appreciative citizens. Speechmaking and applause filled the very room where the vigilantes' kangaroo court had met just two months before. Farris concluded with some irony: "We were now judicially pronounced clean and free from all crime." After their anger cooled, the displaced strikers probably reflected on their strategic mistakes. If they had only recognized that railway workers in the Ozarks could not expect to make the same wages as those in New York or Philadelphia. If only local and national union officials had managed to control the radical element of strikers, those who engaged in sabotage of railroad property. With neither side willing to compromise, the strike became a win-or-lose situation. And the strikers lost.[11]

The M&NA strike had begun in 1921 as a conflict over the place of labor and railroads within the national economy. Usually, the Ozarks as a region were a caboose rather than the engine directing national trends. But this strike and its outcome became a bellwether of broader trends in the American labor movement. In a deflationary economy, the country's railroads were adjusting after the federal government's 1920 lifting of its wartime controls. The political gravity was shifting from President Woodrow Wilson's prolabor position to the business-friendly climate of Warren G. Harding. The M&NA strike began in February 1921, in the twilight of Wilson's presidency, but then for nearly three years it had to contend with the adversarial policies of the Harding administration. The M&NA just happened to be one of the first railroads to test the changing currents with a proposed

20 percent wage cut. National leaders of the railroad brotherhoods could see the handwriting on the wall and determined to take a stand with the M&NA. The Big Four brotherhoods were less courageous a year later, after the Railroad Labor Board (RLB) had shifted its support toward the carriers, leaving the shopmen and maintenance of way workers to go it alone in the great national strike of 1922.

The dismal failure for the M&NA strikers represents the broader decline of a powerful labor movement in the early 1920s. By 1923 membership in unions had shrunk by a third from the high point in 1920. Yet after President Harding's death in 1923 and Calvin Coolidge's dismissal of Harry M. Daugherty as attorney general in March 1924, railroad labor appeared less in crisis. The Railway Labor Act of 1926 revised the Transportation Act of 1920 and replaced the RLB with national boards of adjustments and mediation, whose decisions could be made mandatory by a federal court. The M&NA strike officially ended in December 1923, just as the situation for labor in the national economy had begun to improve. After the contentious early 1920s, the later years of the decade saw some moderation in labor policies from the succeeding Coolidge and Hoover administrations.[12]

But the difficulties that had started with national issues in 1921 quickly became overwhelmed by the situation on the ground. Within weeks the strike effected a rupture within the communities, transforming residents who formerly got along into warring camps. The strike's impact was greatest in the towns of the Arkansas Ozarks. While some damages occurred on the Missouri portion of the line, from Seligman to Joplin, and along the section from Kensett to Helena in eastern Arkansas, these areas had access to other railroads. Business and agricultural concerns there had other options, but the residents from Eureka Springs to Heber Springs utterly depended on the M&NA. The strike especially affected folks in the market towns of the Arkansas Ozarks, from the owners of the big cooperages in Leslie to the teenagers who wanted ice for their soft drinks at the soda fountain. Once people drew their lines, each side demonized the other. With a seeming lack of empathy, nothing but total triumph would satisfy, even if it was a Pyrrhic victory. Actors on both sides could not see past their bitter feelings to imagine a greater good. The Cleburne County judge Brose Massingill said in his testimony before the legislative committee: "Since February 26, 1921, the people of our county have been bull dozed, and bull ragged, and threatened, insulted, and boycotted and intimidated, and we got tired of it . . . and we decided that these strikers would move cheaper than we could. They didn't make that country. They never dug it out of the wilderness as we did and we decided we were going to stay there, and they were going to move—and they moved." Massingill painted a picture of two adversarial sides locked into battle, even as he avoided admitting that strikers were mostly local men too. He strikingly revealed to the legislators his disregard for the law.[13]

Massingill and 1,500 or so other men in Harrison, Leslie, Heber Springs, and Eureka Springs formed mobs willing to use illegal violence to defend, paradoxically, what they saw as law and order. While striker violence had aimed primarily at property, the mob violence by supporters of the railroad, through expulsions, beatings, and a lynching, was directed at people. Their actions may have been a last gasp of the nineteenth-century-style rough justice that had plagued the Ozarks during the Civil War. But in other ways it was modern. The perpetrators were not hillbillies scratching together a living from the soil. They were physicians, clergymen, lawyers, businessmen, and other community leaders who drove automobiles, not wagons. They were fighting to keep their towns moving toward a brighter future, not a rustic past.

As entrenched as the violence was in local issues, the events along the M&NA were hardly exceptional. Chad E. Pearson, in *Capital's Terrorists: Klansmen, Lawmen, and Employers in the Long Nineteenth Century*, argues that employers and their allies consistently used intimidation and violence to put down worker activism in the late 1800s and early 1900s. This long view of the repression of America's labor activism explains, for Pearson and others, why the United States had a less robust and transformative labor movement than did European countries. Pearson uses different case studies to establish the pattern of violence to control labor, starting with the original Ku Klux Klan of Reconstruction, which he sees as an employers' organization formed to control the labor of freedpeople. Other examples include the Law and Order Leagues founded during and after the 1886 Southwest railroad strike; vigilante actions against miners in northern Idaho in the 1890s; the citizens committees that broke a strike of cigar makers in Tampa, Florida, in 1901, even kidnapping

THE SHAME OF ARKANSAS!

Drawn for LABOR, by John M. Baer.

A riot in the name of law and order. *Labor, January 27, 1923.*

the leaders and expelling them to Honduras; and community boosters in Indianapolis who fought unions in the early 1900s.[14]

Pearson does not write about a vigilante attack against striking copper miners in Bisbee, Arizona, that bore eerie resemblances to Harrison's riot five and a half years later. On June 27, 1917, some three thousand miners went on strike to demand better working conditions. The president of the Arizona-based mining company the Phelps Dodge Corporation came to Bisbee on the evening of July 11. By early the next morning the county sheriff had deputized a posse of some two thousand men who went door to door, rounding up more than two thousand strikers. The mob called itself the "Protective League," headed by a "Vigilante Committee." Members wore white cloths around their arms to identify themselves. They beat several men and women. One striker, like Ed Gregor, resisted the vigilantes by shooting when they tried to take him from his home. He was shot and killed. The mob took strikers to the town ballpark, where they received the choice of returning to work or being deported. Some twelve hundred strikers who stood firm were loaded into boxcars of the El Paso and Southwestern Railroad, a subsidiary of Phelps Dodge. Inside the boxcars, the men stood in cow manure in the July heat, going twelve hours without water, as they were shipped to the New Mexico border, 173 miles to the east. In the week that followed, a kangaroo court in Bisbee interrogated sympathizers (mostly merchants who traded with strikers and gave them credit), and expelled dozens as undesirables. Frank Little, an organizer for the Industrial Workers of the World (IWW), was spared deportation because he had a broken ankle resulting from a car crash. He left immediately for Butte, Montana, where copper miners there were striking against the Anaconda Mining Company. On July 19, he spoke to thousands of strikers at a mass meeting in the ballpark. In the early morning hours of August 1, six masked men kicked in the door of his room in a boardinghouse in Butte and dragged him in his underwear behind a car to a railroad trestle outside of town, where he was hanged to his death.[15]

The mob actions along the M&NA line in January 1923 clearly were part of a larger pattern of violence against labor. Unlike in Bisbee and Butte, no evidence suggests a role in the M&NA strike for the IWW, except in the imagination of railroad supporters. But the enactment of specific rituals, the use of language, and the structure of the events suggest that these Arkansas vigilantes were aware of earlier pogroms against striking workers. The white ribbons in Harrison, Leslie, and Heber Springs resembled the white armbands in Bisbee. The expulsion of strikers in Arkansas mimicked the deportations of cigar workers in Tampa and miners in Bisbee. Gregor's lynching reenacted Frank Little's hanging from a railroad trestle in Butte. Mine owners in Idaho in the 1890s had called their impromptu jails for strikers "bullpens," just as the citizens committees did in Harrison and Heber Springs. The innocuous-sounding "Protective League" and "citizens committee" made vigilante violence in Bisbee, Tampa, and Harrison seem like righteous self-defense. Far from original in their actions, the vigilantes fighting the M&NA strike were recycling labels, tropes, and ideas used by other elitist groups. Just as the Klan used the euphemistic phrase "one hundred percent American" to identify Klansmen and billed public presentations as lectures on

"Americanism," probusiness elites cloaked their movements in patriotism. Were not strikers also citizens and Americans?

Pearson, in *Capital's Terrorists*, divides the perpetrators of violence against labor into three groups. He uses the term *terrorists* for those who forcefully repressed people who had committed no crimes. With the riots along the M&NA, the terrorists would include a large collection of people who both planned and executed the attacks on strikers and their supporters. The mob violence in Harrison, Leslie, Heber Springs, and Eureka Springs were clearly planned actions, not knee-jerk reactions. Just who exactly planned the mob actions remains unclear. Pete Venable asserted that the St. Louis owners of the railroad, particularly Festus J. Wade, were privy to the plans for the riots at least a week before they began. The M&NA's general manager in Harrison, Jack Murray, set the stage in December and early January through news releases circulated in local newspapers and posted in depots along the line, calling for citizens to rise up to save the railroad. Murray probably made plans in conjunction with other M&NA officials, such as lead attorney J. Sam Rowland. Murray sent agents up and down the line over the weekend to organize the mob that assembled in Harrison on Monday, January 15. He dispatched a special train to Leslie on Sunday to transport the mob north, ready to depart for Harrison at 6:00 a.m. the next day. John Rogers, the St. Louis reporter who arrived to cover the riot, described Murray as the man in charge, directing the mob's actions by phone or messenger from his office in the Kirby Building. One can imagine that the Klan chapters in Harrison, Berryville, Eureka Springs, Marshall, Leslie, and Heber Springs likely participated in the planning for the riots. In an era without email or social media, a thousand men, coming from towns along a 160-mile stretch of the railroad, could hardly have assembled at a given time and place without some prior organization.

While identities of conspirators remain somewhat obscure, the faces of the terrorists who made up the mobs were clearly known. Newspapers published names of the men on the citizens committees that interrogated and expelled strikers and sympathizers in Harrison, Leslie, Heber Springs, and Eureka Springs. Chief perpetrators in the streets, such as Walter Snapp, George McKinney, Marion Atterberry, Doyle B. Woodruff, Dorsey Treece, and the Reverend Dillard Monroe

Carter, were identified in newspapers and in the voluminous testimony before the legislative committee. Pete Venable alone named 207 people in a list he sent to the ACLU, and he called this group just the "cream" of a mob in Harrison that numbered around 1,000. Many of those on the citizens committees in Harrison and Heber Springs were known members of the Ku Klux Klan, and undoubtedly many other Klansmen were foot soldiers in the mobs. While admitting that most Klansmen in Harrison were part of the mob, contemporaries such as Orville Thrasher Gooden were quick to note that non-Klansmen, too, participated in the riots.[16] Yet the visible role played by Klansmen in the mob actions in the Arkansas Ozarks, despite the fact that Klan officials in Little Rock and Atlanta made no public comment, led the American labor movement to distance itself from the Ku Klux Klan. Similarly, Harrison's Rotary Club, as a group, contributed to the vigilante action. J. Sam Rowland was its founding president, and Jack Murray, Troy Coffman, Luther "Clay" Holt, and Silby Johnson were all members. It is no surprise that the Rotary Club made available its meeting hall for the work of the citizens committee and then two months later as the location for townspeople to fete the legislative committee before the members left town. In all these towns along the M&NA, there was probably considerable overlap between the citizens committees, the chambers of commerce, the men's clubs, and the Ku Klux Klan.

Pearson terms a second group who opposed labor the *enablers*. These were mostly government officials and others who collaborated with, or acquiesced to, the actions of the mob. In this narrative, the enablers would include many officers at various levels of government. County judicial officials James Shinn and Karl Greenhaw, the Arkansas Supreme Court, and federal judge Jacob Trieber all prosecuted strikers while giving members of the mobs a free pass. Governor Thomas McRae sent officers of the Arkansas National Guard to Heber Springs, only for them to distribute weapons from the armory to members of the mob. The legislative committee appointed by the General Assembly to investigate the strike and riots, with the exception of Senator Jacob R. "Jake" Wilson, held no one accountable for the vigilante violence. Even US attorney general Harry Daugherty, when asked for an opinion about the mob violence in Arkansas, claimed not to know whether the M&NA engaged in interstate commerce.

The Harrison Rotary Club in 1923. In the photo are Silby Johnson (third from bottom left, in tall hat), Tom Newman (to the right of Johnson), Jack Murray (near center with cloth cap and bow tie), J. Sam Rowland (second from right in light suit), Troy Coffman (back row behind Murray), and Clay Holt (second row, second from left). At bottom right appears to be the Reverend Walter Bradley. *Courtesy of Boone County Archival Photograph Collection.*

Other government officials, such as Boone County sheriffs Silby Johnson and Bob Shaddox, Heber Springs mayor Marcus E. Vinson, Marshall mayor Stephen W. Woods, and Cleburne County judge Brose Massingill and sheriff Emmett Baldridge functioned as both terrorists and enablers. On the list of enablers we should also include the women of the Harrison Mothers Club and others who brought coffee and food for the mob and even took out-of-towners into their homes to sleep.

Finally, Pearson calls his third category the *narrative creators*, the people who presented the violent actions to the public as necessary and justified. Editors Tom Newman and Jesse Lewis Russell of Harrison's two newspapers, William J. Douglas of Berryville's *North Arkansas Star*, and William Wenrick of the *Marshall Mountain Wave* consistently vilified strikers and defended the actions of the railroad and mob. From the pulpit of Harrison's Presbyterian church, the Reverend Walter F. Bradley preached sermons against the strike, including one on July 2, 1922, so well-advertised through printed handbills that other churches dismissed services so their parishioners could attend. A few days later, the Methodist church's pastor, the Reverend W. T. Martin, gave a similar antistrike oration at a Fourth of July celebration on the courthouse lawn.[17] Bradley managed to get his account of the strike and riot, *An Industrial War*, in print in November 1923, a month before the strike technically ended and several months before the Reverend John Kelly Farris, short-lived successor to Rev. Martin, could release his opposing account, *The Harrison Riot*. And Jesse Russell was still recycling his justification of the Harrison mob twenty-four years after the fact in his memoir, *Behind These Ozark Hills*. Just as the categories of terrorists and enablers overlapped, the distinction between terrorists and narrative creators was fuzzy. Besides creating a narrative about the strike in his book and sermons, Bradley surely was privy to plans for the mob action in his role as exalted cyclops of Harrison's Ku Klux Klan. William Douglas was both a newspaper editor and a member of the citizens committee. And William Wenrick's call for citizens to decorate a few telephone poles with radical strikers went beyond the mere role of crafting a narrative.

For the terrorists, enablers, and narrative creators, the actions taken against strikers and their sympathizers were an exercise in power. The citizens committees met in city hall in Leslie and the county courthouse in Heber Springs. In Harrison, Shinn and Greenhaw remained in the courthouse as the mob surrounded the building. The epicenter of the riot there was the bonfire and speaker's platform at the intersection of Rush and Vine (now North Main). On the southeast corner was the M&NA office, on the second floor of the Kirby Building. Kitty-corner to the northwest was Rotary Hall, where the citizens committee held court. On the other two corners were vestiges of government, the Boone County Courthouse to the southwest and a grand federal building housing the post office to the northeast. The symbolism of this location linked the railroad, the vigilantes, and governmental authority.

Often, mob violence takes place when powerful people "own" civil authorities or simply think that the justice system cannot or will not do anything about it. During the three years of the strike, government at

The Mothers Club of Harrison. *Courtesy of Boone County Library Archival Photo Collection, no. 177.*

nearly all levels stood by the people with some measure of power and wealth, rather than by those who worked for these elites. The strikers were a group of white men, not a down-and-out underclass. They were not Black, Jewish, Catholic, or immigrant, given some degree of second-class citizenship. They were not exactly poor; they earned decent wages pegged to a national wage scale, unlike sharecroppers and transient laborers. The higher end of railroad employees, such as conductors and locomotive engineers, had middle-class incomes and status. But local and state governments and the district, state, and federal courts still sided with the merchants, professional folk, and railroad managers. One exception was the small group of city officials in Harrison who dared to stand behind the strikers: mayors Guy L. Trimble and Jasper L. Clute, a few on the town council, and city marshal William Parr. But the vigilantes ousted them, expelling Clute, Parr, and two councilmen from their homes, replacing them with railroad investor John I. Worthington and known Klansmen Troy Coffman, Clay Holt, and Silby Johnson. For the most part, town, county, judicial district, and state officials facilitated the illegal suppression of the strike and then whitewashed it afterward. One of the saddest conclusions of this book is that government at all levels appeared more concerned about fostering commerce than enforcing the law and protecting constitutional rights for ordinary citizens.

NOTES

CHAPTER 1

1. The only other scholarly work about the M&NA strike is an article by Brooks R. Blevins, "The Strike and the Still: Anti-Radical Violence and the Ku Klux Klan in the Ozarks," *Arkansas Historical Quarterly* 52, no. 4 (Winter 1993): 405–25. Blevins, while a graduate student at Auburn University, wrote this article about the role of the Ku Klux Klan in opposing the M&NA strike. He went on to become the Noel Boyd Professor of Ozark Studies at Missouri State University and arguably the most distinguished historian of the Ozark region. Clifton E. Hull, in *Shortline Railroads of Arkansas* (Norman: University of Oklahoma Press, 1969), 80–98, tells the story of the M&NA strike, based on Gooden's book. James R. Fair Jr., in *The North Arkansas Line: The Story of the Missouri and North Arkansas Railroad* (San Diego, CA: Howell-North Books, 1969), 124–54, also narrates the events of the strike. Fair was a professor of engineering and a railroad enthusiast who had ridden on the M&NA in his childhood years.
2. For the most thorough history of the Ozark region, see Brooks R. Blevins's magisterial three-volume work *A History of the Ozarks* (Urbana: University of Illinois Press, 2018–21). I have particularly relied on volume 2, *The Conflicted Years* (2019).
3. For the population of Eureka Springs and Little Rock in 1880, see *Population of Arkansas by Minor Civil Divisions*, Census bulletin no. 112 (Washington, DC: Government Printing Office, 1891), 2. For more information about the remarkable founding and growth of Eureka Springs, see Fair, *The North Arkansas Line*, 1–8. A two-and-a-half-mile stretch leading out of Eureka Springs that is open seasonally is the only part of the M&NA line that is operational at the point of this writing. From the depot in Eureka Springs, tourists can purchase a scenic round-trip ride complete with narration.
4. Fair, *The North Arkansas Line*, 29–42; Hull, *Shortline Railroads of Arkansas*, 50–53; Walter F. Bradley, *An Industrial War: History of the Missouri and North Arkansas Railroad Strike and a Study of the Tremenduous* [sic] *Issues Involved* (Harrison, AR: Boone County Headlight, 1923), 11. Carroll County is one of several Arkansas counties with two county seats. The county is divided into eastern and western judicial districts, with courthouses in Berryville and Eureka Springs.
5. Fair, *The North Arkansas Line*, 43–50.
6. Fair, *The North Arkansas Line*, 50–61; Hull, *Shortline Railroads of Arkansas*, 72.
7. Fair, *The North Arkansas Line*, 56, 65–83; Hull, *Shortline Railroads of Arkansas*, 63–74. Steamboats would continue to ply the White River through the 1930s; see Duane Huddleston, Sammie Rose, and Pat Wood, *Steamboats and Ferries on the White River: A Heritage Revisited* (Fayetteville: University of Arkansas Press, 1998), 114–16.

8. *Kansas City (MO) Times*, December 26, 1922; Barton Jennings, *Missouri & North Arkansas Railroad: History through the Miles* (Avon, IL: TechScribes, 2019), 156–57, 239–40, 254–55. Jennings's book traces the route of the M&NA from Joplin to Helena, with a description of the surviving remnants of the line and the various stops along the way.
9. Hull, *Shortline Railroads of Arkansas*, 70; Fair, *The North Arkansas Line*, 94; Jennings, *Missouri & North Arkansas Railroad*, 305–6.
10. Lawrence R. Handley, "Settlement across North Arkansas as Influenced by the Missouri and North Arkansas Railroad," *Arkansas Historical Quarterly* 33, no. 4 (Winter 1974): 278–80; Jennings, *Missouri & North Arkansas Railroad*, 249–53; Fair, *The North Arkansas Line*, 91–93.
11. Fair, *The North Arkansas Line*, 95–103; Handley, "Settlement across North Arkansas," 274–75. See Brooks R. Blevins's discussion of the image issue for the Arkansas Ozarks in *Hill Folks: A History of Arkansas Ozarkers and Their Image* (Chapel Hill: University of North Carolina Press, 2002); and *Arkansas/Arkansaw: How Bear Hunters, Hillbillies, and Good Ol' Boys Defined a State* (Fayetteville: University of Arkansas Press, 2009).
12. Jacqueline Froelich and David Zimmerman, "Total Eclipse: The Destruction of the African American Community of Harrison, Arkansas, in 1905 and 1909," *Arkansas Historical Quarterly* 58, no. 2 (Summer 1999): 131–59. The expulsion of Black residents was not unique to Harrison; see also Guy Lancaster, *Racial Cleansing in Arkansas, 1883–1924* (Lanham, MD: Lexington Books, 2014).
13. Stephen J. Lubben, "Railroad Receiverships and Modern Bankruptcy Theory," *Cornell Law Review* 89, no. 6 (2004): 1422–51; Douglas G. Baird and Robert K. Rasmussen, "Control Rights, Priority Rights, and the Conceptual Foundations of Corporate Reorganizations," *Virginia Law Review* 87 (2001): 925–35. New Deal legislation in the 1930s began to replace insiders with impartial third parties as receivers. The legislation also began a transition to the modern Chapter 11 bankruptcy model, whereby other companies, not just railroads, could be reorganized intact rather than having their assets sold to pay off debts.
14. Hull, *Shortline Railroads of Arkansas*, 75; Fair, *The North Arkansas Line*, 103–8; Orville Thrasher Gooden, *The Missouri and North Arkansas Railroad Strike* (New York: Columbia University Press), 19–23. The Eureka Springs depot now anchors the tourist excursion train. In Leslie the depot is used as a warehouse for a lumber company.
15. Fair, *The North Arkansas Line*, 95, 111; Gooden, *The Missouri and North Arkansas Railroad Strike*, 21; Dr. L. Kirby testimony, "Hearings and Report of Missouri & North Arkansas Railroad Strike, Complete Transcription," 993, MG04200, General Microfilm Collection, Arkansas State Archives, Little Rock (hereafter cited as "Hearings and Report").
16. Fair, *The North Arkansas Line*, 61–65. The story of the White River line is well told in Walter M. Adams, *The White River Railway: Being a History of the White River Division of the Missouri Pacific Railroad Company, 1901–1951* (Branson, MO: Ozarks Mountaineer, 1991).
17. Fair, *The North Arkansas Line*, 110; Jennings, *Missouri & North Arkansas Railroad*, 253.

18. Hull, *Shortline Railroads of Arkansas*, 76–79; Fair, *The North Arkansas Line*, 111–16.
19. Adams, *The White River Railway*, 91–94; Fair, *The North Arkansas Line*, 116–21.
20. Gooden, *The Missouri and North Arkansas Railroad Strike*, 21; Fair, *The North Arkansas Line*, 121–26.
21. Shelton Stromquist, in *A Generation of Boomers: The Pattern of Railroad Labor Conflict in Nineteenth-Century America* (Urbana: University of Illinois Press, 1987), examines the big three railroad strikes and smaller strikes between 1877 and 1894. Theresa A. Case's *The Great Southwest Railroad Strike and Free Labor* (College Station: Texas A&M University Press, 2010) describes the strike of 1886, which had a significant impact on Arkansas and Missouri.
22. Paul Michel Taillon, *Good, Reliable, White Men: Railroad Brotherhoods, 1877–1917* (Urbana: University of Illinois Press, 2009), 3–4, 68, 78–79; Colin J. Davis, *Power at Odds: The 1922 National Railroad Shopmen's Strike* (Urbana: University of Illinois Press, 1997), 27.
23. Stromquist, *A Generation of Boomers*, 265–66; Taillon, *Good, Reliable, White Men*, 117–26, 172–77.
24. Taillon, *Good, Reliable, White Men*, 197–201; Jon R. Huibregtse, *American Railroad Labor and the Genesis of the New Deal, 1919–1935* (Gainesville: University Press of Florida, 2010), 23.
25. Robert H. Zieger, *Republicans and Labor, 1919–1929* (Lexington: University of Kentucky Press, 1969), 72; Howell John Harris, *Bloodless Victories: The Rise and Fall of the Open Shop in the Philadelphia Metal Trades, 1890–1940* (Cambridge: Cambridge University Press, 2000), 85–86; Taillon, *Good, Reliable, White Men*, 172, 175–77; Huibregtse, *American Railroad Labor and the Genesis of the New Deal*, 23. Vilja Hulden, in *The Bosses' Union: How Employers Organized to Fight Labor before the New Deal* (Urbana: University of Illinois Press, 2023), examines how employers' associations embraced the open shop and opposed collective bargaining with unions.
26. Fair, *The North Arkansas Line*, 126–33; Huibregtse, *American Railroad Labor and the Genesis of the New Deal*, 24–27; *Harrison (AR) Times*, October 10, 1908, and November 11, 1916; *Arkansas Gazette* (Little Rock), August 13 and 30, 1918, and September 12 and 17, 1918; *St. Louis Daily Globe-Democrat*, September 18, 1918; *St. Joseph (MO) News-Press*, September 20, 1918.
27. *North Arkansas and Carroll Progress* (Berryville), September 13, 1918; *Arkansas Gazette*, September 16, 1918; J. C. Murray testimony, "Hearings and Report," 603.
28. Taillon, *Good, Reliable, White Men*, 204–5; Huibregtse, *American Railroad Labor and the Genesis of the New Deal*, 3–4; Robert H. Zieger, "From Hostility to Moderation: Railroad Labor Policy in the 1920s," *Labor History* 9, no. 1 (Winter 1968): 25–26.
29. Huibregtse, *American Railroad Labor and the Genesis of the New Deal*, 30–35; Zieger, *Republicans and Labor*, 71–74; Harry D. Wolf, *The Railroad Labor Board* (Chicago: University of Chicago Press, 1927), 110, 127–30, 444; *Harrison (AR) Daily Times*, April 19, 1920.
30. *Harrison Times*, July 15, 1916, January 24, 1920, and March 6 and 13, 1920; *Tulsa Democrat*, June 14, 1916.
31. *Harrison Times*, September 4 and 18, 1920, and January 29, 1921; Gooden, *The Missouri and North Arkansas Railroad Strike*, 26–27.

CHAPTER 2

1. James R. Green, *The World of the Worker: Labor in Twentieth-Century America* (New York: Hill and Wang, 1980), 93; Melvin Dubovsky and Foster Rhea Dulles, *Labor in American History*, 8th ed. (Wheeling, IL: Harlan Davidson, 2010), 208–10. For more information about Arkansas's anarchy law and the Elaine massacre, see Joey McCarty, "The Red Scare in Arkansas: A Southern State and National Hysteria," *Arkansas Historical Quarterly* 37, no. 3 (Autumn 1978): 264–77; Grif Stockley, Brian Mitchell, and Guy Lancaster, *Blood in Their Eyes: The Elaine Massacre of 1919* (Fayetteville: University of Arkansas Press, 2020); Guy Lancaster, ed., *The Elaine Massacre and Arkansas: A Century of Atrocity and Resistance, 1819–1919* (Little Rock: Butler Center Books, 2018).
2. Bradley, *An Industrial War*, 15–29; *Harrison Times*, February 17, 1917, and June 16, 1917.
3. For a discussion of shopmen's role in the railroad industry, see Davis, *Power at Odds*, 11–12.
4. *Harrison Times*, February 5, 1921; *Joplin (MO) Globe*, February 5 and 9, 1921; *North Arkansas and Carroll Progress*, February 11, 1921; Gooden, *The Missouri and North Arkansas Railroad Strike*, 25; Bradley, *An Industrial War*, 37; *Labor* (Washington, DC), April 9, 1921. *Labor* was owned and published by the sixteen railroad brotherhoods.
5. Gooden reproduces the entire text of the RLB's ruling; see Gooden, *The Missouri and North Arkansas Railroad Strike*, 30–33. The *Harrison Times*, February 26, 1921, interpreted the ruling as a win for the M&NA.
6. Gooden, *The Missouri and North Arkansas Railroad Strike*, 33–36; *Joplin Globe*, February 26, 1921; *Labor*, April 30, 1921.
7. Gooden, *The Missouri and North Arkansas Railroad Strike*, 36–37; Bradley, *An Industrial War*, 34; *Joplin Globe*, February 27, 1921.
8. *Chillicothe (MO) Constitution*, February 27, 1921; *Kansas City Times*, February 28, 1921; *Arkansas Democrat* (Little Rock), March 2 and 3, 1921; *Joplin Globe*, March 1, 3, and 13, 1921; *St. Louis Post-Dispatch*, April 10, 1921; J. T. Venable affidavit, "Hearings and Report," 1229. Zieger, *Republicans and Labor*, 89, notes that some six million Americans were unemployed in mid-1921; see also Huibregtse, *American Railroad Labor and the Genesis of the New Deal*, 43.
9. Gooden, *The Missouri and North Arkansas Railroad Strike*, 32, 41; Bradley, *An Industrial War*, 19; *Harrison Times*, March 5, 1921; J. T. Venable affidavit, "Hearings and Report," 1295. For a discussion of organized labor's use of boycotts, see Philip Dray, *There Is Power in a Union: The Epic Story of Labor in America* (New York: Doubleday, 2010), 249.
10. Bradley, *An Industrial War*, 33.
11. *Arkansas Democrat*, March 10, 1921; *Harrison Times*, March 12, 1921. The *Times* on March 19, 1921, published a full membership list of the Harrison Protective League, with the amounts that each member had contributed to the public defense fund. W. J. Myers, a local banker, was elected president; J. W. Wallace, vice president; F. M. Garvin, secretary; and R. A. Wilson, treasurer. On the executive committee were Walter L. Snapp, Louis Keck, J. M. Wagley, W. S. Pettit, and R. A. Wilson.

12. Bradley, *An Industrial War*, 35; *Arkansas Gazette*, March 18, 1921, and April 10, 1921; *Harrison Times*, March 19, 1921, and April 2, 1921.
13. Hull, *Shortline Railroads of Arkansas*, 85; *Harrison Times*, March 19 and 26, 1921; *Neosho (MO) Daily Democrat*, March 22, 1921; *Joplin Globe*, March 19, 20, 24, and 25, 1921; *Arkansas Gazette*, March 27, 1921; *Springfield Missouri Republican*, March 22, 1921; Record Book L, 86, Circuit Court Records, 1921–23, Boone County Courthouse, Harrison, AR (hereafter cited as Boone County Circuit Court); *Labor*, April 9, 1921.
14. *Harrison Times*, March 19, 1921, and April 2, 1921; *Joplin Globe*, March 26, 1921.
15. *Joplin Globe*, March 20 and 24, 1921; *Marshall (AR) Mountain Wave*, March 25, 1921; *Harrison Times*, April 2, 1921; *Arkansas Democrat*, March 28, 1921; Bradley, *An Industrial War*, 36; Indictment Book E, 15–49, Boone County Circuit Court.
16. *Labor*, January 27, 1923; *Joplin Globe*, March 25, 1921; *Arkansas Gazette*, March 22 and 24, 1921; *Arkansas Democrat*, March 23 and 25, 1921; *Harrison Times*, March 26, 1921, and April 2, 1921; Bradley, *An Industrial War*, 37–38.
17. *Joplin Globe*, March 20, 1921; *Neosho Daily Democrat*, March 22, 1921; *Arkansas Democrat*, March 22, 1921; *Harrison Times*, March 26, 1921.
18. J. T. Venable, "Restitution not Retaliation," 3, Correspondence—Cases by State, Arkansas, 1924, vol. 256, American Civil Liberties Union Records, subgroup 1: Roger Baldwin Years, Mudd Library, Princeton University, Princeton, NJ (hereafter cited as ACLU Records); *Arkansas Gazette*, March 22, 1921; *Arkansas Democrat*, March 22, 1921; *Marshall Mountain Wave*, March 25, 1921.
19. *Joplin Globe*, March 19 and 20, 1921; Pete Venable to Roger Baldwin, February 28, 1923, Correspondence—Cases by State, Arkansas, 1923–24, vol. 242, ACLU Records; *Marshall Mountain Wave*, March 25, 1921; *Arkansas Democrat*, March 23, 1921; Fair, *The North Arkansas Line*, 139; *Railway Federationist* (Sedalia, MO), June 18, 1921.
20. *Marshall Mountain Wave*, March 25, 1921; *Arkansas Democrat*, March 23, 1921; *Joplin Globe*, March 19, 20, and 25, 1921. The *Boone County Headlight*'s report of the meeting is reproduced in Bradley, *An Industrial War*, 36–37. Issues of the *Headlight* are not extant prior to January 1923, but earlier excerpts appear in *An Industrial War* and editor Jesse Lewis Russell's memoir, *Behind These Ozark Hills: History, Reminiscences, Traditions, Featuring the Author's Family* (New York: Hobson Book Press, 1947).
21. *Harrison Times*, March 26, 1921; Gooden, *The Missouri and North Arkansas Railroad Strike*, 49.
22. *Joplin Globe*, April 7, 1921; Gooden, *The Missouri and North Arkansas Railroad Strike*, 50–51; Bradley, *An Industrial War*, 40–41. Richard H. Dickenhorst, a banker in Heber Springs, said that six or seven men had a pass from the railroad for free passage from Heber Springs to Leslie, where they boarded the special train for Harrison. They repeated this process for the travel back to Heber Springs, paying nothing for the trip. R. H. Dickenhorse [*sic*] testimony, "Hearings and Report," 301–3.
23. Gooden, *The Missouri and North Arkansas Railroad Strike*, 50–52; Bradley, *An Industrial War*, 41; *Joplin Globe*, April 7, 8, and 14, 1921; *Springfield Missouri Republican*, April 8, 1921; George O'Neal testimony, "Hearings and Report," 475. Estimates of the size of the mob on April 6 ranged from six hundred to one thousand. Pete Venable gave a figure of seven hundred in his testimony in "Hearings and Report," 1326.

24. *Springfield (MO) Leader*, April 8, 1921; *Joplin Globe*, April 10 and 17, 1921; *Railway Federationist*, May 7, 1921; Bradley, *An Industrial War*, 41; *St. Louis Post-Dispatch*, April 10, 1921; and, in "Hearings and Report": John Hughey testimony, 98–101; Red Orr testimony, 16–17; Kyle Cook testimony, 175. The weekly newspaper belonging to the railroad brotherhoods, *Labor*, April 16 and 30, 1921, claimed that the mob was supplied with guns and moonshine whiskey upon arrival in Harrison. For an examination of Arkansas's gun laws, see James F. Willis, "Arkansas's Gun Regulation Laws: Suppressing the 'Pistol Toter,' 1838–1925," *Arkansas Historical Quarterly* 81, no. 2 (Summer 2022): 103–26.
25. Woods's remarks are quoted in Bradley, *An Industrial War*, 43–44.
26. Gooden, *The Missouri and North Arkansas Railroad Strike*, 54; Bradley, *An Industrial War*, 42, 48; *Labor*, April 30, 1921. Blue vitriol, or copper sulfate, is a water-soluble inorganic compound that corroded pipes and caused a locomotive's boilers to leak. The engine would struggle to get up steam and had to be withdrawn from service. Emery dust caused moving parts to grind to the point of destruction. The *Railway Federationist*, May 14, 1921, published the list of names and amounts of the warrants paid for guard services in Boone County. See also Russell, *Behind These Ozark Hills*, 131.
27. Gooden, *The Missouri and North Arkansas Railroad Strike*, 56–57; *Harrison Times*, April 23, 1921; *Harrison Daily Times*, April 25, 1921; *Arkansas Democrat*, April 25, 1921; Bradley, *An Industrial War*, 48.
28. Bradley, *An Industrial War*, 49.
29. *Labor*, May 14, 1921; *Railway Federationist*, May 14 and 21, 1921; *Harrison Daily Times*, April 30, 1921.
30. The *Railway Federationist*, June 11, 1921, described the event in great detail, including printing the notarized affidavits of seven strikers who witnessed it. The Harrison newspapers were generally silent. The *Yellville (AR) Mountain Echo*, June 9 and 23, 1921, ran the story and criticized the two Harrison newspapers, along with papers in Leslie and Marshall, for being apologists for the railroad.
31. *Harrison Daily Times*, June 20, 1921; *Railway Federationist*, June 25, 1921, and July 2, 1921; Gooden, *The Missouri and North Arkansas Railroad Strike*, 57–58; Willis, "Arkansas's Gun Regulation Laws," 110.
32. *Harrison Daily Times*, July 7 and 12, 1921; *Harrison Times*, July 22, 1921, and August 12, 1921; *Railway Federationist*, July 9, 1921; Gooden, *The Missouri and North Arkansas Railroad Strike*, 58; Bradley, *An Industrial War*, 49; J. T. Venable, "Restitution not Retaliation," 4, vol. 256, ACLU Records.
33. *Harrison Daily Times*, July 13, 25, 26, and 27, 1921; *North Arkansas Star* (Berryville), July 15, 1921; *Harrison Times*, July 22, 1921; *Arkansas Democrat*, July 27, 1921; *Arkansas Gazette*, July 30, 1921; Gooden, *The Missouri and North Arkansas Railroad Strike*, 61; *Labor*, June 4, 1923. After his resignation, Reddoch took a position as superintendent of the Cuyamel Fruit Company's railway system in Honduras. He died there in 1929; *Springfield Leader*, April 23, 1929.
34. Fair, *The North Arkansas Line*, 141; *Springfield Leader*, December 24, 1923; *Kansas Trades Unionist* (Topeka), January 11, 1924. Mrs. Phelan was still in Harrison on July 5, for the *Harrison Times*, July 8, 1921, reported that she had played cards

that day with Mrs. Murray, Mrs. Reddoch, and other women at a bridge party. In an advertisement that appeared in the September 9, 1921, issue of the *Harrison Daily Times*, Mrs. Phelan, now at 6559 Talman Avenue, Chicago, tried to sell her daughter's horse that was still pastured in the area. A search through Ancestry.com could not find any record of Charles Albert Phelan after his departure from Arkansas. Pete Venable said that he was last seen in 1922, running an employment office in Detroit for strikebreakers during the national shopmen's strike; see J. T. Venable, "Restitution not Retaliation," 4, vol. 256, ACLU Records.

35. J. T. Venable affidavit, "Hearings and Report," 1328. The evolving position of the RLB is described in Wolf, *The Railroad Labor Board*, 141–53, 215–41; Davis, *Power at Odds*, 51–54.
36. *North Arkansas Star*, June 17, 1921. Two brothers, Lloyd and Allen Brown, of Houston, Texas, came to Little Rock to organize the first Klans in Arkansas. See the list of Arkansas chapters of the Ku Klux Klan in Kenneth C. Barnes, *The Ku Klux Klan in 1920s Arkansas: How Protestant White Nationalism Came to Rule a State* (Fayetteville: University of Arkansas Press, 2021), 192–96. For the Joplin and Neosho Klans, see *Joplin Globe*, February 1, 1922; *Neosho Daily Democrat*, September 25, 1922.

CHAPTER 3

1. *Kansas City Times*, August 5, 1921; *Harrison Daily Times*, August 1, 1921; *St. Louis Post-Dispatch*, August 1, 1921; *Springfield Leader*, August 15, 1921.
2. *Arkansas Democrat*, August 26, 1921; *Kansas City Times*, August 6, 1921; *Fayetteville (AR) Daily Democrat*, August 15, 1921.
3. *Arkansas Democrat*, August 4, 1921; *Springfield Leader*, August 8, 1921; *Arkansas Gazette*, December 31, 1921; *Baxter Bulletin* (Mountain Home, AR), December 16, 1921.
4. *Arkansas Democrat*, August 12, 1921, October 6, 1921, and December 2, 1921; *Arkansas Gazette*, September 4, 1921; *St. Louis Post-Dispatch*, August 9, 1921, and October 30, 1921; *Joplin Globe*, August 20, 1921; *Baxter Bulletin*, August 26, 1921, and December 23, 1921; *Harrison Daily Times*, January 11, 1922.
5. *St. Louis Post-Dispatch*, August 1, 1921, and October 30, 1921; *Baxter Bulletin*, August 26, 1921, and December 16, 1921; *Arkansas Democrat*, January 19, 1922, and April 2, 1922; Gooden, *The Missouri and North Arkansas Railroad Strike*, 65.
6. *Neosho Daily Democrat*, August 11, 1921; Bradley, *An Industrial War*, 53–54; *Springfield Leader*, September 22, 1921; *Arkansas Gazette*, September 16, 1921.
7. *Harrison Daily Times*, August 31, 1921; *Arkansas Democrat*, September 6, 1921; Gooden, *The Missouri and North Arkansas Railroad Strike*, 64; Bradley, *An Industrial War*, 54; Russell, *Behind These Ozark Hills*, 134–35.
8. *Crane (MO) Chronicle*, August 11, 1921; *St. Louis Post-Dispatch*, October 30, 1921; *Arkansas Democrat*, March 5, 1922; Gooden, *The Missouri and North Arkansas Railroad Strike*, 65.
9. *Arkansas Democrat*, January 3, 1921; *St. Louis Post-Dispatch*, October 30, 1921.
10. Gooden, *The Missouri and North Arkansas Railroad Strike*, 67–69; Bradley, *An Industrial War*, 56–57; Irene Jones testimony, "Hearings and Report," 847–51.

11. Gooden, *The Missouri and North Arkansas Railroad Strike*, 65; Bradley, *An Industrial War*, 55–57; Russell, *Behind These Ozark Hills*, 136; *Harrison Daily Times*, August 20, 1921; *Arkansas Democrat*, April 13 and 17, 1922.
12. *Harrison Daily Times*, August 25, 1921, September 7, 1921, and October 22, 1921; Russell, *Behind These Ozark Hills*, 135–36; *Arkansas Democrat*, January 5, 1922; Gooden, *The Missouri and North Arkansas Railroad Strike*, 98–99.
13. *Joplin Globe*, September 30, 1921; *Arkansas Gazette*, September 28, 1921; Bradley, *An Industrial War*, 57–58. Gooden prints Wade's written proposal; see *The Missouri and North Arkansas Railroad Strike*, 70–72. The M&NA's indebtedness included nearly $2 million of receivers' certificates, nearly $300,000 still owed to the general director of railroads from the wartime federal control over the line, and approximately $600,000 in other debts and unpaid vouchers. These figures were part of the ICC's final decision regarding the loan, dated April 4, 1922; see *Decisions of the Interstate Commerce Commission of the United States, Finance Reports, January to June 1922* (Washington, DC: Government Printing Office, 1922), 400.
14. *Joplin Globe*, October 11, 1921; *Harrison Daily Times*, October 15, 1921, and November 19 and 21, 1921; *North Arkansas Star*, October 21, 1921; *Harrison Times*, December 2, 1921; Gooden, *The Missouri and North Arkansas Railroad Strike*, 86.
15. *St. Louis Post-Dispatch*, December 20, 1921; *Joplin Globe*, December 21, 1921; *Arkansas Democrat*, December 22, 1921; *Harrison Daily Times*, December 28, 1921. Gooden reproduces much of the correspondence between unions, Murray, and the RLB in *The Missouri and North Arkansas Railroad Strike*, 72–74.
16. *Arkansas Gazette*, December 4, 1921; *Arkansas Democrat*, December 30, 1921; *Springfield Leader*, January 5, 1922.
17. *St. Louis Post-Dispatch*, January 17, 1922, and March 16, 1922; *St. Louis Star*, March 17, 1922; *Arkansas Democrat*, January 17, 1922, and March 17, 1922; *Arkansas Gazette*, January 19, 1922.
18. *Little Rock Daily News*, February 7 and 11, 1922; *Arkansas Gazette*, February 8, 1922; Gooden, *The Missouri and North Arkansas Railroad Strike*, 88. For a discussion of the process of railroad reorganization in the 1920s, see Baird and Rasmussen, "Control Rights, Priority Rights, and the Conceptual Foundations of Corporate Reorganizations," 931–35; Lubben, "Railroad Receiverships and Modern Bankruptcy Theory," 1444–45. In the 1930s, as the bankruptcy system evolved, reorganization took place without the legal fiction of a "sale" of the railroad.
19. *St. Louis Post-Dispatch*, February 19, 1922; Gooden, *The Missouri and North Arkansas Railroad Strike*, 75–81, 90.
20. *Arkansas Gazette*, March 5 and 6, 1922; *Harrison Daily Times*, March 2, 1922; *Decisions of the Interstate Commerce Commission*, 396; Gooden, *The Missouri and North Arkansas Railroad Strike*, 82–87, 90–92, 97. Gooden apparently had access to the M&NA office files; he reproduced letters showing Murray's repeated efforts and stonewalling by strike leaders before March 1.
21. *Harrison Daily Times*, March 15 and 22, 1922, and April 5, 1922; *Decisions of the Interstate Commerce Commission*, 400–403; *Arkansas Democrat*, February 27, 1922, and April 2 and 10, 1922; *Joplin Globe*, April 11, 1922; Bradley, *An Industrial War*, 59; J. T. Venable affidavit, "Hearings and Report," 1312.

22. *Arkansas Democrat*, February 19, 1922, and March 24, 1922; *Harrison Daily Times*, March 25, 1922, and April 5, 1922; *Joplin Globe*, April 11, 1922. Strangely, I have not been able to find any additional information about Pyle through Ancestry.com or in any newspaper, including several St. Louis papers. He is called G. M. Hyle by one paper, G. M. Ryle by another, and G. M. Pyle by three others.
23. *Joplin Globe*, March 19, 1922, and April 20 and 30, 1922; *Harrison Daily Times*, April 26, 1922, and May 5, 1922; *Arkansas Democrat*, April 10 and 23, 1922; Bradley, *An Industrial War*, 60; Russell, *Behind These Ozark Hills*, 139.
24. *Harrison Daily Times*, April 27, 1922, and May 5 and 15, 1922; *Arkansas Democrat*, April 21, 24, and 29, 1922; *Marshall Mountain Wave*, May 5, 1922; *Springfield Leader*, May 29, 1922.

CHAPTER 4

1. Gooden, *The Missouri and North Arkansas Railroad Strike*, 103; *Harrison Daily Times*, May 25, 1922; *Arkansas Democrat*, June 6 and 11, 1922; *Arkansas Gazette*, June 10, 1922; *Joplin Globe*, June 11, 1922.
2. *North Arkansas Star*, June 15, 1922; *Arkansas Gazette*, June 8 and 11, 1922; *Joplin Globe*, June 11, 1922; Gooden, *The Missouri and North Arkansas Railroad Strike*, 104; Bradley, *An Industrial War*, 89–91; Russell, *Behind These Ozark Hills*, 144–45; J. T. Venable affidavit, "Hearings and Report," 1294, 1329.
3. Gooden, *The Missouri and North Arkansas Railroad Strike*, 115–16; *Springfield Leader*, June 23, 1922; *Harrison Daily Times*, August 11 and 14, 1922; Henry Vance Kirby, interview, July 5, 1993, Series 3, Ozark Cultural Resource Center Vertical Files, Arkansas State Archives, Little Rock (hereafter cited as Henry Vance Kirby, interview, ASA); Sam Dennis testimony, "Hearings and Report," 1026; M. E. Vinson testimony, "Hearings and Report," 662; J. K. Farris, *The Harrison Riot, or The Reign of the Mob on the Missouri and North Arkansas Railroad* (Wynne, AR: printed by the author, 1924), 45. The flyer, with heading "What We Have Done to Make the M.&N. A. Run!," can be dated to summer 1922, for it mentions the upcoming primary elections. Orville J. McInturff Collection, Missouri and North Arkansas Strike Folder, Arkansas State Archives, Little Rock.
4. *Arkansas Gazette*, June 23, 1922; *Springfield Leader*, June 21, 1922; *Neosho Daily Democrat*, June 19, 1922; *Wheaton (MO) Journal*, June 16 and 23, 1922; John W. Armstrong affidavit, "Hearings and Report," 1276–77; Bradley, *An Industrial War*, 66; *Arkansas Democrat*, June 22, 1922; *Mountain Air* (St. Paul, AR), June 17, 1922.
5. *Arkansas Democrat*, June 27, 1922; Gooden, *The Missouri and North Arkansas Railroad Strike*, 112–15; *Arkansas Gazette*, October 10, 1922, and December 2, 1922; Record Book L, 261, Boone County Circuit Court.
6. *Venable v. State*, 246 S.W. 544, 156 Ark. 564 (1923), Arkansas Supreme Court opinion, January 22, 1923, https://opinions.arcourts.gov; *Venable v. State*, folder 2753, box 80, series 4, Arkansas Supreme Court Briefs and Records, Bowen School of Law Library/Pulaski County Law Library, Little Rock, AR (hereafter cited as ASCBR). For an examination of the Herrin massacre, see Paul M. Angle, *Bloody Williamson: A Chapter in American Lawlessness* (New York: Alfred A. Knopf, 1983).

For the cases of Barnett, Stevens, and Selby, see *Harrison Daily Times*, January 9, 12, and 24, 1923; *Arkansas Democrat*, January 22, 1923. Selby argued that he intended to sell the cartridges in his store, while his opponents countered that he ran a restaurant. The 1920 US manuscript census shows Selby as a merchant operating a grocery store.

7. In "Hearings and Report": Dr. Kirby testimony, 996; J. C. Murray testimony and list of indictments of strikers, 618; J. T. Venable affidavit, 1295.
8. Farris, *The Harrison Riot*, 53–56; *Harrison Times*, February 17, 1917, and June 16, 1917; *McAlester (OK) News-Capital*, March 29, 1926; *Arkansas Gazette*, September 23, 1956; Murray testimony, "Hearings and Report," 626.
9. *Arkansas Gazette*, June 29 and 30, 1922, and July 2, 1922; *Arkansas Democrat*, June 28 and 29, 1922.
10. *Joplin Globe*, February 1, 1922; *Neosho Daily Democrat*, September 25, 1922; Sean Rost, "A Call to Citizenship: Anti-Klan Activism in Missouri, 1921–1928" (PhD diss., University of Missouri, 2018), 79–81, 103. It is unclear what town in Missouri had the alpha chapter of the Klan.
11. Harrison City Council Minutes, June 5, 1922, 58, Office of the Mayor, Harrison, AR; *North Arkansas Star*, July 21, 1922, September 1, 1922, and November 3, 1922; *Arkansas Democrat*, August 5, 1922; *Searchlight* (Atlanta), October 7, 1922, and November 11, 1922; *Harrison Daily Times*, August 24, 1922. No newspapers from Heber Springs are extant for the early 1920s to provide documentation about the Klan there, but the charter for Klan no. 126 is held in the museum of the Cleburne County Historical Society in Heber Springs. The information about Klansmen whipping strikers originated from a victim, Charles Kuykendall, who told his nephew Dale Lee. Lee shared this information with local historian James Johnston, a communication of February 8, 1996. In June or July 1923, the Klans of Marshall and Leslie held a joint meeting attended by three hundred Klansmen at which they initiated a large class of new members. *Marshall Mountain Wave*, July 6, 1923.
12. See Donald B. Holley, "A Look behind the Masks: The 1920s Klan in Monticello, Arkansas," *Arkansas Historical Quarterly* 60, no. 2 (Summer 2001): 131–50; Kenneth C. Barnes, "Another Look behind the Masks: The Ku Klux Klan in Bentonville, Arkansas, 1922–1926," *Arkansas Historical Quarterly* 76, no. 3 (Autumn 2017): 191–217; Barnes, *The Ku Klux Klan in 1920s Arkansas*, 17–22; *Lonoke (AR) Democrat*, March 9, 1922.
13. The Heber Springs Klan officers are listed on the charter. The 1920 manuscript census schedules, available through Ancestry.com, enabled the identification of their occupations. By 1924, the Klan was abandoning some of the secrecy about its members. The *Harrison Times*, August 8, 1924, identified Klansmen marching or riding unmasked in a parade through downtown the day before. On August 1, 1924, the newspaper also listed attendees from Harrison at a Klan event in Valley Springs. For Venable's comments about Snapp, see J. T. Venable affidavit, "Hearings and Report," 1292. Dr. Kirby said that the Klan meeting place on Shaddox's farm was on the east side of a knoll, just south of what is today the Robinwood II subdivision in Harrison. Henry Vance Kirby, "Missouri and

North Arkansas Railroad Strike: A Review of Personal Experiences" (typescript, c. 1989), 1, 7–8, Boone County Heritage Museum, Harrison, AR. See also Walter Snapp testimony, "Hearings and Report," 863–69.

14. *Harrison Daily Times*, August 24, 1922; *Searchlight*, February 25, 1922, and November 11, 1922; Charles Finger to Roger Baldwin, June 27, 1923, vol. 242, ACLU Records; Bradley, *An Industrial War*, 71–78. See the broader discussion of Klan ideology in Barnes, *The Ku Klux Klan in 1920s Arkansas*, 93–111. For a thorough discussion of the IWW and its repression by political and economic elites, see Ahmed White, *Under the Iron Heel: The Wobblies and the Capitalist War on Radical Workers* (Oakland: University of California Press, 2022).
15. Huibregtse, *American Railroad Labor and the Genesis of the New Deal*, 43–48; Zieger, "From Hostility to Moderation," 28–30; Zieger, *Republicans and Labor*, 129–42.
16. Davis, *Power at Odds*, 85–86, 94, 97. On the Harding administration's opposition to the shopmen's strike, see David Montgomery, *The Fall of the House of Labor: The Workplace, the State, and American Labor Activism, 1865–1925* (New York: Cambridge University Press, 1987), 408; Dubovsky and Dulles, *Labor in American History*, 218–20. For an interesting take on the scandals involving Attorney General Daugherty and his roommate, Jess Smith, see Nathan Masters, *Crooked: The Roaring Twenties Tale of a Corrupt Attorney General, a Crusading Senator, and the Birth of the American Political Scandal* (New York: Hachette Books, 2023).
17. *Arkansas Democrat*, July 5 and 24, 1922, and August 18, 1922; *North Arkansas Star*, July 7, 1922; *Arkansas Gazette*, August 18, 1922.
18. *Arkansas Gazette*, July 4, 1922; *Little Rock Daily News*, July 6 and 14, 1922; *Springfield Leader*, August 3, 1922; *Joplin Globe*, December 5, 1922; *Arkansas Democrat*, December 8 and 9, 1922; Russell, *Behind These Ozark Hills*, 142–43. McMahan's district, the eleventh district of chancery court, extended from Eureka Springs to Marshall. Two strikers in Helena, John Ruffel and Fred Surman, were indicted for picketing in defiance of McMahan's injunction; *Harrison Daily Times*, September 23, 1922.
19. Gooden, *The Missouri and North Arkansas Railroad Strike*, 116–17; *Harrison Daily Times*, May 10 and 18, 1922, and August 15, 1922; *Marshall Mountain Wave*, July 21 and 28, 1922; *Arkansas Democrat*, August 20 and 25, 1922; *Arkansas Gazette*, October 5, 1922.
20. Fair, *The North Arkansas Line*, 25; *Arkansas Gazette*, July 6, 1922; *Yellville Mountain Echo*, July 27, 1922; *Harrison Daily Times*, August 15, 1922.
21. *Harrison Daily Times*, April 29, 1922, May 10 and 17–18, 1922, and August 15, 1922; Blevins, "The Strike and the Still," 420; *Arkansas Democrat*, October 3, 1922; *Arkansas Gazette*, October 5, 1922; J. T. Venable, "Restitution not Retaliation," 5, vol. 256, ACLU Records.
22. *Harrison Daily Times*, August 21, 1922, and September 2, 1922; *Springfield Leader*, August 21, 1922; *Madison County Record* (Huntsville, AR), August 24, 1922; *Joplin Globe*, August 22, 1922; Bradley, *An Industrial War*, 68.
23. *North Arkansas Star*, September 1 and 15, 1922; Bradley, *An Industrial War*, 68, 93. A note on terminology: in this book I have used various terms for the destruction of railroad property during the strike. The management of the railroad,

antistrike newspapers, and other opponents of the unions used the term *depredations*, signifying plunder, as in war. Strikers, conversely, used the term *sabotage*. Coming from French slang for "botched work," the term entered the vocabulary of the American labor movement after 1910 to refer to destruction of property as a means of legitimate protest, somewhat like what Luddite revolts had signified in the English Industrial Revolution. The IWW particularly was identified with this strategy, even publishing a pamphlet celebrating sabotage in 1913. See the discussion of the term and pamphlet in White, *Under the Iron Heel*, 29, 42–43. Finally, the more neutral term *damages* gestures toward the disputed cause of some of the fires on bridges and mechanical failures of engines.

24. *Arkansas Gazette*, October 29, 1922; *North Arkansas Star*, November 3, 1922; *Arkansas Democrat*, September 20, 1922.
25. Farris, *The Harrison Riot*, 24–26, 28–30; Clyde R. Newman, *One Hundred Years, 1873–1973: A History of the Methodist Church in Harrison, Arkansas* (Harrison, AR: printed by the author, 1973), 51–55.
26. Farris, *The Harrison Riot*, 33–36, 53–56.
27. Farris, *The Harrison Riot*, 25, 43–52.
28. *Labor*, November 25, 1922.
29. Bradley reproduces the November 25 *Labor* article, which he in error dates as November 21, in *An Industrial War*, 94. The *North Arkansas Star*, December 8, 1922, says that the train car with cotton was burned at Aubrey, but this actually happened at Fargo, where the M&NA intersected with the Cotton Belt line. See list of depredations given by J. C. Murray in his testimony, "Hearings and Report," 615–17. Gooden discusses the Tulsa plan in *The Missouri and North Arkansas Railroad Strike*, 224–25; Pete Venable described his role in a letter to a Tulsa lawyer, Charles West, August 1, 1924, vol. 256, ACLU Records.
30. Murray's letter was printed verbatim in the *North Arkansas Star*, December 15, 1922; the *Neosho Daily Democrat*, December 7, 1922; and the *Wheaton Journal*, December 15, 1922. See the discussion of the letter in the *Joplin Globe*, December 3, 1922; *Arkansas Democrat*, December 11, 1922.

CHAPTER 5

1. Bradley, *An Industrial War*, 96; Gooden, *The Missouri and North Arkansas Railroad Strike*, 121; J. C. Murray testimony, "Hearings and Report," 567; *Arkansas Democrat*, January 8 and 11, 1923.
2. *Harrison Daily Times*, January 11 and 12, 1923; *Little River News* (Ashdown, AR), January 17, 1923.
3. In "Hearings and Report": J. T. Venable affidavit, 1330–34; B. B. Montague testimony, 344–45; D. J. Williams testimony, 158–61; W. O. VanPelt testimony, 1119–29; H. E. Littleton affidavit, 1163–67; "Bureau of Locomotive Inspection Report," 1260–73.
4. In "Hearings and Report": John Devaney testimony, 522–62; J. C. Murray testimony with affidavits of Rosen and Raynor and Eugenia Nager, 628–34. Gooden, in *The Missouri and North Arkansas Railroad Strike*, 203–6, reproduces the Rosen-Raynor affidavit and Eugenia Nager's affidavit. The Rosen-Raynor affidavit refers to Devaney as "Jack" rather than "John."

5. Gooden, *The Missouri and North Arkansas Railroad Strike*, 184–90; *Pritchett v. State*, 254 S.W. 544, 160 Ark. 233 (1923), bound transcript of trial in Madison County Circuit Court, folder 2804, box 82, series 4, ASCBR. The description of Pritchett is from the report of Charles Finger filed following Margaret Germann to Gentlemen of ACLU, January 2, 1924, vol. 256, ACLU Records. Pritchett's given name was variously reported as Ollie, Owen, Omer, Omar, O. M., and O. N. His gravestone and selective service records identify him as Omar Newell Pritchett.
6. Gooden, *The Missouri and North Arkansas Railroad Strike*, 182–84; *Arkansas Democrat*, January 15, 1923.
7. Mrs. L. A. Wise testimony, "Hearings and Report," 33; Bradley, *An Industrial War*, 114–16; Gooden, *The Missouri and North Arkansas Railroad Strike*, 156–57, 162–63; *Southwest American* (Fort Smith, AR), January 14, 1923. According to Indictment Book E, 124, Boone County Circuit Court, Jack Halter was the witness for the state in both the Stevens and the Orr cases.
8. Indictment Book E, 126–27, Boone County Circuit Court; and, in "Hearings and Report": Bryan Holt testimony, 836–38; J. M. Shinn testimony, 811–12.
9. *Springfield Missouri Republican*, January 14, 1923. Gooden reproduces the entirety of Shinn's speech of January 12 in *The Missouri and North Arkansas Railroad Strike*, 157–59.
10. *Arkansas Democrat*, January 13 and 15, 1923; *Arkansas Gazette*, January 14 and 15, 1923; S. W. Woods testimony, "Hearings and Report," 742; *Marshall Mountain Wave*, January 12 and 19, 1923.
11. George O'Neal testimony, "Hearings and Report," 474; *Arkansas Gazette*, January 14, 1923; *Harrison Daily Times*, January 8 and 13, 1923; Pete Venable to Charles West, August 1, 1924, vol. 256, ACLU Records; Venable to Roger Baldwin, February 16, 1923, and October 13, 1924, vol. 242, ACLU Records; Venable to West, July 30, 1924, vol. 242, ACLU Records.
12. Farris, *The Harrison Riot*, 75, 134; Pete Venable to Charles West, August 1, 1924, vol. 242, ACLU Records; Venable to Charles Finger, September 7, 1923, vol. 242, ACLU Records; J. C. Murray testimony, "Hearings and Report," 632; *Arkansas Gazette*, January 18, 1923. Murray admitted that a man in Leslie had ordered and paid for the train, but he would not name the person and the committee did not compel him to do so.
13. Russell, *Behind These Ozark Hills*, 148; *Joplin Globe*, January 16, 1923; *St. Louis Post-Dispatch*, January 16 and 19, 1923; and, in "Hearings and Report": D. E. Decker testimony, 968; S. W. Woods testimony, 742; C. M. Routh testimony, 1032. Farris, *The Harrison Riot*, 82, says that the train was scheduled to arrive at midnight the night before and was twelve hours, not two hours, late.
14. *Joplin Globe*, January 16, 1923; Bradley, *An Industrial War*, 98; and, in "Hearings and Report": Sam Dennis testimony, 876–77; S. W. Woods testimony, 743; W. J. Douglas testimony, 689–90; William Parr testimony, 445; George O'Neal testimony, 469. Luther Wise, from the state penitentiary in July 1923, filed a petition for writ of error coram nobis, in which he said that Walter Snapp was chair of the committee that directed the squads that detained strikers and searched their homes. See *Luther Wise v. State of Arkansas*, case no. 1154, Criminal Box 113, Boone County Circuit Court. Jackson Henley lived in St. Joe

but practiced law in Marshall. Orville McInturff said that Henley opposed the Ku Klux Klan; see his notes in the Orville J. McInturff Collection, Missouri and North Arkansas Railroad Strike Folder, Arkansas State Archives, Little Rock.

15. Bradley, *An Industrial War*, 98–99; and, in "Hearings and Report": S. W. Woods testimony, 744; Karl Greenhaw testimony, 911, 925.
16. Pete Venable to Charles West, August 1, 1924, vol. 256, ACLU Records; Farris, *The Harrison Riot*, 82; and, in "Hearings and Report": Dr. L. Kirby testimony, 997–98; C. L. Iegoche [*sic*] testimony, 370–71; G. W. Roberts affidavit, 1251–52; Mrs. Charlie DeGoche testimony, 1283–84; C. M. Routh testimony, 1032.
17. Bradley, *An Industrial War*, 99; and, in "Hearings and Report": Mrs. Tillman Jines affidavit, 1245; George McKinney testimony, 981–84; Jenniel Venable affidavit, 1343–47.
18. Farris, *The Harrison Riot*, 90–92; *Arkansas Democrat*, January 16, 1923; and, in "Hearings and Report": Bailey McManus affidavit, 179; R. L. Mills affidavit, 181; Albert Raash testimony, 187–89. Orville Gregor graduated from the Naval Academy in 1924 and had a distinguished career as a navy officer. In World War II he commanded landing craft in the invasion of Anzio, Italy, and in southern France, and he retired from the navy as a rear admiral in 1947.
19. Mrs. Gregor written statement [not notarized],"Hearings and Report," 1048–53. John Worthington, who was in the crowd, admitted that Phifer was asked to leave the square, and that when he did not leave quickly enough someone struck him. See Worthington testimony, "Hearings and Report," 1023–25.
20. Farris, *The Harrison Riot*, 111; Henry Vance Kirby, interview, ASA; and, in "Hearings and Report": George McKinney testimony, 985; Arvin Moore testimony, 970–71; Bob Shattock [*sic*] testimony, 1005; Mrs. Gregor written statement, 1053–54.
21. Gooden, *The Missouri and North Arkansas Railroad Strike*, 132; and, in "Hearings and Report": Mrs. Gregor written statement, 1055–56; J. S. Johnson testimony, 1018; S. W. Woods testimony, 746–47. This section of Vine Street is now North Main Street.
22. *St. Louis Post-Dispatch*, January 19, 1923; Mrs. Metz Louck affidavit, "Hearings and Report," 1279; G. W. Roberts affidavit, "Hearings and Report," 1252; Farris, *The Harrison Riot*, 125–27. Reverend Farris said that Mrs. Stevens was a member of his church.
23. In "Hearings and Report": Mrs. Metz Louck affidavit, 1279–80; John Hughey testimony, 73; Mrs. Tillman Jines affidavit, 1245–47.
24. A. B. Arbaugh testimony, "Hearings and Report," 893; G. W. Roberts affidavit, "Hearings and Report," 1254–55; Ralph Rea, *Boone County and Its People* (Van Buren, AR: Press-Argus, 1955), 176; Gooden, *The Missouri and North Arkansas Railroad Strike*, 129.
25. In "Hearings and Report": George O'Neal testimony, 465–68; William Parr testimony, 445–48.
26. *Arkansas Democrat*, January 16, 1923; *St. Louis Post-Dispatch*, January 16, 1923; J. R. Curnutt affidavit, "Hearings and Report," 1172; Farris, *The Harrison Riot*, 87.

27. *Boone County Headlight* (Harrison, AR), January 18, 1923; *Arkansas Democrat*, January 17, 1923; *Kansas City (MO) Star*, January 17, 1923; and, in "Hearings and Report": Clay Holt testimony, 982; William Parr testimony, 446–48.
28. Bradley, *An Industrial War*, 102; Albert Raash testimony, "Hearings and Report," 187–203; *Kansas Leader* (Salina), February 8, 1923; *Mid-West Labor News* (Omaha, NE), February 2, 1923.
29. Farris, *The Harrison Riot*, 87. The *Arkansas Democrat* posted temperatures for 3:00 a.m. on January 16, 1923, as 32 degrees in Fort Smith, and 36 degrees in Springfield, Missouri. Harrison's temperature was likely somewhere in between. *Labor*, January 27, 1923.
30. In "Hearings and Report": J. R. Curnutt testimony, 1169–70; John Hughey testimony, 66–68, 71–72; C. L. Iegoche [*sic*] testimony, 373–75. Henry Grady Crutchfield, a striking machinist in the M&NA shops, presented an affidavit to the legislative committee from his exile in Branson, Missouri, asserting that Shaddox had conspired with the mob that took Gregor away. The affidavit failed to make it into the "Hearings and Report." It was reported in the *Kansas Trades Unionist*, February 9, 1923; and *Labor*, February 3, 1923.
31. In "Hearings and Report": James Taylor testimony, 45–47; D. E. Decker testimony, 965–69. Decker made no mention in his testimony that he was in the mob that searched Gregor's house. He said that he did not even know that a special train was taking people to Harrison until his mother woke him in his hotel room at around 5:00 or 5:30 a.m., telling him that the train was leaving at 6:00. This story is hardly credible, given that the special train arrived in Leslie on Sunday, with plans then made for the train's departure for Harrison the next morning. Alda Treece's recollections come from her great-nephew James J. Johnston, in an email to the author, July 8, 2020. Decker had served time in the Arkansas State Penitentiary for a counterfeiting scheme whereby he manufactured fake five-dollar gold pieces. By 1908 he had moved to Leslie, where he operated a photography studio. But again, he ran afoul of the law; he was indicted, tried, and found not guilty of producing and disseminating lewd pictures of two local women. *Monticellonian* (Monticello, AR), October 27, 1899; *Arkansas Democrat*, October 19, 1899, and December 13, 1908.
32. Henry Vance Kirby, interview, ASA; James J. Johnston, in an interview with the author, January 27, 2023, said that his father had heard similar stories when working in Harrison some decades after the event.
33. *Arkansas Democrat*, January 17, 1923; *Joplin Globe*, January 17, 1923; Bob Shattock [*sic*] testimony, "Hearings and Report," 1007; J. M. Shinn testimony, "Hearings and Report," 814; Farris, *The Harrison Riot*, 94, 106–7. Farris observed the marks on Gregor when he viewed the body as it was being embalmed. Josie Gregor tasked Farris with removing her husband's Masonic ring to give to his son, Orville.
34. George O'Neal testimony, "Hearings and Report," 464, 468–72; *Labor*, February 17, 1923. Farris, *The Harrison Riot*, 120, said that the preacher who whipped O'Neal later participated in religious services with Farris's friend and church member Andrew McAllen, who was newly ordained. In April 1923 McAllen, a Methodist,

assisted the Reverend D. M. Carter with a two-week long revival in the Baptist church in Berryville, resulting in forty baptisms; see *Harrison Daily Times*, April 21 and 28, 1923.

35. Farris, *The Harrison Riot*, 98; and, in "Hearings and Report": J. R. Curnutt testimony, 1171; George O'Neal testimony, 468–69.
36. Farris, *The Harrison Riot*, 102–5, 108–16; and, in "Hearings and Report": Mrs. Gregor written statement, 1058–60; Rev. J. K. Farris testimony, 1014–17.
37. *Labor*, February 3, 1923. Stephenson's statement can be found in the *Pittsburgh (PA) Press*, April 8, 1928; for a discussion of Klan violence in Arkansas and the Mer Rouge case, see Barnes, *The Ku Klux Klan in 1920s Arkansas*, 79–92; for further examination of the Klan's use of black masks, see John Ruiz, *The Black Hood of the Ku Klux Klan* (Bethesda, MD: Austin and Winfield, 1998).
38. Pete Venable to Roger Baldwin, February 16, 1923, vol. 242, ACLU Records; J. T. Venable, "Restitution not Retaliation," 11, vol. 256, ACLU Records; Farris, *The Harrison Riot*, 95–96, 107.
39. John Hughey testimony, "Hearings and Report," 96.

CHAPTER 6

1. See the description of the town in *Arkansas Democrat*, January 16, 1923; *Springfield Leader*, January 16, 1923; and *Joplin Globe*, January 17, 1923.
2. J. M. Shinn testimony, "Hearings and Report," 821; *Arkansas Gazette*, January 17, 1923; Record Book L, 298, Boone County Circuit Court, has the names of forty-one special deputies sworn in on January 16, 1923.
3. Message of Governor Thomas C. McRae to the Forty-Fourth General Assembly of the State of Arkansas, 1923, folder 3, box 3, series 3: Speeches, Thomas C. McRae Papers, M244, Special Collections, Mullins Library, University of Arkansas, Fayetteville; *St. Louis Post-Dispatch*, January 16, 1923; *Arkansas Democrat*, January 17, 1923; *Pine Bluff (AR) Daily Graphic*, January 17, 1923; *Arkansas Gazette*, January 18, 1923; J. M. Shinn testimony, "Hearings and Report," 821.
4. *Kansas City Star*, January 17, 1923; *Daily News* (New York), January 18, 1923; *St. Louis Post-Dispatch*, January 17, 1923; *Marshall Mountain Wave*, January 19, 1923; *Harrison Daily Times*, January 22, 1923; *Southwest American*, January 18, 1923.
5. *Kansas City Star*, January 17, 1923; *Kansas City Times*, January 18, 1923; *Pine Bluff Daily Graphic*, January 17, 1923; Indictment Book E, 130, 133, Boone County Circuit Court; and, in "Hearings and Report": Troy Coffman testimony, 881; Dock Keeter statement before grand jury, read in testimony by Karl Greenhaw, 930.
6. *St. Louis Post-Dispatch*, January 19, 1923; and, in "Hearings and Report": Mrs. Tillman Jines affidavit, 1245–49; Jenniel Venable affidavit, 1343–51; Dr. Leonidas Kirby testimony, 999–1000.
7. *Labor*, January 27, 1921, described the treatment of Mrs. Johnson. The February 17, 1923, issue of the *Boone County Headlight* printed Judge Shinn's denial of the story and then also his nephew's letter, written from Muskogee, Oklahoma, on February 11, contradicting Shinn's account.

8. *Pine Bluff Daily Graphic*, January 17, 1923; *Arkansas Democrat*, January 17, 1923; *Joplin Globe*, January 17, 1923; Farris, *The Harrison Riot*, 78; J. M. Shinn testimony, "Hearings and Report," 821.
9. Gooden, *The Missouri and North Arkansas Railroad Strike*, 159–61. Gooden devotes a whole chapter to the Orr-Wise court case and reproduces much of the documentation surrounding the case, including Shinn's speeches and grand jury testimony.
10. *Harrison Daily Times*, July 20, 1920; Gooden, *The Missouri and North Arkansas Railroad Strike*, 163, 168–69; *Springfield Leader*, January 19, 1923. Cooper's statement was presented during the appeal of the Orr-Wise case to the Arkansas Supreme Court in July.
11. In "Hearings and Report": J. M. Shinn testimony, 812–13; V. D. Orr testimony, 5–8; Luther Wise testimony, 25–30. E. G. Mitchell's statement in the Arkansas Supreme Court proceeding is reproduced in Gooden, *The Missouri and North Arkansas Railroad Strike*, 165–67. For more information about Mitchell, see Barnes, *The Ku Klux Klan in 1920s Arkansas*, 146–47; Nita Gould, *Remembering Ella: A 1912 Murder and Mystery in the Arkansas Ozarks* (Little Rock: Butler Center Books, 2018), 115.
12. Mrs. Gregor written statement, "Hearings and Report," 1060. Walter Casey's membership in the Klan was identified by the national Klan journal, the *Imperial Night-Hawk* (Atlanta), August 8, 1923, in reporting on Casey's tragic death. Casey was assisting Sheriff Shaddox and Silby Johnson in apprehending an escaped prisoner at the Boone County jail on July 16, when the prisoner grabbed Casey's gun and shot him dead. See also reporting about the incident in the *Harrison Daily Times*, July 16 and 19, 1923. The *Imperial Night-Hawk* erroneously said that Casey was a resident of Heber Springs.
13. *Arkansas Democrat*, January 17, 1923; *Arkansas Gazette*, January 18 and 20, 1923; *Kansas City Star*, January 18, 1923; *Harrison Daily Times*, January 18 and 19, 1923; Pete Venable to Roger Baldwin, February 16, 1923, vol. 242, ACLU Records.
14. *Arkansas Democrat*, January 17, 1923; *Arkansas Gazette*, January 17–18, 1923.
15. *Kansas City Star*, January 17, 1923; *Arkansas Democrat*, January 17, 1923; *Arkansas Gazette*, January 16 and 20, 1923; *St. Louis Post-Dispatch*, January 16, 1923; *Kansas City Times*, January 19, 1923. The newspaper of the railroad brotherhoods, *Labor*, on January 27, 1923, contradicted the other newspaper accounts. Its reporter had called at the White House inquiring about a federal response to the reign of terror in Harrison. He was told that President Harding was leaving the matter with Attorney General Daugherty. The newspaperman then asked for a response from Daugherty, who said that he did not know whether the federal government had jurisdiction. He was uncertain whether the M&NA was an interstate or intrastate railroad, and whether the receivership was under a federal or state court. The reporter made bold to reply that the name alone or any map would imply that the railroad was interstate and thus under the direction of a federal court. When asked whether he had sent a representative to Arkansas to investigate, Daugherty said no.

16. *Arkansas Democrat*, January 21, 1923; *Kansas City Times*, January 18, 1923; *Springfield Leader*, January 19, 1923.
17. John Rogers described the trip to Harrison in the *St. Louis Post-Dispatch*, January 18, 1923; and in his testimony in "Hearings and Report," 349–56. See also Jack Carberry testimony, "Hearings and Report," 785–87.
18. In "Hearings and Report": John Rogers testimony, 357; Jack Carberry testimony, 787–90.
19. In "Hearings and Report": Jack Carberry testimony, 787–90; John Rogers testimony, 358–62.
20. John Rogers testimony, "Hearings and Report," 357–67; *St. Louis Post-Dispatch*, January 18–19, 1923.
21. *Arkansas Democrat*, January 21, 1923; *Arkansas Gazette*, January 19, 20, and 21, 1923; *Memphis Commercial Appeal*, January 19 and 21, 1923. The *Harrison Daily Times*, February 9, 1923, reprinted Travis's article accusing Venable of graft; the original in the *Memphis Commercial Appeal* could not be found at the time of this writing. The *Boone County Headlight*, February 1, 1923, also carried the story of how Venable profited from the strike. For Douglas's discussion of Gregor, see his article of February 9, 1923, in Berryville's *North Arkansas Star*.
22. *Memphis Commercial Appeal*, January 19, 1923; *Arkansas Gazette*, January 19, 1923; *Kansas City Star*, January 19, 1923; *Kansas City Times*, January 19, 1923; Russell, *Behind These Ozark Hills*, 151.
23. *Kansas City Times*, 19 and 20, 1923; *Harrison Daily Times*, January 20, 1923. The entire list included (first name chair, second secretary): Harrison—W. L. Snapp, Troy Coffman; Leslie—W. W. Fendley, N. G. Sawyer; Marshall—S. W. Woods, Z. V. Ferguson; St. Joe—W. L. Henley, H. M. Walker; Everton—B. Killebrew, F. M. Jones; Alpena—J. A. Centers, Dr. D. L. Watkins; Green Forest—A. L. Kinney, W. G. Coxie; Berryville—Tom Morris, Oscar Johnson; Eureka Springs—C. E. Sweeney, Floyd Walker; Western Grove—C. E. Shinn (younger brother of Judge J. M. Shinn), Horace Magness; and Jasper—J. W. Moore, Ab Arbaugh.
24. *Harrison Daily Times*, January 23, 1923; *San Antonio Evening News*, January 20, 1923; *Kansas City Times*, January 20, 1923. When he was before the legislative committee, Karl Greenhaw read into the record the testimony of George Roberts and other strikers given before the grand jury, "Hearings and Report," 930–32. Roberts provided an affidavit from exile in Oklahoma detailing his treatment by the citizens committee and his false statement before Greenhaw and the grand jury, "Hearings and Report," 151–57.
25. *Belvidere (IL) Daily Republican*, January 20, 1923; *Arkansas Gazette*, January 19, 1923; Farris, *The Harrison Riot*, 134; Bradley, *An Industrial War*, 101; *Harrison Daily Times*, January 23, 1923; Harrison City Council Minutes, January 22, 1923, and February 5, 1923, Office of the Mayor, Harrison, AR. George Cline's brother Ralph was the undertaker who embalmed Ed Gregor. The brothers were proprietors of the combined furniture store/funeral parlor on the east side of the downtown square.
26. *Arkansas Democrat*, January 17, 1923; *St. Louis Post-Dispatch*, January 17, 1923; *Kansas City Star*, January 17, 1923; *Harrison Daily Times*, January 23, 1923. The *Harrison Times*, on January 26, 1923, published the names of all donors to the

expense fund, which could be taken as a list of members of the mob on the street on January 16.

27. Farris, *The Harrison Riot*, 128–44, 150, 155–56. Farris titled his chapter about the relief efforts, "A Relief Committee That Did Not Relieve." Farris was careful not to use names in his book, but the identities of most persons are clear from other sources. *Harrison Daily Times*, February 2, 1923; and, in "Hearings and Report": Dr. D. E. Evans testimony, 1012–13; Jenniel Venable affidavit, 1349.
28. *Springfield Leader*, January 19, 1923; J. T. Venable, "Restitution not Retaliation," 10, vol. 256, ACLU Records; Pete Venable to Roger Baldwin, February 16, 1923, vol. 242, ACLU Records; Russell, *Behind These Ozark Hills*, 146.
29. *Harrison Times*, August 1, 1924; *Harrison Daily Times*, August 5, 8, 11, and 24, 1924; J. T. Venable, "Restitution not Retaliation," 11, vol. 256, ACLU Records. The Harrison Klan took the Kerr-Harrell name from two members who were original members of the Reconstruction Klan. Most likely these two men were Rufus Kerr and William Harrell, both born in 1844. For the term *100 percent Americans*, see *Harrison Daily Times*, January 24, 1923; John Hughey testimony, "Hearings and Report," 68; Thomas R. Pegram, *One Hundred Percent American: The Rebirth and Decline of the Ku Klux Klan in the 1920s* (Chicago: Ivan R. Dee, 2011).

CHAPTER 7

1. In "Hearings and Report": Ed Treece testimony, 505–8; James Taylor testimony, 39–43.
2. In "Hearings and Report": S. W. Woods testimony, 549–53; A. L. Barnett testimony, 845; James Taylor testimony, 43; A. G. Killebrew testimony, 766.
3. Gooden, *The Missouri and North Arkansas Railroad Strike*, 145; and, in "Hearings and Report": Ed Treece testimony, 511–16; Grover C. Leslie testimony, 1143.
4. Abe Treece testimony, "Hearings and Report," 563–66. Abe Treece said that others who participated in his flogging were Atterberry, Richard W. Highland, Jerome Cotton, and Henry Nation.
5. In "Hearings and Report": J. R. Clay testimony, 761; A. G. Killebrew testimony, 767–68; A. L. Barnett testimony, 844–47; D. E. Decker testimony, 966–67; D. M. Carter testimony, 975–80. The *Harrison Times*, January 19, 1923, reported that twenty strikers or sympathizers were whipped in Leslie.
6. In "Hearings and Report": S. W. Woods, 754; M. E. Vinson, 664–66; Chester Casey, 207–8; R. H. Dickenhorse [*sic*], 287–88.
7. *Kansas City Star*, January 19, 1923; *Arkansas Democrat*, January 19, 1923; and, in "Hearings and Report": Chester Casey testimony, 210; M. E. Vinson testimony, 666–67, 683; B. Massingill testimony, 712; O. B. Robbins testimony, 234–36; A. N. Hilger testimony, 735–36; Frank Stewart testimony, 393–94.
8. In "Hearings and Report": O. B. Robbins testimony, 243–45; Mortimer Frauenthal testimony, 411; M. E. Vinson testimony, 653–58, 668.
9. In "Hearings and Report": Mortimer Frauenthal testimony, 408, 410; Neill Reed testimony, 962–64; M. E. Vinson testimony, 669; O. B. Robbins testimony, 266; Chester Casey testimony, 210–11.

10. In "Hearings and Report": Mortimer Frauenthal testimony, 430; Frank Stewart testimony, 388–90; O. B. Robbins testimony, 246. Cleburne County Court Records, Book 11, 129–33, 146, Cleburne County Courthouse, Heber Springs, AR, shows that Emmett Baldridge deputized the five men on January 18, 1923, and annulled the deputizations on March 16, 1923.
11. In "Hearings and Report": Mortimer Frauenthal testimony, 411; M. E. Vinson testimony, 686; Frank Stewart testimony, 396–97, 401, 406; Odie Logan testimony, 436–38. Colt 45 pistols were standard issue to soldiers in World War I.
12. In "Hearings and Report": Mortimer Frauenthal testimony, 413; Frank Stewart testimony, 387; T. J. Garner testimony, 117–20; M. E. Vinson testimony, 669.
13. In "Hearings and Report": B. Massingill testimony, 709; O. B. Robbins testimony, 247–48, 256; Emmett Baldridge testimony, 827–29; R. H. Dickenhorse [*sic*] testimony, 291–92; Frank Stewart testimony, 388–90; S. W. Woods testimony, 796; Neill Reed testimony, 962–64.
14. In "Hearings and Report": B. Massingill testimony, 713; M. E. Vinson testimony, 667; Ura Russell testimony, 110–16; C. E. Black testimony, 569–77; W. C. Webb testimony, 329–33; Emmett Crosby testimony, 487–503.
15. In "Hearings and Report": O. B. Robbins testimony, 265; Ura Russell testimony, 110–16; C. L. Woolard testimony, 90–95; Mortimer Frauenthal testimony, 414–19; Odie Logan testimony, 439–43; John Byes testimony, 149–58; C. E. Black testimony, 569–77; C. L. Goff testimony, 77–89.
16. In "Hearings and Report": Chester Casey testimony, 210–20; J. A. Casey testimony, 226–27; O. B. Robbins testimony, 264; Dorsey Treece testimony, 768–72.
17. Chester Casey testimony, "Hearings and Report," 207–9.
18. In "Hearings and Report": B. Massingill testimony, 710–11; Chester Casey testimony, 217; J. A. Casey testimony, 225–30.
19. In "Hearings and Report": Joe Phillips testimony, 1145–50; D. I. DeBusk testimony, 1153–55.
20. Chester Casey testimony, "Hearings and Report," 214, 217. Testimony by R. Moor Stewart and Henry Newman, and another farmer organizer, I. V. Morgan, apparently given before the legislative committee in Little Rock on February 28, 1923, was inserted between pages 579 and 580 in "Hearings and Report."
21. In "Hearings and Report": M. E. Vinson testimony, 660, 669; O. B. Robbins testimony, 247–48, 266; C. E. Black testimony, 572; C. L. Woolard testimony, 90–95.
22. In "Hearings and Report": Ura Russell testimony, 111; John Byes testimony, 150; C. L. Goff testimony, 79.
23. *Arkansas Democrat*, January 19, 1923; and, in "Hearings and Report": Odie Logan testimony, 439–43; A. N. Hilger testimony, 735–36; S. W. Woods testimony, 796; R. H. Dickenhorse [*sic*] testimony, 280–81.
24. In "Hearings and Report": C. E. Black testimony, 572; M. E. Vinson testimony, 686; J. B. Davis testimony, 51; C. L. Goff testimony, 80; T. J. Garner testimony, 121–22; Woodrow Wilson testimony, 136–38; Emmett Crosby testimony, 498–99.
25. In "Hearings and Report": M. E. Vinson testimony, 653, 669–72, 677–78; T. J. Garner testimony, 120; C. L. Woolard testimony, 94; Woodrow Wilson testimony, 136; Emmett Crosby testimony, 492–93; A. N. Hilger testimony, 735–36.

26. In “Hearings and Report”: Emmett Crosby testimony, 487–503; Dewey Webb testimony, 305–13; W. C. Webb testimony, 329–33.
27. In “Hearings and Report”: M. E. Vinson testimony, 656–61; Mortimer Frauenthal testimony, 429; O. B. Robbins testimony, 926; Emmett Baldridge testimony, 827–29.
28. *Arkansas Democrat*, January 19 and 21, 1923; *Arkansas Gazette*, January 19, 1923; *Hot Springs (AR) New Era*, January 20, 1923; and, in “Hearings and Report”: M. E. Vinson testimony, 681; Arch Cathey testimony, 566–68. While it is difficult from present times to imagine small farmers identifying with labor struggles, Arkansas and neighboring states had a long history of agrarian radicalism in the late 1800s and early 1900s. See James R. Green, *Grass-Roots Socialism: Radical Movements in the Southwest, 1895–1943* (Baton Rouge: Louisiana State University Press, 1978); Matthew Hild, *Arkansas's Gilded Age: The Rise, Decline, and Legacy of Populism and Working-Class Protest* (Columbia: University of Missouri Press, 2018); Matthew Hild, *Greenbackers, Knights of Labor, and Populists: Farmer-Labor Insurgency in the Late-Nineteenth-Century South* (Athens: University of Georgia Press, 2007).
29. *Arkansas Democrat*, January 19 and 21, 1923; *Arkansas Gazette*, January 20, 1923; J. T. Venable, “Restitution not Retaliation,” 10, vol. 256, ACLU Records; Pete Venable to Roger Baldwin, dated January 10, 1923 [but the actual date was January 24], vol. 242, ACLU Records; and, in “Hearings and Report”: O. B. Robbins testimony, 738; John Q. Adams testimony, 646; Ben Allen testimony, 1139–40.
30. S. W. Woods testimony, “Hearings and Report,” 749–53; F. O. Butt testimony, “Hearings and Report,” 772–81; *Eureka Springs (AR) Daily Times-Echo*, January 29, 1923, typescript copy in “Hearings and Report,” 780; *Harrison Times*, January 19, 1923; *Harrison Daily Times*, January 26, 1923; *Joplin Globe*, January 23, 1923; *Springfield Missouri Republican*, January 23, 1923.
31. T. J. Garner testimony, “Hearings and Report,” 119; Evalena Berry, *Time and the River: A History of Cleburne County* (Little Rock: Rose, 1982), 259–60. The charter is part of the collection of the Cleburne County Historical Society in Heber Springs. The namesake of the Klan chapter was a Confederate general from Helena, Arkansas, Patrick R. Cleburne, who was killed at the Battle of Franklin, Tennessee, in 1864. The Arkansas General Assembly named the county for Cleburne when it was created in 1883. Arthur Allen Hodges, the exalted cyclops, formerly an automobile salesman in Heber Springs, had just returned to the town in September 1922 from Cabot, having bought a grocery and variety store from Lee Davis. *Arkansas Democrat*, September 10, 1922.
32. Compare the membership listings provided in testimonies before the legislative committee and recorded in “Hearings and Report.” For citizens committee and squad members' accounts, see: R. H. Dickenhorse [*sic*], 300; M. E. Vinson, 668; O. B. Robbins, 243–45; and Mortimer Frauenthal, 411. For strikers' accounts, see: Woodrow Wilson, 137; C. L. Goff, 83; Ura Russell, 110; John Byes, 150; C. L. Woolard, 91; and T. J. Garner, 122–23. The *Arkansas Democrat*, January 19 and 21, 1923, and the *Arkansas Gazette*, January 19, 1923, reported about a committee of fifteen. Walter Snapp had become exalted cyclops by August 1924. When exactly the baton was passed from the Reverend Bradley is unclear.

33. Berry, *Time and the River*, 260; Hallie Ormond, "The Awful M&NA Strike," *White County Heritage* 36 (1998): 55–56; email from James J. Johnston, great-nephew of Abe Treece, to author, August 30, 2020. Mr. Johnston also shared a communication from Dale Lee to him, dated February 1996. Mollie Thomas was interviewed for Mary Frances Harrell, ed., *History and Folklore of Searcy County, Arkansas* (Harrison, AR: New Leaf Press, 1977), 84. Thomas lived in Leslie to her death in 1982, at the age of ninety-four.
34. Ed Treece testimony, "Hearings and Report," 515; *North Arkansas Star*, September 28, 1923, and March 7, 1924; *Marshall Mountain Wave*, January 19, 1923. Orville J. McInturff, the author of *Searcy County, My Dear: History of Searcy County, Arkansas* (Marshall, AR: Marshall Mountain Wave, 1963), makes no mention of the strike in his book, although he was twenty-eight and living in Marshall when the strike ended. His father, Dan McInturff, was the assistant secretary of Marshall's Protective League; *Marshall Mountain Wave*, January 26, 1923. Dale Lee said that it was Dan McInturff who came to his uncle's home and summoned him to appear before the committee in Leslie. Orville McInturff collected a folder of materials about the M&NA strike and scrawled in the margin of a newspaper clipping the notation that Hugh Treece, the exalted cyclops of the Marshall Klan, resigned his membership after he learned about his brother's whipping. Orville J. McInturff Collection, Missouri and North Arkansas Railroad Strike Folder, Arkansas State Archives, Little Rock.

CHAPTER 8

1. For more on Klan involvement with the 1922 elections, see Barnes, *The Ku Klux Klan in 1920s Arkansas*, 114–21.
2. J. T. Venable, "Restitution not Retaliation," 5–6, vol. 256, ACLU Records; Barnes, *The Ku Klux Klan in 1920s Arkansas*, 116, 120.
3. *Arkansas Gazette*, December 10 and 12, 1922, and January 7, 11, and 15, 1923; *Arkansas Democrat*, December 11 and 12, 1922, and January 10 and 14, 1923. For more examples of the Klan's attempt to control juries, see Barnes, *The Ku Klux Klan in 1920s Arkansas*, 61–65.
4. For a discussion of the McKennon bill, which became Arkansas Act 430, see Willis, "Arkansas's Gun Regulation Laws," 122–23.
5. For more information about the Klan's influence over the Forty-Fourth General Assembly, see Barnes, *The Ku Klux Klan in 1920s Arkansas*, 121–23.
6. *Arkansas Democrat*, January 18, 1923; and February 19, 1923; *Arkansas Gazette*, January 18, 1923; and March 14, 1923. The language of the act to create the legislative committee comes from the committee's report, as published in Bradley, *An Industrial War*, 138. Wilson's membership in the Klan was asserted by John Martineau, his opponent in the 1924 Democratic gubernatorial primary. Wilson neither confirmed nor denied the assertion; see Martineau's ad in the *Arkansas Gazette*, August 3, 1924; J. T. Venable, "Restitution not Retaliation," 18, vol. 256, ACLU Records. An undated document sent to the ACLU from the Marion Hotel, room 673, in July 1923, apparently authored by railway union representative

John Rives, also asserted that the investigative committee "was composed of KKK men with no exception." Response to this document sent July 17, 1923, vol. 242, ACLU Records.

7. *Arkansas Democrat*, January 23 and 24, 1923; *Arkansas Gazette*, January 23, 1923; statement by Chairman Norfleet, "Hearings and Report," 186.
8. Clipping from unidentified newspaper, February 6, 1923, Clippings File, vol. 235, ACLU Records; *Arkansas Gazette*, February 1, 1923; and, in "Hearings and Report": Albert Raash testimony, 202–3, 318–19; John T. Rogers testimony, 355–56, 365. The *St. Louis Post-Dispatch*, February 1, 1923, ran a lengthy article about Bogle's behavior in questioning Rogers.
9. John Hughey testimony, "Hearings and Report," 72; *Arkansas Democrat*, January 23, 25, 26, 29, and 30, 1923; *Springfield Missouri Republican*, January 30, 1923.
10. *Arkansas Gazette*, March 1 and 6, 1923; *Arkansas Democrat*, February 2 and 21, 1923; *Kansas City Times*, February 20, 1923; "Hearings and Report," nonpaginated section inserted into the record between pages 579 and 580.
11. *Arkansas Gazette*, March 14 and 20, 1923, and May 9, 1923; *Hot Springs New Era*, March 19, 1923; *Harrison Daily Times*, March 20, 1923.
12. M. B. Norfleet statement, "Hearings and Report," 599–600.
13. *Kansas City Times*, March 22, 1923; *Journal and Tribune* (Knoxville, TN), March 22, 1923; *Tulsa Tribune*, March 21, 1923. The reporter for the *Arkansas Gazette*, March 22, 1923, reported Woods's statement and noted the applause that Chairman Norfleet allowed unchecked. The transcript in "Hearings and Report" does not record this comment or the applause.
14. In "Hearings and Report": Karl Greenhaw testimony, 904–58; Robert Shattock (*sic*) testimony, 1004–11.
15. *Harrison Daily Times*, March 22, 1923; *Arkansas Gazette*, March 24 and 25, 1923; *Marshall Mountain Wave*, July 13, 1923; Chairman Norfleet address and response by Anna Fitzpatrick, "Hearings and Report," 1033–34.
16. *Hot Springs New Era*, April 13, 1923; and, in "Hearings and Report": minutes of meeting of March 26, 1923, 839; additional material submitted on behalf of strikers appears on pages 1145–355. The railway brotherhoods may have been responsible for the preservation of the only extant transcription of the legislative hearings, a copy originally belonging to John R. T. Rives, deputy president of the Order of Railway Conductors. Rives lived in Birmingham, Alabama, but was in Arkansas in April 1923, collecting materials to present to the legislative committee. His copy appears to have come into the possession of Orville Gooden, for it was presented by Matt Ellis, president of Hendrix College, to the Arkansas History Commission, now the Arkansas State Archives, on August 25, 1960. A handwritten note on the manuscript says that only three copies were made.
17. *Harrison Daily Times*, April 30, 1923; *Springfield Leader*, April 30, 1923. The committee's report is printed in its entirety in "Hearings and Report," 1356–68; Bradley, *An Industrial War*, 138–43; and *Arkansas Gazette*, May 6, 1923.
18. *Arkansas Gazette*, May 9 and 10, 1923, June 25, 1924, and July 24, 1924; *Hot Springs New Era*, May 9, 1923. For more about the 1924 Democratic primary, see Barnes, *The Ku Klux Klan in 1920s Arkansas*, 126–29.

19. *Arkansas Gazette*, January 19, 1923; *St. Louis Post-Dispatch*, January 19, 1923; *Kansas City Star*, January 22, 1923; *Recorder* (San Francisco), January 25, 1923; *North Arkansas Star*, January 26, 1973; *New York Times*, January 24, 1923; Peter J. Albert and Grace Palladino, eds., *The Samuel Gompers Papers*, vol. 12, *The Last Years, 1922–1924* (Urbana: University of Illinois Press, 2010), 192–97; *Fall River (MA) Globe*, March 10, 1923; *Railway Federationist*, May 19, 1923.
20. Thomas R. Pegram, "The Ku Klux Klan, Labor, and the White Working Class during the 1920s," *Journal of the Gilded Age and Progressive Era* 17 (2018): 374–75, 384–85, 389; *Labor*, January 27, 1923.
21. Robert C. Cottrell, *Roger Nash Baldwin and the American Civil Liberties Union* (New York: Columbia University Press, 2000), 137; for another account of Baldwin's life and work in the ACLU, see Peggy Lamson, *Roger Baldwin, Founder of the American Civil Liberties Union: A Portrait* (Boston: Houghton Mifflin, 1976).
22. Roger Baldwin to Thomas C. McRae, telegram, January 17, 1923; McRae to Baldwin, telegram, January 17, 1923; L. W. Lowry to Baldwin, January 21, 1923; ACLU Executive Committee Minutes, February 13, 1923; Baldwin to Pete Venable, February 5, 1923; Venable to Baldwin, February 16, 1923; all items in vol. 242, ACLU Records.
23. L. W. Lowry to Roger Baldwin, February 5, 1923; Pete Venable to Baldwin, February 16, 1923; Baldwin to Thomas C. McRae, February 17, 1923; Baldwin to McRae, February 26, 1923; all items in vol. 242, ACLU Records. McRae's answer was printed in the *Pine Bluff Daily Graphic*, February 23, 1923.
24. Roger Baldwin to Thomas C. McRae, April 6, 1923, vol. 242, ACLU Records.
25. Roger Baldwin to Pete Venable, April 6, 1923; Baldwin to John T. Rogers, April 16, 1923; ACLU Executive Committee Minutes, May 21, 1923; all items in vol. 242, ACLU Records. Rogers had just published a similar pamphlet taken from his reporting about the infamous Mer Rouge, Louisiana Klan murders, titled *The Murders of Mer Rouge: The True Story of an Atrocity Unparalleled in the Annals of Crime* (St. Louis: Security, 1923).
26. Cottrell, *Roger Nash Baldwin*, 80, 122; ACLU Executive Committee Minutes, October 1, 1923, Correspondence—Organizational Matters, 1920–24, vol. 229, ACLU Records; and, in vol. 242, ACLU Records: Roger Baldwin to Charles Finger, May 29, 1923; Pete Venable to Finger, September 7, 1923; Venable to Robert Dunn, September 27, 1923. For the interesting biography of Finger, see Elizabeth Findley Shores, *Shared Secrets: The Queer World of Newberry Medalist Charles J. Finger* (Fayetteville: University of Arkansas Press, 2021), 1–72.
27. The report follows the letter by Margaret Germann (Finger's secretary) to Gentlemen of ACLU, January 2, 1924, vol. 256, ACLU Records; *Arkansas Gazette*, October 28, 1923.
28. In vol. 256, ACLU Records: Pete Venable to Roger Baldwin, January 11, 1924; Robert J. Boone to Baldwin, January 12, 1924. In vol. 242, ACLU Records: Baldwin to Venable, April 16, 1924; E. C. Marianelli to Baldwin, July 10, 1924; Baldwin to Marianelli, July 14, 1924.
29. *Topeka Plaindealer*, January 30, 1925; and, in vol. 242, ACLU Records: Pete Venable to Charles J. West, August 1, 1924; West to Venable, July 31, 1924; Venable to Roger Baldwin, August 2, 1924, September 15 and 23, 1924, and

October 6, 13, and 21, 1924; ACLU to Venable, October 14, 1924; West to Venable, December 12, 1924; West to Baldwin, telegram, December 13, 1924.

CHAPTER 9

1. *Arkansas Democrat*, February 9, 1923; *Pine Bluff Daily Graphic*, February 8, 1923; *Arkansas Gazette*, February 8, 1923.
2. *Arkansas Democrat*, February 12 and 16, 1923; *Arkansas Gazette*, February 12, 1923; *Buffalo (NY) Labor Journal*, February 8, 1923; C. P. Ruff affidavit, "Hearings and Report," 1285–86.
3. *Oakland (CA) Tribune*, March 21, 1923; *Logansport (IN) Pharos-Tribune*, March 21, 1923; *Shreveport (LA) Times*, March 22, 1923; Jack Carberry testimony, "Hearings and Report," 785–90.
4. *Nevada County Picayune* (Prescott, AR), May 3, 1922; *Arkansas Gazette*, January 28, 1923; J. G. Brown testimony, "Hearings and Report," 337–38, 342.
5. In "Hearings and Report": Joe Phillips testimony, 1150; J. G. Brown testimony, 1151–54; Ura Russell testimony, 585–88; Fred Bell testimony, 590–94; Joe Taylor testimony, 929; M. E. Vinson testimony, 684. Wilmer's testimony is missing from the transcripts, but was reported in the *Arkansas Democrat*, February 22, 1923.
6. W. C. Webb testimony, "Hearings and Report," 1036–42; *Railway Federationist*, March 31, 1923.
7. *Arkansas Gazette*, April 25, 1923; *San Antonio Light*, April 24, 1956; *Nevada County Picayune*, May 3, 1923; *Labor*, May 12, 1923.
8. Gooden, *The Missouri and North Arkansas Railroad Strike*, 182–84; *Arkansas Democrat*, February 7, 8, 9, and 10, 1923; *Arkansas Gazette*, February 8, 10, 11, and 14, 1923; J. T. Venable, "Restitution not Retaliation," 9, vol. 256, ACLU Records.
9. *Harrison Daily Times*, August 29, 1923; *Arkansas Gazette*, July 22, 1923, August 5, 15, and 22, 1923, and February 13 and 14, 1924.
10. *Harrison Daily Times*, February 10, 1923; *Arkansas Gazette*, March 10 and 12, 1923; Gooden, *The Missouri and North Arkansas Railroad Strike*, 184–91. Gooden corresponded with Judge Dickson in collecting information for his account.
11. Gooden, *The Missouri and North Arkansas Railroad Strike*, 190–92; *Arkansas Gazette*, March 12, 1923; *Labor*, March 17, 1923; Charles Finger, "Report on Harrison, Arkansas, Case of Mob Violence," 3, vol. 256, ACLU Records.
12. *Arkansas Gazette*, March 30, 1923, and April 2, 1923; *Washington (DC) Evening Star*, April 9, 1923; *Hot Springs New Era*, April 9, 1923; *Lebanon (PA) Daily News*, April 10, 1923; Men of Monette, Barry County, Missouri, affidavit, "Hearings and Report," 1259; *Labor*, April 21, 1923.
13. Gooden, *The Missouri and North Arkansas Railroad Strike*, 190; *Arkansas Gazette*, October 2, 1923; *Pritchett v. State*, 254 S.W. 544, 160 Ark. 233 (1923), https://www.westlaw.com; *Pritchett v. State*, folder 2804, box 82, series 4, ASCBR.
14. *Arkansas Gazette*, July 10, 12, and 15, 1923; Gooden, *The Missouri and North Arkansas Railroad Strike*, 164–72; *Wise et al. v. State*, 253 S.W. 1119, 158 Ark. 639 (1923), folder 2833, box 83, series 4, ASCBR. Gooden devotes an entire chapter to the Orr and Wise trials and reproduces many depositions verbatim.

15. For more information about Trieber, see Gerald W. Heaney, "Jacob Trieber," in *United States District Courts and Judges of Arkansas, 1836–1960*, ed. Frances Ross (Fayetteville: University of Arkansas Press, 2016), 107–56.
16. *Harrison Times*, February 16, 1923, and July 20, 1923; Pete Venable to Robert Dunn, July 21, 1923, vol. 242, ACLU Records; *Joplin Globe*, July 18, 1923; *Arkansas Gazette*, July 18, 1923; *St. Louis Post-Dispatch*, July 18, 1923; J. T. Venable, "Restitution not Retaliation," 17, vol 256, ACLU Records. Sixty years after Judge Shinn said he saw only one armed man, Henry Vance Kirby, who had been a Harrison schoolboy on the day of the riot of January 15, 1923, remembered that all the men marching around the courthouse were armed. Henry Vance Kirby, interview, ASA.
17. Venable attached Trieber's entire ruling to the back of his narrative; J. T. Venable, "Restitution not Retaliation," 18–35, vol. 256, ACLU Records. Gooden reproduced most of Trieber's ruling in *The Missouri and North Arkansas Railroad Strike*, 172–80.
18. *Harrison Daily Times*, July 24, 1923; C. D. Allison to Robert W. Dunn, July 29, 1923, vol. 242, ACLU Records.
19. *Kansas City Star*, August 20, 1923; *Mid-West Labor News*, August 24, 1923; *New Yorker Volkszeitung*, August 26, 1923; *Labor*, August 25, 1923. The latter two newspapers were reporting from a news release by the ACLU. This information did not appear in the Arkansas papers. Benjamin Hudgins had formerly served as Boone County circuit judge, representative to the General Assembly, and chairman of the Arkansas Railroad Commission. See Gould, *Remembering Ella*, 86.
20. *New Yorker Volkszeitung*, August 26, 1923; *Mid-West Labor News*, August 24, 1923; *Harrison Daily Times*, August 3, 1923, and July 31, 1924. In its internal records, the ACLU listed Lean's death in August 1923 as a lynching; "Report on Civil Liberties Situation for the Week Ending. . . . August 18," vol. 229, ACLU Records. According to manuscript census schedules, Ewing Sansing resided in 1930 and 1940 in the Arkansas State Hospital for Nervous Disorders in Little Rock.
21. *Harrison Daily Times*, July 27, 1923, and August 3, 1923; Harrison City Council Minutes, June 5, 1923, Office of the Mayor, Harrison, AR; *Boone County Headlight*, May 31, 1923.
22. *Arkansas Gazette*, August 6, 1923; *Harrison Daily Times*, August 7, 10, and 13, 1923; *Joplin Globe*, August 11 and 12, 1923; Pete Venable to Robert Dunn, August 13, 1923, vol. 242, ACLU Records.
23. *Harrison Daily Times*, August 20, 1923, and June 4, 1924; *Boone County Headlight*, November 15, 1923; Pete Venable to Roger Baldwin, December 12, 1923, vol. 242, ACLU Records.
24. *West Virginia Federationist* (Charleston), December 13, 1923, vol. 235, ACLU Records; J. T. Venable, "Restitution not Retaliation," 11, vol. 256, ACLU Records; Pete Venable to Roger Baldwin, January 4, 1924, vol. 242, ACLU Records; *Boone County Headlight*, November 8, 1923; *Arkansas Gazette*, November 6, 1923; *Southern Standard* (Arkadelphia, AR), November 15, 1923; *North Arkansas Star*, November 9, 16, and 30, 1923.

25. *Fayetteville Daily Democrat*, September 20, 1923; *Minneapolis Labor Review*, November 23, 1923, vol. 235, ACLU Records.
26. *Minneapolis Labor Review*, November 23, 1923, vol. 235, ACLU Records; *Arkansas Gazette*, October 28, 1923; *Harrison Daily Times*, August 2 and 17, 1923.
27. F. L. Mulholland to D. B. Robertson (president of the Brotherhood of Locomotive Firemen and Enginemen), December 24, 1923, M&NA Railroad Room, Strike Folder, Boone County Heritage Museum, Harrison, AR (hereafter cited as M&NA Railroad Room); "Termination of the Railroad Strike on the Missouri & Northern Arkansas R. R.," *Railway Maintenance of Way Employes Journal* 33, no. 2 (February 1924): 9–10; *Labor*, December 29, 1923.
28. Karl Greenhaw to Thomas McRae, December 21, 1923, M&NA Railroad Room; *Baxter Bulletin*, December 28, 1923; *Tulsa Tribune*, February 1, 1924.
29. *Labor*, January 19, 1924; *Springfield Leader*, December 21, 1923; Eugene Lyons (publicity director for ACLU) to Editor, January 4, 1924, vol. 256, ACLU Records; and, in M&NA Railroad Room: Brotherhoods to Frank Mulholland, December 15, 1923; J. C. Murray to Frank L. Mulholland, December 21, 1923. Both the Springfield newspaper and Lyons used the term *hostages*.
30. Frank Reeves to Dear Sir, July 15, 1923, vol. 242, ACLU Records; *Marshall Mountain Wave*, June 26, 1923, and July 6, 1923.
31. See Barnes, *The Ku Klux Klan in 1920s Arkansas*, 150–51. Sadly only a few issues of the *Eagle* have survived, for the summer and fall of 1924, and one issue in 1926.
32. *Marshall Mountain Wave*, November 2, 1923; *Arkansas Gazette*, October 28, 1923; *Yellville Mountain Echo*, November 1, 1923.
33. *Marshall Mountain Wave*, March 7 and 14, 1924; *Harrison Daily Times*, February 25, 1924; *Arkansas Gazette*, August 31, 1924; *Eagle* (Marshall, AR), September 5, 1924.
34. *Eagle*, July 4, 1924, and October 25, 1926; James J. Johnston, email to author, August 24, 2018; *Marshall Mountain Wave*, June 13, 1924; Nancy Hensley, interview with author, December 12, 2022; *Harrison Daily Times*, June 8, 1924; *Arkansas Gazette*, June 25, 1924; *Yellville Mountain Echo*, June 12, 1924.
35. *Harrison Times*, April 4, 1924; *Marshall Mountain Wave*, April 4, 1924, July 18, 1924, and August 22, 1924.
36. *Harrison Daily Times*, April 16 and 25, 1924, July 1 and 23, 1924, and August 11 and 13, 1924; *Boone County Headlight*, July 24, 1924; *Yellville Mountain Echo*, March 13 and 20, 1924; "Speech of E. G. Mitchell, Harrison, April 15, 1924," printed pamphlet in the possession of Nita Gould, shared with author.
37. *Harrison Daily Times*, July 21 and 30, 1924, and August 13, 1924; *Marshall Mountain Wave*, August 22, 1924; *Southern Standard*, August 21, 1924. For the gubernatorial primary, see also Barnes, *The Ku Klux Klan in 1920s Arkansas*, 126–29; the Democratic primary vote tally is in *Arkansas Gazette*, August 15, 1924.
38. *Harrison Times*, August 1 and 8, 1924; *Boone County Headlight*, August 7 and 14, 1924; Henry Vance Kirby, interview, ASA.
39. *Eureka Springs Daily Times-Echo*, quoted in *Eagle*, September 5, 1924; *Boone County Headlight*, June 6, 1924.

CONCLUSION

1. Fair, in *The North Arkansas Line*, 196–97, 227, describes the M&NA's two streamliners. For the crash of the McRae, see Charlton S. Stanley, *The Wreck of the Thomas C. McRae: M&NA Motorrailer #705 at Harrison, Arkansas, on August 23, 1946: A Personal Account* (Elizabethton, TN: printed by the author, 2006).
2. *Marshall Mountain Wave*, April 10, 1925, and June 25, August 20, and October 15, 1926; *Harrison Times*, July 9, 1926.
3. *Harrison Daily Times*, May 14, 1925; *Marshall Mountain Wave*, August 24, 1925. For a longer account of the precipitous decline of the Klan in Arkansas and nationally, see Barnes, *The Ku Klux Klan in 1920s Arkansas*, 157–79. For a readable account of Stephenson's misdeeds, see Timothy Egan, *A Fever in the Heartland: The Ku Klux Klan's Plot to Take Over America, and the Woman Who Stopped Them* (New York: Viking, 2023).
4. Froelich and Zimmerman, "Total Eclipse." Charles Stinnett, the Black man found guilty of rape of a white woman, was assisted in his legal pleas by Guy L. Trimble and Elbridge G. Mitchell, two Harrison lawyers who stood by the strikers in the early 1920s. Dr. Charles Routh declared him dead after his hanging on March 24, 1909.
5. Hull, *Shortline Railroads of Arkansas*, 99; Fair, *The North Arkansas Line*, 155–88; *Harrison Daily Times*, June 16, 1933.
6. "Biographical Sketch—L. A. Watkins," Lewie A. Watkins Papers, MC782, box 1, Special Collections, Mullins Library, University of Arkansas, Fayetteville; Hull, *Shortline Railroads of Arkansas*, 101–2; Russell, *Behind These Ozark Hills*, 156. Fair discusses the last years of the M&A in *The North Arkansas Line*, 187–228.
7. The *Harrison Daily Times* reported activities of the local lodge of the Brotherhood of Railroad Trainmen on May 8, 1935, and February 11, 1936. The brotherhoods' role in the strike was reported in the *Blytheville (AR) Courier News*, September 6, 1946, and *Arkansas Gazette*, September 8 and 11, 1946. The return of railroad unions to the M&A may have resulted from amendments passed during the New Deal in 1934, which strengthened the position for unions laid out in the 1926 Railway Labor Act. See Huibregtse, *American Railroad Labor and the Genesis of the New Deal*, 89–90. Besides being arguably the most capable manager of the railroad in its history, Lewie Watkins appears to have been a decent human being. Following the crash of the Thomas C. McRae on August 23, 1946, Watkins personally took care of Charlton Stanley, an eleven-year-old boy who was traveling alone from Eureka Springs to his home in Heber Springs. Watkins took the boy to a Harrison physician, who stitched up a head wound, then brought young Stanley home and bathed and fed him, while they waited for the boy's father to arrive to take him back to Heber Springs. Stanley, *The Wreck of the Thomas C. McRae*.
8. *Arkansas Gazette*, September 23, 1956; *Harrison Daily Times*, August 28, 1933; *Marshall Mountain Wave*, July 9, 1926. Additional biographical information in this and the following paragraphs came from various sources in Ancestry.com.

9. *McAlester News-Capital*, March 29, 1926; *Orlando Morning Sentinel*, March 27, 1926; *Harrison Daily Times*, April 1, 1926; "Conductor Venable Meets Tragic Death," *International Brotherhood of Blacksmiths, Drop Forgers and Helpers Bi-Monthly Journal* 28, no. 4 (April–May 1926): 7. According to a deed search in the Boone County Clerk's Office, the Venables' home at 410 North Willow Street in Harrison was sold on April 9, 1923, to a dentist, Dr. Walter W. Cecil, for $3,250. Pete Venable named Dr. Cecil as one of the 207 members of the January 15 mob, on a list Venable prepared for the planned lawsuit through the ACLU; Pete Venable to Roger Baldwin, January 11, 1924, vol. 256, ACLU Records.
10. *Marshall Mountain Wave*, April 23, 1926; *Harrison Daily Times*, August 19, 1926.
11. Russell, *Behind These Ozark Hills*, 154; Bradley, *An Industrial War*, 103; Farris, *The Harrison Riot*, 183.
12. See the comments about the collapse of labor activism in Montgomery, *The Fall of the House of Labor*, 7; Dubovsky and Dulles, *Labor in American History*, 220; and Green, *The World of the Worker*, 101. For more information about the moderation of Republican labor policies after 1923, see Huibregste, *American Railroad Labor and the Genesis of the New Deal*, 66–91; Zieger, *Republicans and Labor*, 190–215.
13. Brose Massingill testimony, "Hearings and Report," 715.
14. Chad E. Pearson, *Capital's Terrorists: Klansmen, Lawmen, and Employers in the Long Nineteenth Century* (Chapel Hill: University of North Carolina Press, 2022). Robert Justin Goldstein, in *Political Repression in Modern America from 1870 to 1976* (Urbana: University of Illinois Press, 2001), xxiv, 3–19, argues that the United States had the most violent record of labor repression in the late 1800s and early 1900s, explaining why labor movements failed to reshape society as in many European countries. Chapter 2 of Pearson's book describes J. West Goodwin, owner of a print shop and newspaper in Sedalia, Missouri, who organized Law and Order Leagues to oppose the Knights of Labor in the 1886 railroad strike. A similar Law and Order League was founded in Little Rock, Arkansas, in May 1886 to fight the strike. However, over the following thirty-five years, as Law and Order Leagues were established in numerous communities in Arkansas and Missouri, they generally morphed into organizations to fight public immorality: gambling, bawdy houses, illegal liquor, Sabbath breaking, and so forth. By the early 1920s, Law and Order Leagues operated in El Dorado and Newport, Arkansas, and along the Louisiana border, as unmasked auxiliaries to the Ku Klux Klan. See *Arkansas Gazette*, May 4, 1886; Barnes, *The Ku Klux Klan in 1920s Arkansas*, 71–73, 87–88.
15. James Byrkit, "The Bisbee Deportation," in *American Labor in the Southwest: The First Hundred Years*, ed. James C. Foster (Tucson: University of Arizona Press, 1982), 86–102; *Anaconda (MT) Standard*, July 20, 2017; *Washington Post*, August 2, 1917. See also James Byrkit, *Forging the Copper Collar: Arizona's Labor-Management War, 1901–1921* (Tucson: University of Arizona Press, 1982); Arnold Stead, *Always on Strike: Frank Little and the Western Wobblies* (Chicago: Haymarket Books, 2014). White discusses Frank Little and the Bisbee deportation in *Under the Iron Heel*, 83–92.

16. Gooden, in *The Missouri and North Arkansas Railroad Strike*, 112, 256, said that Klansmen who were personal friends and men of integrity assured him that the Klan did not plan or carry out "the movement." In fact, Gooden credits Klansmen in the crowd with preventing bloodshed by holding more radical citizens in check.
17. Russell describes the preachers' orations in *Behind These Ozark Hills*, 1443.

BIBLIOGRAPHY

PRIMARY SOURCES

ARCHIVAL MATERIAL

Arkansas State Archives, Little Rock

"Hearings and Report of Missouri & North Arkansas Railroad Strike, Complete Transcription." MG04200, General Microfilm Collection.

Kirby, Henry Vance. Interview, July 5, 1993. Series 3, Ozark Cultural Resource Center Vertical Files.

McInturff, Orville J. Collection. Missouri and North Arkansas Strike Folder.

Boone County Courthouse, Harrison, Arkansas

Circuit Court Records, 1921–23.

County Clerk Records: Deeds.

Boone County Heritage Museum, Harrison, Arkansas

Kirby, Henry Vance. "Missouri and North Arkansas Railroad Strike: A Review of Personal Experiences," c. 1989.

M&NA Railroad Room. Strike Folder.

Bowen School of Law Library/Pulaski County Law Library, Little Rock, Arkansas

Pritchett v. State, 1923. Folder 2804, box 82, series 4. Arkansas Supreme Court Briefs and Records (ASCBR).

Venable v. State, 1923. Folder 2753, box 80, series 4. ASCBR.

Wise et al. v. State, 1923. Folder 2833, box 83, series 4. ASCBR.

Cleburne County Courthouse, Heber Springs, Arkansas

Cleburne County Court Records, 1923.

Mudd Library, Princeton University, Princeton, New Jersey

Clippings File. Vol. 235, American Civil Liberties Union (ACLU) Records, subgroup 1: Roger Baldwin Years.

Correspondence—Cases by State, Arkansas, 1923–24. Vol. 242, ACLU Records, subgroup 1.

Correspondence—Cases by State, Arkansas, 1924. Vol. 256, ACLU Records, subgroup 1.

Correspondence—Organizational Matters, 1920–24. Vol. 229, ACLU Records, subgroup 1.

Office of the Mayor, Harrison, Arkansas
Harrison City Council Minutes, 1921–23.

Special Collections, Mullins Library, University of Arkansas, Fayetteville
McRae, Thomas C. Papers. M244, series 3: Speeches, box 3.
Watkins, Lewie A. Papers. MC782, box 1.

JUDICIAL DECISIONS

Pritchett v. State, 254 S.W. 544, 160 Ark. 233 (October 1, 1923).
Venable v. State, 246 S.W. 860, 156 Ark. 564 (January 22, 1923).
Wise et al. v. State, 253 S.W. 1119, 158 Ark. 639 (July 9, 1923).

NEWSPAPERS

Anaconda (MT) Standard
Arkansas Democrat (Little Rock)
Arkansas Gazette (Little Rock)
Baxter Bulletin (Mountain Home, AR)
Belvidere (IL) Daily Republican
Blytheville (AR) Courier News
Boone County Headlight (Harrison, AR)
Buffalo (NY) Labor Journal
Chillicothe (MO) Constitution (digitized as *Chillicothe Constitution-Tribune*)
Crane (MO) Chronicle
Daily News (New York)
Eagle (Marshall, AR)
Eureka Springs (AR) Daily Times-Echo
Fall River (MA) Globe
Fayetteville (AR) Daily Democrat
Harrison (AR) Daily Times
Harrison (AR) Times
Hot Springs (AR) New Era
Imperial Night-Hawk (Atlanta)
Joplin (MO) Globe
Journal and Tribune (Knoxville, TN)
Kansas City (MO) Star
Kansas City (MO) Times
Kansas Leader (Salina)
Kansas Trades Unionist (Topeka) (digitized as the *Kansas State News*)
Labor (Washington, DC)
Lebanon (PA) Daily News
Little River News (Ashdown, AR)
Little Rock Daily News
Logansport (IN) Pharos-Tribune

Lonoke (AR) Democrat
Marshall (AR) Mountain Wave
McAlester (OK) News-Capital
Memphis Commercial Appeal
Mid-West Labor News (Omaha, NE)
Minneapolis Labor Review
Monticellonian (Monticello, AR)
Mountain Air (St. Paul, AR)
Neosho (MO) Daily Democrat (digitized as *Neosho Daily News*)
Nevada County Picayune (Prescott, AR)
New York Times
New Yorker Volkszeitung
North Arkansas and Carroll Progress (Berryville) (digitized as *Star Progress*)
North Arkansas Star (Berryville) (digitized as *Star Progress*)
Oakland (CA) Tribune
Orlando Morning Sentinel
Pine Bluff (AR) Daily Graphic
Pittsburgh (PA) Press
Railway Federationist (Sedalia, MO)
Recorder (San Francisco)
San Antonio Evening News
San Antonio Light
Searchlight (Atlanta)
Shreveport (LA) Times
Southern Standard (Arkadelphia, AR)
Southwest American (Fort Smith, AR)
Springfield (MO) Leader (digitized as *Springfield Leader and Press*)
Springfield Missouri Republican (digitized as *Springfield News-Leader*)
St. Joseph (MO) News-Press
St. Louis Daily Globe-Democrat
St. Louis Post-Dispatch
St. Louis Star (digitized as *St. Louis Star and Times*)
Topeka Plaindealer
Tulsa Democrat
Tulsa Tribune
Washington (DC) Evening Star
Washington Post
West Virginia Federationist (Charleston)
Wheaton (MO) Journal
Yellville (AR) Mountain Echo

PUBLISHED PRIMARY MATERIAL

Albert, Peter J., and Grace Palladino, eds. *The Samuel Gompers Papers*. Vol. 12, *The Last Years, 1922–24*. Urbana: University of Illinois Press, 2010.

Bradley, Walter F. *An Industrial War: History of the Missouri and North Arkansas Railroad Strike and a Study of the Tremenduous [sic] Issues Involved.* Harrison, AR: Boone County Headlight, 1923.

"Conductor Venable Meets Tragic Death." *International Brotherhood of Blacksmiths, Drop Forgers and Helpers Bi-Monthly Journal* 28, no. 4 (April–May 1926): 7.

Decisions of the Interstate Commerce Commission of the United States, Finance Reports, January to June 1922. Washington, DC: Government Printing Office, 1922.

Farris, J. K. *The Harrison Riot, or The Reign of the Mob on the Missouri and North Arkansas Railroad.* Wynne, AR: printed by the author, 1924.

Population of Arkansas by Minor Civil Divisions. Census bulletin no. 112. Washington, DC: Government Printing Office, 1891.

Russell, Jesse Lewis. *Behind These Ozark Hills: History, Reminiscences, Traditions, Featuring the Author's Family.* New York: Hobson Book Press, 1947.

Stanley, Charlton S. *The Wreck of the Thomas C. McRae: M&NA Motorrailer #705 at Harrison, Arkansas, on August 23, 1946: A Personal Account.* Elizabethton, TN: printed by the author, 2006.

"Termination of the Railroad Strike on the Missouri & Northern Arkansas R. R." *Railway Maintenance of Way Employes Journal* 33, no. 2 (February 1924): 9–10.

SECONDARY SOURCES

Adams, Walter M. *The White River Railway: Being a History of the White River Division of the Missouri Pacific Railroad Company, 1901–1951.* Branson, MO: Ozarks Mountaineer, 1991.

Angle, Paul M. *Bloody Williamson: A Chapter in American Lawlessness.* New York: Alfred A. Knopf, 1983.

Baird, Douglas G., and Robert K. Rasmussen. "Control Rights, Priority Rights, and the Conceptual Foundations of Corporate Reorganizations." *Virginia Law Review* 87 (2001): 921–59.

Barnes, Kenneth C. "Another Look behind the Masks: The Ku Klux Klan in Bentonville, Arkansas, 1922–1926." *Arkansas Historical Quarterly* 76, no. 3 (Autumn 2017): 191–217.

———. *The Ku Klux Klan in 1920s Arkansas: How Protestant White Nationalism Came to Rule a State.* Fayetteville: University of Arkansas Press, 2021.

Berry, Evalena. *Time and the River: History of Cleburne County.* Little Rock: Rose, 1982.

Blevins, Brooks R. *Arkansas/Arkansaw: How Bear Hunters, Hillbillies, and Good Ol' Boys Defined a State.* Fayetteville: University of Arkansas Press, 2009.

———. *A History of the Ozarks*. 3 vols. Urbana: University of Illinois Press, 2018–21.

———. *Hill Folks: A History of Arkansas Ozarkers and Their Image*. Chapel Hill: University of North Carolina Press, 2002.

———. "The Strike and the Still: Anti-Radical Violence and the Ku Klux Klan in the Ozarks." *Arkansas Historical Quarterly* 52, no. 4 (Winter 1993): 405–25.

Brecher, Jeremy. *Strikes!* Boston: South End Press, 1972.

Brenner, Aaron, Benjamin Day, and Immanuel Ness, eds. *The Encyclopedia of Strikes in American History*. Armonk, NY: M. E. Sharpe, 2009.

Byrkit. James. "The Bisbee Deportation." In *American Labor in the Southwest: The First Hundred Years*, edited by James C. Foster, 86–102. Tucson: University of Arizona Press, 1982.

———. *Forging the Copper Collar: Arizona's Labor-Management War, 1901–1921*. Tucson: University of Arizona Press, 1982.

Case, Theresa A. *The Great Southwest Railroad Strike and Free Labor*. College Station: Texas A&M University Press, 2010.

Cottrell, Robert C. *Roger Nash Baldwin and the American Civil Liberties Union*. New York: Columbia University Press, 2000.

Davis, Colin J. *Power at Odds: The 1922 National Railroad Shopmen's Strike*. Urbana: University of Illinois Press, 1997.

DeVore, Anthony, and Thereisa Housley. *All Aboard the Missouri and North Arkansas Train: The Legends and Tales of Searcy County*. Marshall, AR: printed by the authors, 2022.

Dray, Philip. *There Is Power in a Union: The Epic Story of Labor in America*. New York: Doubleday, 2010.

Dubovsky, Melvin, and Foster Rhea Dulles. *Labor in American History*. 8th ed. Wheeling, IL: Harlan Davidson, 2010.

Egan, Timothy. *A Fever in the Heartland: The Ku Klux Klan's Plot to Take Over America, and the Woman Who Stopped Them*. New York: Viking, 2023.

Fair, James R., Jr. *The North Arkansas Line: The Story of the Missouri and North Arkansas Railroads*. San Diego, CA: Howell-North Books, 1969.

Fine, Sidney. *"Without Blare of Trumpets": Walter Drew, the National Erectors' Association, and the Open Shop Movement, 1903–57*. Ann Arbor: University of Michigan Press, 1995.

Froelich, Jacqueline, and David Zimmerman. "Total Eclipse: The Destruction of the African American Community of Harrison, Arkansas, in 1905 and 1909." *Arkansas Historical Quarterly* 58, no. 2 (Summer 1999): 131–59.

Goldstein, Robert Justin. *Political Repression in Modern America from 1870 to 1976*. Urbana: University of Illinois Press, 2001.

Gooden, Orville Thrasher. *The Missouri and North Arkansas Railroad Strike*. New York: Columbia University Press, 1926.

Gould, Nita. *Remembering Ella: A 1912 Murder and Mystery in the Arkansas Ozarks*. Little Rock: Butler Center Books, 2018.

Grant, H. Roger. *Railroads and the American People*. Bloomington: University of Indiana Press, 2012.

Green, James R. *Grass-Roots Socialism: Radical Movements in the Southwest, 1895–1943*. Baton Rouge: Louisiana State University Press, 1978.

———. *The World of the Worker: Labor in Twentieth-Century America*. New York: Hill and Wang, 1980.

Handley, Lawrence R. "Settlement across North Arkansas as Influenced by the Missouri and North Arkansas Railroad." *Arkansas Historical Quarterly* 33, no. 4 (Winter 1974): 273–92.

Harrell, Mary Frances, ed. *History and Folklore of Searcy County, Arkansas*. Harrison, AR: New Leaf Press, 1977.

Harris, Howell John. *Bloodless Victories: The Rise and Fall of the Open Shop in the Philadelphia Metal Trades, 1890–1940*. Cambridge: Cambridge University Press, 2000.

Heaney, Gerald W. "Jacob Trieber." In *United States District Courts and Judges in Arkansas, 1836–1960*, edited by Frances Ross, 107–56. Fayetteville: University of Arkansas Press, 2016.

Hild, Matthew. *Arkansas's Gilded Age: The Rise, Decline, and Legacy of Populism and Working-Class Protest*. Columbia: University of Missouri Press, 2018.

———. *Greenbackers, Knights of Labor, and Populists: Farmer-Labor Insurgency in the Late-Nineteenth-Century South*. Athens: University of Georgia Press, 2007.

Holley, Donald B. "A Look behind the Masks: The 1920s Klan in Monticello, Arkansas." *Arkansas Historical Quarterly* 60, no. 2 (Summer 2001): 131–50.

Huddleston, Duane, Sammie Rose, and Pat Wood. *Steamboats and Ferries on the White River: A Heritage Revisited*. Fayetteville: University of Arkansas Press, 1998.

Huibregtse, Jon R. *American Railroad Labor and the Genesis of the New Deal, 1919–1935*. Gainesville: University Press of Florida, 2010.

Hulden, Vilja. *The Bosses' Union: How Employers Organized to Fight Labor before the New Deal*. Urbana: University of Illinois Press, 2023.

Hull, Clifton E. *Shortline Railroads of Arkansas*. Norman: University of Oklahoma Press, 1969.

Jennings, Barton. *Missouri & North Arkansas Railroad: History through the Miles*. Avon, IL: TechScribes, 2019.

Lamson, Peggy. *Roger Baldwin, Founder of the American Civil Liberties Union: A Portrait*. Boston: Houghton Mifflin, 1976.

Lancaster, Guy, ed. *The Elaine Massacre and Arkansas: A Century of Atrocity and Resistance, 1818–1919*. Little Rock: Butler Center Books, 2018.

———. *Racial Cleansing in Arkansas, 1883–1924*. Lanham, MD: Lexington Books, 2014.

Lubben, Stephen J. "Railroad Receiverships and Modern Bankruptcy Theory." *Cornell Law Review* 89, no. 6 (2004): 1420–75.

Masters, Nathan. *Crooked: The Roaring Twenties Tale of a Corrupt Attorney General, a Crusading Senator, and the Birth of the American Political Scandal*. New York: Hachette Books, 2023.

McCarty, Joey. “The Red Scare in Arkansas: A Southern State and National Hysteria.” *Arkansas Historical Quarterly* 37, no. 3 (Autumn 1978): 264–77.

McInturff, Orville J. *Searcy County, My Dear: History of Searcy County, Arkansas*. Marshall, AR: Marshall Mountain Wave, 1963.

Montgomery, David. *The Fall of the House of Labor: The Workplace, the State, and American Labor Activism, 1865–1925*. New York: Cambridge University Press, 1987.

———. “Strikes in Nineteenth-Century America.” *Social Science History* 4, no. 1 (Winter 1980): 81–104.

Newman, Clyde R. *One Hundred Years, 1873–1973: A History of the Methodist Church in Harrison, Arkansas*. Harrison, AR: printed by the author, 1973.

Ormond, Hallie. “The Awful M&NA Strike.” *White County Heritage* 36 (1998): 55–56.

Pearson, Chad E. *Capital's Terrorists: Klansmen, Lawmen, and Employers in the Long Nineteenth Century*. Chapel Hill: University of North Carolina Press, 2022.

———. *Reform or Repression: Organizing America's Anti-Union Movement*. Philadelphia: University of Pennsylvania Press, 2016.

Pegram, Thomas R. “The Ku Klux Klan, Labor, and the White Working Class during the 1920s.” *Journal of the Gilded Age and Progressive Era* 17 (2018): 373–96.

———. *One Hundred Percent American: The Rebirth and Decline of the Ku Klux Klan in the 1920s*. Chicago: Ivan R. Dee, 2011.

Rea, Ralph. *Boone County and Its People*. Van Buren, AR: Press-Argus, 1955.

Rost, Sean. “A Call to Citizenship: Anti-Klan Activism in Missouri, 1921–1928.” PhD diss., University of Missouri, 2018.

Ruiz, John. *The Black Hood of the Ku Klux Klan*. Bethesda, MD: Austin and Winfield, 1998.

Salmond, John A. *Gastonia, 1929*. Chapel Hill: University of North Carolina Press, 1995.

Shores, Elizabeth Findley. *Shared Secrets: The Queer World of Newberry Medalist Charles J. Finger*. Fayetteville: University of Arkansas Press, 2021.

Stead, Arnold. *Always on Strike: Frank Little and the Western Wobblies*. Chicago: Haymarket Books, 2014.

Stockley, Grif, Brian Mitchell, and Guy Lancaster. *Blood in Their Eyes: The Elaine Massacre of 1919*. Fayetteville: University of Arkansas Press, 2020.

Stromquist, Shelton. *A Generation of Boomers: The Pattern of Railroad Labor Conflict in Nineteenth-Century America*. Urbana: University of Illinois Press, 1987.

Taillon, Paul Michel. *Good, Reliable, White Men: Railroad Brotherhoods, 1877–1917*. Urbana: University of Illinois Press, 2009.

Wakstein, Allen M. “The Origins of the Open-Shop Movement, 1919–1920.” *Journal of American History* 51, no. 3 (December 1964): 460–75.

White, Ahmed. *Under the Iron Heel: The Wobblies and the Capitalist War on Radical Workers*. Oakland: University of California Press, 2022.

Willis, James F. "Arkansas's Gun Regulation Laws: Suppressing the 'Pistol Toter,' 1838–1925." *Arkansas Historical Quarterly* 81, no. 2 (Summer 2022): 103–26.

Wolf, Harry D. *The Railroad Labor Board*. Chicago: University of Chicago Press, 1927.

Zieger, Robert H. "From Hostility to Moderation: Railroad Labor Policy in the 1920s." *Labor History* 9, no. 1 (Winter 1968): 23–38.

———. *Republicans and Labor, 1919–1929*. Lexington: University of Kentucky Press, 1969.

INDEX

J

K